WAR OF THE
WHITE DEATH

The Stackpole Military History Series

THE AMERICAN CIVIL WAR

Cavalry Raids of the Civil War
Ghost, Thunderbolt, and Wizard
In the Lion's Mouth
Pickett's Charge
Witness to Gettysburg

WORLD WAR I

Doughboy War

WORLD WAR II

After D-Day
Airborne Combat
Armor Battles of the Waffen-SS, 1943–45
Armoured Guardsmen
Army of the West
Arnhem 1944
Australian Commandos
The B-24 in China
Backwater War
The Battle of France
The Battle of Sicily
Battle of the Bulge, Vol. 1
Battle of the Bulge, Vol. 2
Beyond the Beachhead
Beyond Stalingrad
The Black Bull
Blitzkrieg Unleashed
Blossoming Silk against the Rising Sun
Bodenplatte
The Brandenburger Commandos
The Brigade
Bringing the Thunder
The Canadian Army and the Normandy Campaign
Coast Watching in World War II
Colossal Cracks
Condor
A Dangerous Assignment
D-Day Bombers
D-Day Deception
D-Day to Berlin
Destination Normandy
Dive Bomber!
A Drop Too Many
Eagles of the Third Reich
The Early Battles of Eighth Army
Eastern Front Combat
Europe in Flames
Exit Rommel
The Face of Courage
Fist from the Sky
Flying American Combat Aircraft of World War II
For Europe
Forging the Thunderbolt
For the Homeland

Fortress France
The German Defeat in the East, 1944–45
German Order of Battle, Vol. 1
German Order of Battle, Vol. 2
German Order of Battle, Vol. 3
The Germans in Normandy
Germany's Panzer Arm in World War II
GI Ingenuity
Goodwood
The Great Ships
Grenadiers
Guns against the Reich
Hitler's Nemesis
Hold the Westwall
Infantry Aces
In the Fire of the Eastern Front
Iron Arm
Iron Knights
Japanese Army Fighter Aces
JG 26 Luftwaffe Fighter Squadron War Diary, Vol. 1
Kampfgruppe Peiper at the Battle of the Bulge
The Key to the Bulge
Knight's Cross Panzers
Kursk
Luftwaffe Aces
Luftwaffe Fighter Ace
Luftwaffe Fighter-Bombers over Britain
Luftwaffe Fighters and Bombers
Massacre at Tobruk
Mechanized Juggernaut or Military Anachronism?
Messerschmitts over Sicily
Michael Wittmann, Vol. 1
Michael Wittmann, Vol. 2
Mountain Warriors
The Nazi Rocketeers
Night Flyer / Mosquito Pathfinder
No Holding Back
On the Canal
Operation Mercury
Packs On!
Panzer Aces
Panzer Aces II
Panzer Aces III
Panzer Commanders of the Western Front
Panzergrenadier Aces
Panzer Gunner
The Panzer Legions
Panzers in Normandy
Panzers in Winter
Panzer Wedge
The Path to Blitzkrieg
Penalty Strike
Poland Betrayed

Red Road from Stalingrad
Red Star under the Baltic
Retreat to the Reich
Rommel's Desert Commanders
Rommel's Desert War
Rommel's Lieutenants
The Savage Sky
Ship-Busters
The Siege of Küstrin
The Siegfried Line
A Soldier in the Cockpit
Soviet Blitzkrieg
Stalin's Keys to Victory
Surviving Bataan and Beyond
T-34 in Action
Tank Tactics
Tigers in the Mud
Triumphant Fox
The 12th SS, Vol. 1
The 12th SS, Vol. 2
Twilight of the Gods
Typhoon Attack
The War against Rommel's Supply Lines
War in the Aegean
War of the White Death
Winter Storm
Wolfpack Warriors
Zhukov at the Oder

THE COLD WAR / VIETNAM

Cyclops in the Jungle
Expendable Warriors
Fighting in Vietnam
Flying American Combat Aircraft: The Cold War
Here There Are Tigers
Land with No Sun
MiGs over North Vietnam
Phantom Reflections
Street without Joy
Through the Valley
Two One Pony

WARS OF AFRICA AND THE MIDDLE EAST

Never-Ending Conflict
The Rhodesian War

GENERAL MILITARY HISTORY

Carriers in Combat
Cavalry from Hoof to Track
Desert Battles
Guerrilla Warfare
Ranger Dawn
Sieges
The Spartan Army

WAR OF THE WHITE DEATH

Finland against the Soviet Union, 1939–40

Bair Irincheev

STACKPOLE
BOOKS

Copyright © 2011 by Bair Irincheev

Published in paperback in the U.S. in 2012 by
STACKPOLE BOOKS
5067 Ritter Road
Mechanicsburg, PA 17055
www.stackpolebooks.com

Cover design by Tracy Patterson

Printed in the United States of America

10 9 8 7 6 5 4 3 2 1

Library of Congress Cataloging-in-Publication Data

Irincheev, Bair.
  War of the white death : Finland against the Soviet Union, 1939–40 / Bair Irincheev.
      pages ; cm. — (Stackpole military history series)
  Includes bibliographical references and index.
   ISBN 978-0-8117-1088-6
   1. Russo-Finnish War, 1939–1940. 2. Russo-Finnish War, 1939–1940—Campaigns. 3. Russo-Finnish War, 1939–1940—Personal narratives. I. Title. II. Series: Stackpole military history series.
   DL1099.I75 2012
   948.9703'2—dc23
                                    2012000335

Contents

List of Maps

Note: more precise maps can be found on the author's webpages at www.bair-travels.com in the Downloads section.

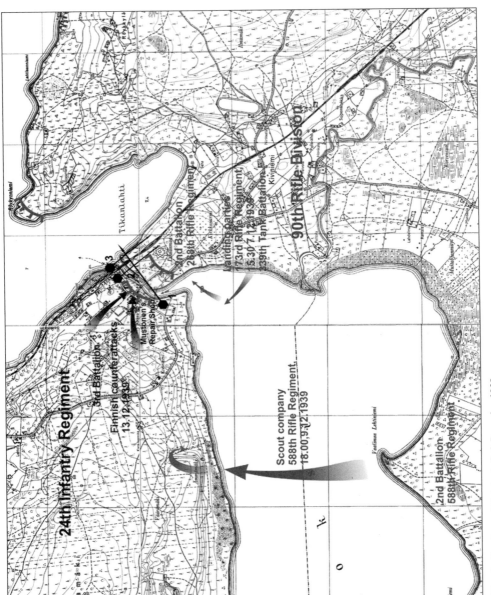

Map 1. Crossing at Kiviniemi, 7–9 December 1939.

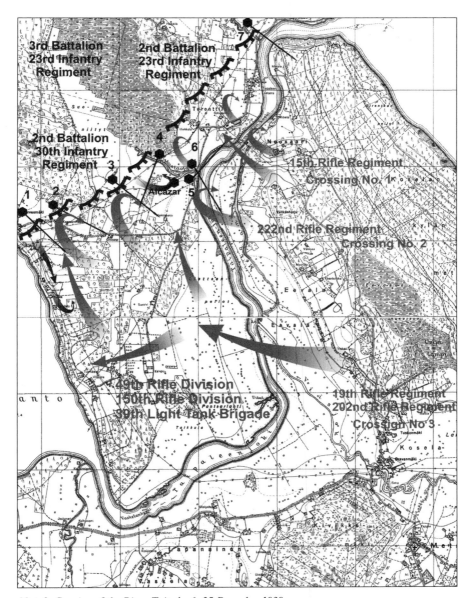

Map 2. Crossing of the River Taipale, 6–25 December 1939.

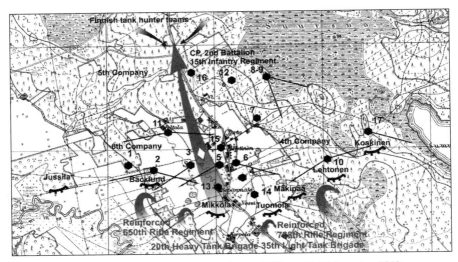

Map 3. Offensive of the 138th Rifle Division at Summa Village, 17–19 December 1939.

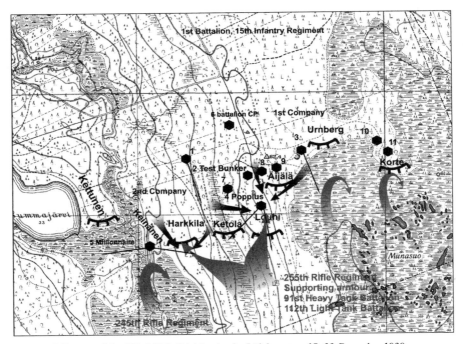

Map 4. Offensive of the 123rd Rifle Division in the Lähde sector, 17–23 December 1939.

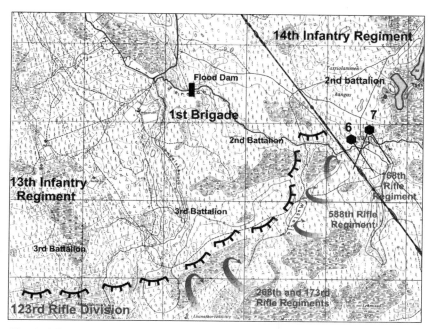

Map 5. Offensive of the 90th Rifle Division at Merkki, December 1939.

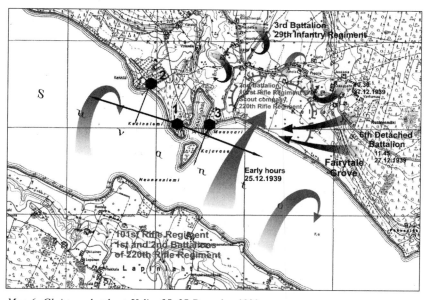

Map 6. Christmas battle at Kelja, 25–27 December 1939.

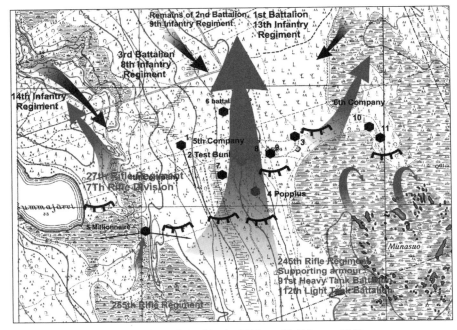

Map 7. Breakthrough of the Mannerheim Line in Lähde on 11 February 1940.

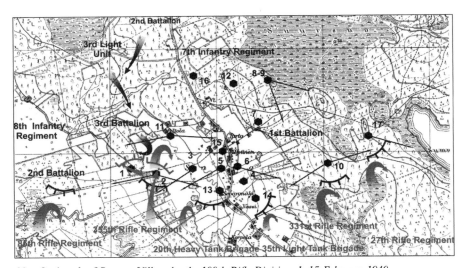

Map 8. Assault of Summa Village by the 100th Rifle Division, 1–15 February 1940.

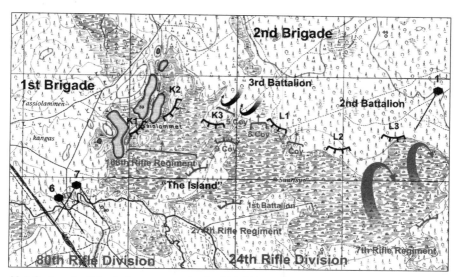

Map 9. *Assault of Tassionlammet sector by the 24th Rifle Disivion, 11–15 February 1940.*

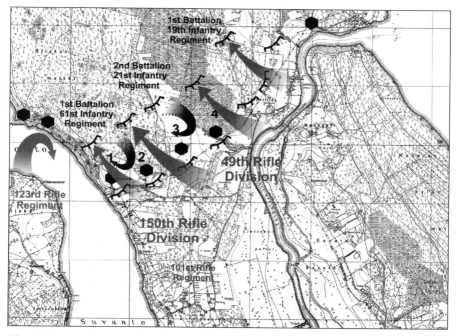

Map 10. *Soviet offensive at Taipale Bridgehead, 11–18 February 1940.*

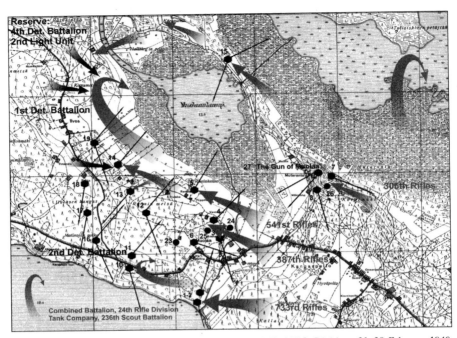

Map 11. Assault of Muolaa fortified area by the 136th and 62nd Rifle Divisions, 21–28 February 1940.

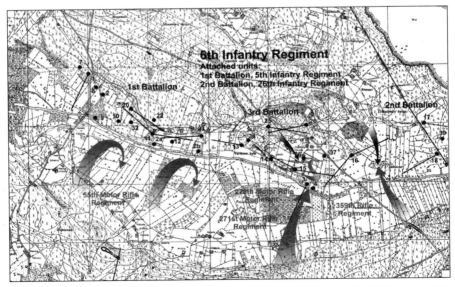

Map 12. Assault of Salmenkaita fortified line by the 17th Motor Rifle Division, 21–28 February 1940.

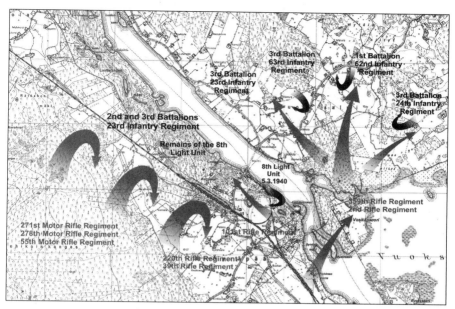

Map 13. The last battles at Äyräpää Ridges, 1–13 March 1940.

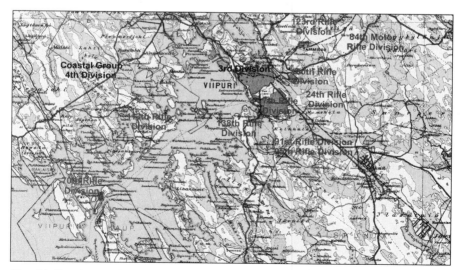

Map 14. Situation around Vyborg at the end of hostilities, 13 March 1940.

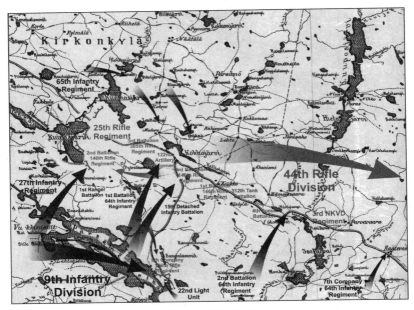

Map 15. Finnish offensive against the 44th Rifle Division at Suomussalmi.

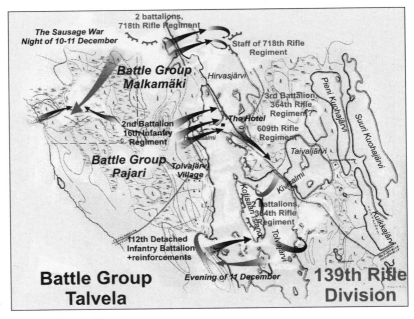

Map 16. Battle of Tolvajärvi.

Preface

The year 2010 marked the 70th anniversary of the Winter War between Finland and the Soviet Union. It is traditionally called the 'Winter War' in the West, while in the former USSR it is called the 'Finnish War' or the 'Soviet–Finnish War'. The war lasted for just 105 days but left a deep trace in the history of Finland and the USSR. The war united Finnish society, which was still suffering from the scars of civil war. For the USSR and the Red Army, the war became a costly but valuable lesson: a sort of exam before the war with a far more formidable enemy – Nazi Germany.

After the end of the Second World War, Soviet researchers paid little attention to the Winter War. In Finland, the war was researched thoroughly via Finnish documents, as Soviet archives were kept secret from all. Even now, this is probably the least researched campaign of the Second World War. Books about the war in Russian, Finnish and English are full of myths and incorrect information. This is only natural, as Finnish and Russian are not the most commonly studied languages in the world (and not the world's easiest!). I spent eight years of my life studying Finnish in order to research the Finnish military archives. In our times, the Russian archives are finally open for researchers from all over the world. Nevertheless, language and distance remain a serious barrier. All these factors contributed to the one-sided view of the Winter War in the West. The purpose of this book is to correct that view to some extent. In this book, I would also like to give the view from both the Soviet and the Finnish sides. It is also crucial for me to make voices of ordinary soldiers from the Winter War heard.

It is not possible to give a comprehensive description of each battle and skirmish that was fought along a front of over 1,300 kilometres. Some battles will be described in brief, some in the greatest possible detail. Both Finnish and Soviet viewpoints are in the book. This is one more purpose of the book – to explain the actions of the Red Army and see the reason for its failures in the Winter War. Everyone knows the Soviet invasion plan went terribly wrong; but few know the precise reasons why.

In this book, the campaign on land is stressed. Naval and air combat are largely omitted, as this is a topic for a whole different book. Whenever possible, descriptions of battles are augmented by memories of veterans from both sides.

It is widely known that the war was fought in extreme winter conditions, but it is important to know what that felt like for rank-and-file soldiers of both sides.

The terrain of the theatre of operations – tundra and forest-covered wilderness – dictated the nature of the war. Red Army units advanced along roads from the USSR into Finland with a continuous front line existing only on the Karelian Isthmus. The war disintegrated into a series of isolated battles, often many miles away from each other. A Soviet division or rifle corps advanced along a road into Finland, with Finnish units trying their best to stop them. The width of the front was 5–10 kilometres from the road at most. The rest was just *taiga* forest and swamps. Both sides used flanking manoeuvres as best they could, according to their training, expertise and resources. That is why the book is split into chapters by theatre of operations and timeline of the campaign.

Finally, in order to avoid confusion, all events mentioned in the book are given according to Moscow time.

Bair Irincheev
Spring–summer 2009, Helsinki–St Petersburg–Karelian Isthmus
bair@bair-travels.com

CHAPTER 1

Plans and Preparations

Finland and Russia shared a troubled history in the 1900s, with the roots of the conflict going back to the Middle Ages. Starting from the thirteenth century, the Karelian Isthmus, Finland and the Baltics became a battlefield for two rising superpowers – Sweden and Russia. Borders were moved in favour of the country that had a winning hand or better army at any given moment. Wars and border skirmishes repeated themselves regularly throughout the Middle Ages. The Swedes founded the castle of Vyborg in 1293 and continued to expand their influence in Karelia and the Baltic.

Finland was traditionally a domain of Sweden, but with the rise of the Russian Empire in the 1700s the border moved closer and closer to Stockholm. Finally, the war of 1808–1809 changed the fate of Finland: Sweden lost the last major war against Russia and Finland was incorporated into the Russian Empire as the Grand Duchy of Finland. The new province retained vast autonomy and privileges, granted by Alexander I of Russia. Alexander even granted Vyborg to the Grand Duchy. Towards the end of the 1800s the new Russian Tsar, Alexander III, abolished most of these privileges in a project to make his vast empire more homogeneous in terms of language, government, bureaucracy and other aspects. The Finnish intellectual elite saw this as a threat to their national culture and autonomy. As in many other European empires, an independence movement began to grow.

The First World War, the Russian Revolution and the collapse of the Russian Empire gave Finland a chance to become independent for the first time in its history. On 6 December 1917 the country officially split with the Russian Empire or, rather, what was left of it.

However, independence did not bring peace. A bloody civil war was fought in 1918. The Whites were supported by Sweden and Germany, while the Reds were supported by Soviet Russia. The war ended with the defeat of the Reds and their flight to Russia or extermination. During the civil war Mannerheim, Commander-in-Chief of the White forces, gave his famous 'Drawn Sword' speech, in which he claimed that his sword would be drawn as long as Eastern Karelia remained in Soviet hands. Some ultra right-wing White officers made

1

several raids into Soviet Karelia in order to annex these territories to Finland. Such raids were made on several occasions in 1918 and 1920. However, the local Karelian population was scared off by the atrocities that the Whites committed during these raids and mostly did not support them.

Peace between Soviet Russia and Finland was signed in 1920 in Tartu, Estonia. Russia was still torn and weakened by civil war and Finland received very favourable borders. On the strategically important Karelian Isthmus, the border was drawn along the Sister river ('Raja-joki' or 'Border river' in Finnish). At the closest point the border was only 32 kilometres from Petrograd (later Leningrad), the second-largest city of Soviet Russia. Proximity and lack of certainty regarding the Finnish border caused Lenin to shift the capital from Petrograd to Moscow in 1918.

It is important to note that, although diplomatic relations between the two countries were established and borders set, relations remained cool to say the least. Ideological differences, the imperial past and a nationalistic anti-Russian campaign triggered in Finland all contributed to this.

As the Soviet Union regained its status as a great European military power, Stalin started a project to expand Soviet influence in the Baltic. Soviet leaders approached the governments of Latvia, Lithuania and Estonia, requesting land and naval bases for the Soviet Armed Forces. A similar request was sent to Finland. In addition to the request to rent Hanko as a naval base, Soviet leaders demanded a shift of the border north from the Sister river, beyond Vyborg. The Soviets were offering an area three times larger in Karelia as compensation. However, such an exchange would have meant a loss of the Karelian Isthmus with all its fortifications and Vyborg – the second-largest city of Finland at that time. Several rounds of negotiations were held in Moscow but politicians failed to reach a compromise. Finally, in early November 1939, Stalin and his close associates decided to resolve the matter by war. Hasty preparation for a military campaign began. On the political front, Stalin formed a puppet government from surviving Finnish communists in the USSR and created the Finnish People's Army. At the same time the regular Finnish Army had been secretly mobilized in October 1939, during the extraordinary exercises of the reservists, and was standing ready at the main defence line.

The *casus belli* appeared on 26 November 1939. The Soviet side claimed that Finnish artillery had fired across the border at Mainila village, killing seven Red Army men. The Finns denied all accusations and called for an international investigation but the USSR would not comply. A propaganda campaign was unleashed in the Soviet Union, calling on the Red Army to deal with the 'troublesome' neighbour's rulers once and for all. The Red Army was to stretch out a helping hand to the oppressed Finnish people and bring freedom and democracy to Finland.

On 30 November 1939 the Soviet Air Force delivered several strikes on targets in Finland, including Helsinki, and the Red Army crossed the border. All this was done without an official declaration of war. The whole world believed the campaign would only last a couple of weeks and would end with the hoisting of the red banner atop the presidential palace in Helsinki. But things would turn out differently. The world looked on with awe as Finland defended its independence, stopping and defeating the Red Army. The course of events regarding the struggle on land is described in the pages that follow.

The Opposing Forces

The Winter War is often described as a 'David and Goliath' battle and indeed the contrast between the resources and equipment of the two armies is staggering. Nevertheless, it is important to note that the over-optimistic Soviet plan was to crush Finland with units of the Leningrad Military District only. Resources available in the Leningrad District were rather limited, and it would be wrong to state that, at the outbreak of the Winter War, Finland was facing the entire Red Army.

A basic unit in both armies was the infantry division, called a 'rifle division' in the Red Army. The basic composition of both Finnish and Soviet divisions was the same: each division had three regiments with supporting artillery and other units. The most important difference between Finnish and Soviet divisions was in their firepower and the equipment of supporting units. A Finnish infantry division had one artillery regiment of three battalions. Two-thirds of the artillery pieces were light 3-inch guns, most of them inherited from the Russian Imperial Army. Heavy howitzers made up the rest. Each Finnish division also had a light unit, comprising a cavalry squadron, a bicycle company, and a heavy machine-gun platoon.

A Soviet division had an artillery regiment and a howitzer regiment, with a greater share of large-calibre artillery pieces. Each division also had an anti-tank battalion with twelve 45mm anti-tank guns. In addition to division-level artillery, each rifle regiment had its own regimental battery of four regimental 3-inch guns and an AT battery of six 45mm anti-tank guns. Thus the superiority of a Soviet division over its Finnish opponent was more than twofold. Each Soviet rifle division had a tank battalion, but their composition varied greatly. A tank battalion could have from ten to forty tanks. The equipment of the tank battalions was light: T-37 and T-38 amphibious tanks and T-26 tanks of all models. Equivalent to a Finnish light unit in Soviet divisions was a scout battalion, with cavalry squadron, armoured car company and motor-cycle company. The composition of Finnish and Soviet divisions is presented at the end of the book in Appendix II.

Four detached heavy artillery battalions represented the Finnish Army's heavy artillery branch. Heavy, corps and supreme command reserve artillery regiments and independent battalions represented the Red Army's artillery branch. These heavy units were attached to rifle corps and armies to strengthen the direction of the main axis of advance. Artillery units had guns and mortars up to 280mm in calibre.

The detached tank company represented Finnish tank units, with thirty-two Vickers 6-ton tanks and a bunch of outdated Renault FT-17 tanks. The 20th Heavy Tank Brigade (named after S. M. Kirov) and numerous light tank brigades represented Soviet tank units. Each brigade had from three to five tank battalions and fielded from 100–200 tanks with support and supply units.

Soviet tank battalions fielded specialized armoured vehicles known as 'chemical tanks' and 'teletanks'. Chemical tanks, built on the chassis of the T-26 light tank, were armed with a compressed-air-operated thrower, which could spray poisonous chemicals, gases, burning liquids or decontaminating liquids onto the surrounding terrain. Detached tank battalions fielded some thirty to forty chemical tanks. In the Winter War they were used only as flame-thrower tanks. The range of flame-throwers was 50–100 metres, depending on the tank's model.

Teletanks were probably the most unusual and high-tech Soviet armoured weapon of the late 1930s. Teletanks were radio-operated chemical tanks, which could be deployed in battle without a crew. Each teletank had a control vehicle, from which the crew directed the world's first battle robot. A teletank and a control vehicle formed a battle pair. A teletank could also be manned as a regular chemical tank. From the outside, a teletank looked like a regular chemical tank: the only difference was the presence of a second antenna on the turret. The 217th Detached Tank Battalion fielded eight battle pairs in the Battle of Summa in December 1939–February 1940. Detached tank battalions were attached either to tank brigades or to rifle divisions.

It is important to note the explosive growth of the Red Army in the 1930s and the purges that took place in the same period. This led to a degradation in the training level of commanders. Majors, not colonels, led regiments. There was a consistent lack of division-level commanders. However, it is important to note that most of the Soviet colonels, *kombrigs* and commanders of higher rank were not new to war: they all had battle experience from the First World War as non-commissioned officers or privates in the Russian Imperial Army, rising to commanders in the Red Army during the Russian Civil War.

In this book I do not use the terms 'officers' and 'NCOs' when referring to the Red Army. These terms were not officially used in the Red Army until 1943, as the words were connected with the Russian Imperial Army. The Red Army tried to distance itself from its imperial predecessor as much as possible. The term 'senior commander' or 'commander' was used for a commanding officer, and 'junior commander' was used for a non-commissioned officer.

The political branch of the Red Army was established during the Russian Civil War in order to ensure the loyalty of certain former Tsarist officers to the Soviet state. As time moved on, however, the role of political workers and commissars changed to encompass political education, morale and propaganda. At company and battalion level, political workers took part in combat together with their unit and often replaced a killed or wounded commander in battle. In fact, the casualty rate of company-level political workers was sometimes as high as that of commanders.

Red Army Plans

The Red Army had certain plans in case of war with Finland, just like any army. However, in autumn 1939 all plans were scrapped and a new plan for a military campaign against Finland was developed. The order to develop new invasion plans was issued to Kirill Meretskov, Commander of Leningrad Military District, shortly before the war, when it became obvious to the Soviet leadership that there would be no peaceful solution following negotiations with Finland.

The whole invasion of Finland was planned as a local military operation by the Leningrad Military District. The basic assumption of the plan was that the Finnish Army would not be able to resist due to its limited resources. Meretskov's plan was to destroy the Finnish Army in a battle at the border and quickly march into the Finnish heartland via main roads leading from the USSR. The plan was hastily developed in November 1939 and was only completed in mid-November. Four armies were earmarked for the invasion; they were to operate along the entire length of the Finnish border, from the Gulf of Finland in the south to the tundra landscapes of Petsamo.

The Seventh Army, under Komandarm 2nd Class V. F. Yakovlev, attacked Finnish positions on the Karelian Isthmus. At the outbreak of hostilities the Seventh Army fielded nine rifle divisions (70th, 24th, 43rd, 49th, 90th, 123rd, 138th, 142nd and 150th) and four tank brigades (20th Heavy Tank Brigade, 35th Light Tank Brigade, 39th Light Tank Brigade and 40th Light Tank Brigade). The army was reinforced with several heavy artillery regiments. The X Tank Corps (with the 1st Light Tank, 13th Light Tank and 15th Motor Rifle Brigades) was in the army's reserve, ready to exploit the success of the rifle units at the front. The mission of the Seventh Army was to break through the Finnish defences on the Karelian Isthmus, destroy Finnish units and reach the Viipuri–Vuoksi line. After this, the army was to continue its offensive in the direction of Lappeenranta, Lahti and finally Helsinki.

Although the Red Army was aware of the Finnish defences on the Karelian Isthmus, the latest intelligence dated back to 1937 and was incomplete, as the most important fortifications were built after that date. Furthermore, maps of the Finnish fortifications were sent to the troops too late or were too inaccurate to be of use.

The whole campaign was to last no more than three weeks. This meant the Seventh Army had to advance at a pace of 20 kilometres a day – almost the same pace as a peacetime march for a rifle division in those days.

The Eighth Army, under Komdiv Khabarov, was to advance north from Lake Ladoga. This army fielded the 139th, 56th, 168th, 18th and 155th Rifle Divisions, as well as the 34th Light Tank Brigade. The army was reinforced with several heavy artillery regiments. The mission of the Eighth Army was to reach the Sortavala–Joensuu line and continue west and south-west into the heartland of Finland. This also meant getting into the rear of the Finnish defences on the Karelian Isthmus.

The Ninth Army, under Komkor M. P. Dukhanov, was founded on 15 November even further to the north. The army fielded four rifle divisions: the 44th, 54th (Mountain), 122nd and 163rd. At the outbreak of war the 44th Rifle Division was still on its way to the front from Zhitomir, Ukraine. The mission of the army was to capture Kajani and then Oulu, thus cutting Finland in two at its narrowest spot.

The Fourteenth Army, under Komandarm V. A. Frolov, was to advance in the extreme north. The army fielded two rifle divisions and one mountain rifle division, with most of the units still on the way to the front. The mission of the Fourteenth Army was to capture Petsamo in cooperation with the Northern Fleet and prevent possible landings by the Western Allies on the Kola Peninsula, as well as any Allied offensive from Norway.

Soviet plans were so hastily prepared that, even before the start of the campaign, some commanders had their doubts. However, an atmosphere of self-confidence in the Red Army prevailed. The Red Army had just defeated Japanese units at Khalkin-Gol in Mongolia, and successfully incorporated the Western Ukraine and Western Byelorussia into the USSR. All the campaigns of the Red Army before the Winter War were victorious and Soviet propaganda described the Red Army as 'legendary and unbeatable'. The Red Army was well equipped with the newest military equipment and it was the pride of the Soviet Union. However, the purges of the 1930s had left their mark on morale.

Some commanders were promoted too quickly without proper experience, some disappeared, but the worst consequence of the purges was an atmosphere of distrust and fear among the commanders, who feared that their subordinates would complain to the political workers or NKVD: consequently, in some cases, commanders followed the will of their men.

Finnish Options

The Finnish general staff developed plans for the country's defence during the twenty years of independence. By 1939 two plans were in place, designed to cope with different political and military situations in Europe. These plans were designated VK 1 (Russian Concentration 1) and VK 2 (Russian Concentration 2).

VK 1 assumed a very favourable situation for Finland. This scenario assumed that the armed forces of the Soviet Union were tied up in battles all along the USSR's western borders with Europe, preventing deployment of sufficient forces against Finland. In such a situation, the Finnish Army was planning not only to defend the country's independence but also to bite off some chunks of land from its mighty eastern neighbour. According to this plan, advancing Red Army units would be stopped on Finland's Karelian Isthmus at Inkilä–Hatjalahdenjärvi–Summa–Muolaanjärvi–Yskjärvi–Lipola–Rautu–Taipale. Then the Finns were to counter-attack and regain the state border, or even cross it, in order to gain better defensive ground.

To the north, from Lake Ladoga, Finnish units were to counter-attack from the area of Pitkäranta–Suojärvi and advance into Soviet Karelia and the area of Tuloksa–Vedlozero–Syamozero.

Further to the north, the Finns were to counter-attack from the Lieksa–Kuhmo area, capturing Reboly and continuing deep into Soviet territory towards Rugozero. At Suomussalmi Finnish ski units were to cross the border, capture Voknavolok and continue towards the Murmansk railway. This plan was, to a great extent, implemented in the summer campaign of 1941, when the USSR was embraced in a deadly fight with Nazi Germany and could not deploy large numbers of troops against the Finnish offensive.

VK 2 was a more pessimistic plan, assuming unfavourable conditions for Finland: consequently, its nature was more defensive. The plan implied a rigid defence of the Inkilä–Hatjalahdenjärvi–Muolaanjärvi–Vuoksi–Suvanto–Taipale line. North of Ladoga, three options for the Finnish main defence line could be chosen, depending on the situation at the front. Nevertheless, Finnish action north of Ladoga implied repelling the Soviet offensive and launching a counter-offensive. Units in the north of Finland had no special plan and they were to act according to the VK 1 plan.

The most important step that Finland undertook in autumn 1939 was the decision to carry out what became known as 'extraordinary manoeuvres' (YH) for all reservists. In effect, the manoeuvres meant a secret mobilization of the Finnish Army. The term 'mobilization' could not be used for obvious reasons in those days (mobilization of an army was almost equal to a declaration of war), and yet the Finns managed to concentrate their forces on the main defence line. Throughout October and November Finnish troops built additional fortifications and performed intensive combat training at squad–platoon–company–battalion level, with live ammunition firing and advanced tactics courses. Counter-attacks against Soviet breaches of the main defence line were rehearsed time and again. When war began, the main defence line was indeed home turf for Finnish troops: they knew every inch of the battlefield like their back garden. These two months of training and preparation played a crucial role in the battles of December 1939, largely contributing to the Soviet failure.

During autumn 1939 the Finnish Field Army was formed, as well as delaying troop units. The main task of the Field Army was to hold the main defence line and carry out counter-attacks. The Field Army consisted of infantry divisions with supporting artillery and was stationed along the main defence line as early as October 1939. The main task of the delaying troops was to fight a delaying action in the area between the border and the main defence line, winning time, inflicting losses, and depriving the Red Army of the element of surprise. Reservists that lived in border areas became the backbone of the delaying troops. The basic unit of delaying troops was a detached battalion, normally formed from reservists from one village or parish. Along with reservists, delaying troops also had mobile units – Jaeger battalions and bicycle battalions, as well as the Uusimaa Dragoon Regiment and the Häme Cavalry Regiment. These units were supported by weak and obsolete artillery in detached batteries. The delaying troops were well trained, mobile and highly motivated. The most important dilemma for Finnish generals and the Commander-in-Chief, Mannerheim, was the use of the delaying troops – should they hold their ground as long as possible or carry out a fast delaying action and quickly withdraw behind the main defence line? The latter option was implemented, as Finnish generals wanted the delaying troops intact at the main defence line as mobile reserves.

Finnish units were distributed in accordance with the importance of the theatre of operations. The Karelian Isthmus was defended with the bulk of Finnish forces. The western part of the Isthmus was the responsibility of the II Army Corps, under Lieutenant-General Harald Ökvist. The Eastern Isthmus was defended by the III Army Corps, which comprised the 8th and 10th Infantry Divisions.

The IV Army Corps defended the area north from Lake Ladoga. Other theatres of operations in the north were considered unimportant in Finnish pre-war plans and were defended by small forces of delaying troops.

The Finnish defence plan in the Winter War was simple. The main defence line was to be held at all costs. Lack of anti-tank weapons influenced tactics: the main task of Finnish defenders was to separate Soviet tanks and infantry, as tanks alone could not hold captured terrain. Strongpoints that were lost were to be recaptured in counter-attacks by platoon-, company-, or battalion-sized task forces.

In all Finnish plans the Karelian Isthmus was the main theatre of operations. The mainstay of the Finnish defences on the Karelian Isthmus was the main defence line, built during the twenty years of Finland's independence. The Mannerheim Line could easily be the subject of a separate book. The reader can find more detailed information on the Line at the author's web page: www. mannerheim-line.com.

CHAPTER 2

December 1939: Soviet Failure on the Karelian Isthmus

The commander of the Seventh Army, Yakovlev, had two rifle corps and a tank corps at his disposal on 30 November 1939. His units were to advance on the Isthmus towards Viipuri and Käkisalmi along two strategic axes. The XIX Rifle Corps, under Komdiv Starikov, advanced towards the main objective, Viipuri. This corps was reinforced with two howitzer regiments and one heavy artillery regiment. The L Rifle Corps, under Komdiv Gorelenko, with two artillery regiments of the Stavka Reserve, advanced on Käkisalmi. The Soviet units were to engage the Finns' main defence line within four to five days. The same amount of time was allocated for penetrating the line. After the breakthrough, the Seventh Army had some five days to spend pursuing the enemy before capturing Viipuri and Käkisalmi. The X Tank Corps was to enter the battle after the main defence line had been breached. One week after capturing Viipuri, units of the Seventh Army were to enter Helsinki, the Finnish capital, supposedly ending the military campaign.

The pace of advance was set at 20 kilometres a day. Soviet commanders did not expect any strong opposition from the Finnish Army. Soviet ideological statements suggested that Finnish workers and peasants would not fire on their 'class brothers' and would join the Red Army. This proved completely wrong: all Finns fought with great determination, regardless of their political views.

It is also important to mention that the Seventh Army had almost the same number of infantrymen as the Finnish II and III Army Corps combined. This meant that, even if the Seventh Army managed to penetrate the Finnish main defence line on the Isthmus, it would have no additional forces to develop the offensive operation. On the other hand, Finnish forces on the Karelian Isthmus had enough reserves to plug gaps and also carry out counter-attacks in case of a Soviet breakthrough.

Another crucial weakness in the Soviet plan was that it completely ignored the nature of Finland's terrain. Due to the country's dense forests, Soviet tank units could only advance along roads but even the well developed road network of the Karelian Isthmus could not bear all the tanks, gun tractors, armoured cars and trucks that crossed the border on 30 November 1939. Traffic jams, confusion and delays ensued, severely compromising Soviet logistics. This, in turn, led to the failure of the first assault on the Mannerheim Line on the Karelian Isthmus while, north of Lake Ladoga, a catastrophe was to unfold.

The Eastern Isthmus: Vanished Hopes

According to the original plan, the main thrust of the Seventh Army was towards Viipuri, then Hamina and Kotka and on to Helsinki. However, the action of the Finnish delaying troops was much more effective than Yakovlev expected. The distance from the border to the Finnish main defence line was also larger on the west of the isthmus. In the east of the isthmus there were just 25 kilometres from the border to the main defence line, and Finnish delaying troops were few in number.

The L Rifle Corps quickly advanced in the east and reached the Finnish main defence line in six days. This fast pace caused Meretskov to shift the main thrust of the Seventh Army to the Rautu–Kiviniemi–Käkisalmi axis, along the highway and along the western bank of Lake Ladoga. Additional units were dispatched to this area. Meretskov ordered the formation of a spearhead group, named 'Right Group', under Komkor V. D. Grendal. Before this appointment, Grendal was inspector of artillery of the Seventh Army. The Right Group comprised the 150th Rifle Division, under Kombrig S. A. Knyazkov, and the 49th Rifle Division, under Kombrig P. I. Vorobyev, as well as the 19th Rifle Regiment from the 142nd Rifle Division.

Battle order No. 11, issued by Leningrad Military District on 5 December 1939, set objectives for the L Rifle Corps and the Right Group. These large units were to cross Lake Suvanto at Kiviniemi and the River Taipale at Koukkuniemi. The 142nd and 90th Rifle Divisions were to advance from Kiviniemi to Räisälä and then turn to the Kirvu–Hiitola railway. Units of the Right Group were to get both rifle divisions immediately to the northern bank of the river and advance into the flank and rear of Finnish defences. The X Tank Corps was ready behind the L Rifle Corps and the Right Group, waiting to exploit the success.

General-Major Heinrich's III Army Corps defended the Eastern Isthmus. The corps comprised Colonel Winel's 8th Infantry Division at Kiviniemi and Colonel Kauppila's 10th Infantry Division at Suvanto and Taipale. Lieutenant-Colonel Merikallio's 24th Infantry Regiment was defending Kiviniemi. Lieutenant-Colonel Warttiovaara's 29th Infantry Regiment held a wide front from Haitermaa to Vilakkala. The Taipale sector was held by the 28th Infantry Regiment, under Lieutenant-Colonel Sihvonen. Lieutenant-Colonel Laurila's

23rd Infantry Regiment was in the corps' reserve. (This is the regiment depicted in the famous Finnish war movie *Talvisota* (*Winter War*), which came out in 1989.)

Units from the Finnish Navy were responsible for defending the banks of the Ladoga and its islands. The Ladoga sector was under the command of the III Army Corps. The so-called 'Isthmus sector' was formed at Taipale. It comprised the coastal batteries of Järisevä, Kaarnajoki and the artillery forts at Lake Suvanto.

The 28th Infantry Regiment was supported by strong artillery (by Finnish standards of 1939). The artillery comprised the 1st and 2nd Battalions of the 10th Artillery Regiment and the 4th Heavy Detached Artillery Battalion, as well as the Kaarnajoki and Järisevä coastal batteries. Thus, the Finnish defences were supported by twelve 6-inch guns (four in stationary positions at Kaarnajoki), eight 122mm howitzers, sixteen Russian 3-inch guns and one 120mm stationary gun of the Järisevä battery. It is important to stress the stationary character of the Kaarnajoki battery, as its tables of fire were prepared well before the outbreak of war. The battery's fire was deadly accurate and the battery was dubbed 'the Angel of Taipale' as the war progressed.

After the Metsäpirtti delaying group had withdrawn to the main defence line, the 2nd Detached Battery with six 87mm guns (dating back to 1895) was also at the disposal of the 28th Regiment, but the battle value of these guns in 1939 was questionable. Nevertheless, such a quantity of artillery pieces was a luxury for the Finnish Army of 1939. The accurate and concentrated fire of Finnish artillery was one of the contributing factors to their defensive victory at Taipale in December 1939.

The Finnish Army order of 7 November stressed that the main defence line was along the northern bank of the River Taipale. This meant that the Finns were to prohibit Red Army landings on the northern bank of the river. The vast fields of Koukkuniemi were to be defended at all costs. But despite these clear instructions, the 10th Division permitted the 28th Infantry Regiment to ignore the order due to the topography of the cape: the main defence line ran from Kirvesmäki to Terenttilä, with only forward positions left on the Koukkuniemi fields. Consequently, if the Army's order were followed, the 28th Infantry Regiment would have had its flanks exposed to Soviet fire across the river. Such a position would have been difficult to defend.

The width of the River Taipale at Cape Koukkuniemi is around 200 metres. A fast current and the lack of covered approaches to the river were more serious challenges for the crossing parties. Wide fields famous for their fertility lay along the southern and northern banks of the river. In the winter of 1939–1940 they received a more morbid fame, due to the heavy fighting that raged along the fields during the entire period of the Winter War.

A River Fast and Cold: Crossing the Taipaleenjoki

The crossing of Taipaleenjoki by the Soviet 49th and 150th Rifle Divisions began in the afternoon of 6 December 1939. The crossing was carried out in three places on a wide front.

Finnish forward units on Koukkuniemi quickly withdrew to the main defence line and Finnish batteries opened devastating fire on the advancing Red Army units – the sappers and pontoon engineers that provided the crossings (sapper battalions of the 49th and 150th Rifle Divisions plus the 6th and 7th Pontoon Battalions) took heavy casualties. The approaches to the river were open fields that stretched along the southern bank. Cape Koukkuniemi was also covered with fields, which made for a perfect killing ground.

Despite heavy casualties, units of the 49th and 150th Rifle Divisions managed to cross the river and establish a bridgehead on Cape Koukkuniemi and at School Grove in Terenttilä village. From 6–11 December Red Army units expanded the bridgehead while the Finns tried to push them back into the river. Battles in the fields of Koukkuniemi raged until 13 December, when the Finns finally retreated to the main defence line.

The 15th Rifle Regiment was to cross the river at a ferry crossing, code-named Crossing No. 1. The officer commanding was Captain I. A. Zykin of the 1st Sapper Battalion.

The 222nd Rifle Regiment was to cross at Kosela, code-named Crossing No. 2. The officer commanding was Senior Lieutenant A. E. Shelkov, Chief of Staff of the 1st Sapper Battalion.

The 212th and 49th Rifle Regiments were to cross at the mouth of the River Viisjoki, code-named Crossing No. 3. The officer commanding was Chief of Staff of the Sapper Battalion of the 142nd Rifle Division.

According to the original plan, all three crossings were to begin at noon, 6 December 1939. However, Finnish artillery hit the crossing parties way before they reached the southern bank, causing delays, casualties and confusion.

Captain Zykin's sappers were hit at their jump–off positions at 1300 hours and two trucks with crossing equipment were destroyed. Eighteen men were badly wounded and two men were killed. Confusion and chaos followed. Captain Zykin and the battalion's Commissar Markelov managed to rally their men as late as 1500 hours. Zykin and Markelov led the trucks to the crossing in person. It turned out that all the rubber boats had been hit by shrapnel and were no longer usable. Trucks of the 7th Pontoon Battalion made it to the river under heavy Finnish fire and the crossing began with a joint effort of pontoon operators and sappers. Two companies of the 15th Rifle Regiment made it to the opposite bank by 1800 hours, at which point the crossing was called off. These two companies held a tiny foothold on the Finnish side of the river in the so-called Pärssinen Grove.

The 3rd Battalion, 28th Infantry Regiment, under Captain Karl Lagerlöf, immediately attacked the two companies and tried to drive them into the river, but without success. Then the regimental reserve, the 2nd Battalion under Captain Mauno von Scroewe, was thrown into action. The battle lasted all night and in the morning the Finns reported that the grove was free of enemy troops. But according to Russian archive sources, companies of the 222nd Rifle and 15th Rifle Regiments still held out in Pärssinen Grove and School Grove.

At Crossing No. 2, Soviet sappers carrying rubber boats were hit by concentrated machine-gun fire from the Musta-oja bunkers even as they approached the river, taking heavy casualties. Despite this, the sappers pressed on with the crossing. As they entered the river, they were carried downstream right into the gun sights of the bunkers. According to Second Lieutenant Kähönen, who commanded the two bunkers, the River Taipale in a moment turned into a 'River Styx' – the river that takes men to the underworld. Rubber boats with men inside were blasted at a range of 50 metres. Out of twenty boats only three were left intact. The sappers lost seventeen men wounded and two men killed: the riflemen's losses are unknown. The operation at Crossing No. 2 was also called off at 1800 hours.

At Crossing No. 3, riflemen made it across the river after incurring heavy casualties. V. V. Tkachev, Sergeant-Major of the 19th Rifle Regiment, wrote:

> It was like this. We were crossing the river in the middle, the two other crossings were dummy. There was an open field in front of the river, some kilometre-and-a-half wide. There was a freshly dug trench across the field to the crossing. The assault began. Our men ran into the field towards the river, and Finnish artillery immediately hit them with shrapnel. Everyone was pinned down. I was next to the trench at that moment. We rushed to the river along the trench. We reached the bank and saw the bodies of our dead sappers lying in heaps, and there was no crossing ready! The bank was steep, so we dived down to the river. There were several row boats below. 'Move, fellows, move!' We jumped into the boats and rowed like crazy, although what could we do on the other bank? Each one of us had fifteen rifle rounds and one F-1 hand grenade. Not much of a soldier! Thirty-two of us made it to the other bank. There were piles of logs there. I ordered: 'Disperse!' We took cover behind the logs, and the

Finns hit them hard with artillery! An artillery round went through three rows and the rest flew into the river. I thought that the whole mass of logs would crash into the river and take us down too.

Nevertheless, the Soviet units made it over the river at Viisjoki and advanced across the fields into some woods. By the end of the day a pontoon bridge was operational and two rifle regiments marched across, accompanied by the 116th Howitzer Regiment. At Kirvesmäki Hill, on the shore of Lake Suvanto, Soviet units made contact with the Finnish main defence line.

Lieutenant-Colonel Sihvonen ordered the 8th and 9th Detached Companies to counter-attack towards Cape Koukkuniemi (the two companies were formed from Metsäpirtti border guards). The Finnish border guards charged forward at 1815 hours and were soon pinned down by intense Soviet fire. Captain Reino Inkinen, commander of Unit Metsäpirtti, ordered his men to attack again at midnight but the attack failed once more. As the Finnish border guards were making their fruitless attempts to move forward, the 10th Division brought the reserves closer to the front line. The 30th Infantry Regiment of Lieutenant-Colonel Armas Kemppi marched some 30 kilometres to the front line and went straight on the counter-attack.

Major Jaakko Sohlo's 1st Battalion was the first to arrive at Kirvesmäki. Two companies attacked at five o'clock in the morning on 7 December, as the 3rd Company was still on the march. As the attack progressed, it turned out that Läämäki Farm was already in Soviet hands, although Major Sorri informed the 30th Regiment that the area was under Finnish control. Finnish companies pushed the Soviet infantry back in the chaos of a night battle, but later were forced to withdraw to the main defence line. Only the 2nd Company of the battalion continued its advance, making it 1.5 kilometres south to Nuutila Farm. Major Sohlo did not spot the withdrawal of his own companies and proudly reported that his battalion had advanced 2 kilometres, encountering only sporadic resistance, and continued the attack. Only at midday of 7 December did Major Sohlo see the real situation and then he ordered a general withdrawal to the main defence line. Sohlo's battalion lost thirty-three men killed, thirty-six wounded and eight missing in action. The Metsäpirtti border guards lost fifteen men killed and twenty-two wounded. The 2nd Battalion, 30th Infantry Regiment, arrived in Kirvesmäki on the afternoon of 7 December, but its attack was cancelled.

Soviet reinforcements, the 469th and 674th Rifle Regiments (150th Rifle Division) arrived at the bridgehead on 8 December. Four artillery battalions from the 331st Cannon Regiment and 334th Artillery Regiment were also sent across the river. The 3rd Battalion of the 19th Rifle Regiment, which had suffered heavy casualties, was withdrawn from the front line. The rotation of troops took place without proper concealment and organization. Withdrawing units and reinforcements formed a huge traffic jam on the fields of Koukkuniemi. The Finns immediately hit the mass of troops with artillery. The 150th Rifle Division's Chief of Staff, Colonel Levin, and Chief of Communications, Major Zorin, were killed during the Finnish barrage. Several staff commanders were wounded.

A new Soviet offensive began on 9 December and was repelled. A further attack next day also failed. The 469th Rifle Regiment suffered exceptionally high losses as it charged against the Finnish lines without proper reconnaissance. The regiment was hit with concentrated fire from the Finnish main defence line. At 1900 hours on 10 December the regiment's men left the battlefield in disorder. Captain Duben, Acting Regimental Commander, was severely wounded in the battle and died later. The Chief of Staff, Captain Semenov, was wounded and left on the battlefield during the rout: he froze to death. All three battalion commanders were either killed or wounded, as were most company commanders. As a result, the regiment had to be withdrawn from the line to be replaced by the 756th Rifle Regiment.

The only Soviet success of the day was the capture of three Finnish bunkers in the mouth of Musta-oja Brook by Captain Netreba's battalion, 222nd Rifle Regiment. All Finnish attempts to recapture the bunkers on 10 and 11 December failed. The loss of Musta-oja Brook meant that Grendal's infantry and tanks had a perfect jump-off position for an assault across the Terenttilä fields. In the meantime, a large armoured unit, the 39th Light Tank Brigade, was arriving at the bridgehead. The grand Soviet offensive at Taipale started five days later.

The Rapids of Kiviniemi

According to the augmented offensive plan of the Seventh Army, the thrust of the Soviet advance was shifted to the Eastern Isthmus, towards Taipale and Kiviniemi. Additional units were dispatched in that direction. The 90th Rifle Division and the 24th Corps Artillery Regiment were sent towards Kiviniemi. The chief of staff of the L Rifle Corps issued the order to the 90th Rifle Division by phone at 0300 hours on 6 December 1939. According to the order, regiments of the 90th Rifle Division were to turn east and march 15–20 kilometres to arrive in Kiviniemi at dawn on 7 December.

In Kiviniemi itself, the lead elements of the 142nd Rifle Division reached the village in the early hours of 6 December, exchanging fire with Finnish delaying parties from the Rautu Group. The Finns blew up the railway bridge and highway bridge at 0535 hours and withdrew behind the rapids. The highway bridge was completely destroyed and fell into the rapids, but the railway bridge remained partially intact and one could still get across.

Around 0700 hours on 7 December the staff of the 90th Rifles received a verbal order from the chief of staff of the L Rifle Corps to be ready for the crossing by 1100 hours. The crossing was to start in the following manner: the 461st Rifle Regiment was to cross the river first, followed by the 35th Light Tank Brigade and then the 90th Rifle Division. The corps' chief of staff informed all units that the southern bank of the rapids was already clear of Finnish units and under the control of the 461st Rifle Regiment. The 90th Rifle Division's staff and the 173rd Rifle Regiment had made it to Kiviniemi by the dawn of 7 December. The 286th Regiment was about to arrive as well. However, the division's artillery was lagging behind due to traffic jams.

The Commander of the Seventh Army, Yakovlev, and the staff of the L Rifle Corps, as well as the Army's Chief of Engineers, Khrenov, were all present at Kiviniemi. The poet Alexander Tvardovski was among the military reporters accompanying the Army staff.

For some strange reason the 461st Regiment reported that the houses of Kiviniemi village on the southern bank and Suvorov's Fort were still held by Finnish delaying parties. Was this a mistake or were there indeed some Finns left in the village? It is hard to say but Finnish archive sources claim that all Finns had retreated across the rapids the previous morning. The Commander of the 461st Rifle Regiment, Major Vasiliev, was newly appointed and often lost control due to lack of experience. The commander of the 142nd Rifle Division personally led the 461st Rifle Regiment into the assault to correct the situation. Battalions of the 461st Regiment reached the southern bank of the rapids. They were the first Soviet battalions to reach the main defence line. At the same moment the Finns poured down machine-gun, mortar and artillery fire on the regiment. Previous to this, the 461st Regiment had only dealt with small Finnish delaying parties. Consequently, the Finnish fire shocked the men. For the first time on the Karelian Isthmus the Finns demonstrated their determination to fight and defend their country. The men of the 461st Regiment could not stand the unexpected and concentrated fire and withdrew from the rapids in disorder. Major Vasiliev, commander of the 461st Regiment, again lost control of his unit.

Kombrig Zaitzev, Commander of the 90th Rifle Division, saw the panic and ordered the 2nd Battalion of the 286th Rifles Regiment to take positions at the fort. Despite all attempts, the 461st Regiment could not be brought back to order, although staff of the Seventh Army also took part in the effort. It became obvious that it would take a long time to make the regiment a fighting unit again. At the same time, Yakovlev was running out of time – the Right Group of the Army started crossing the River Taipaleenjoki on 6 December.

Confusion and delay at Kiviniemi caused Yakovlev to make a fateful decision: instead of the demoralized 461st Rifle Regiment, two regiments of the 90th Rifle Division were to start the crossing immediately. Yakovlev gave this order in a conversation with Kombrig Zaitzev. The division's staff had very little time for planning, as Yakovlev ordered the crossing to start immediately after the arrival of the 5th Pontoon Battalion, which was still fighting its way through traffic jams from Leningrad. Kombrig Zaitzev and his staff only managed to visit the site of the crossing and issue preliminary orders. There was no time to wait for artillery, reconnaissance and cooperation between all arms of the division.

Anyone who has ever visited Kiviniemi – now called Losevo – and seen the rapids (a favourite place for white-water rafting) would ask this question: who would issue orders to cross the rapids on pontoons? Why didn't Zaitzev and his chief of staff immediately refuse? The report on the crossing made after the war reveals that the place of the crossing was some 500 metres upstream from the rapids, at a wider part of the Vuoksi. The report of the division stated: 'the speed of the current is insignificant, not visible'. Apparently, Zaitzev thought that if a crossing took place far enough from the rapids, the pontoons and amphibious tanks would not be drawn into them. Zaitzev did not dare make a crossing further west across the frozen lake – he had no time to send sappers to investigate the thickness of the ice.

Kombrig Zaitzev issued the following orders for the crossing: the 1st Battalion, 173rd Rifle Regiment, escorted by a company of amphibious T-37 tanks from the 339th Tank Battalion of the division, were to lead the operation. The regimental battery and anti-tank guns, as well as T-26 tanks from the 339th Tank Battalion, were to provide covering fire over open sights. All the artillery and the tanks were gathered on the bank, at the place of the crossing. After capturing a bridgehead, the battalion was to fire signal flares. The main force of the regiment and the division were to follow.

The division's artillery, as well as the corps' artillery, was still on the way. Only three artillery battalions were in position on the morning of 7 December. One more artillery battalion took up firing positions at noon. The rest of artillery was still on the move, with only 50 per cent of daily ammunition requirements at hand. There was no reconnaissance made, no phone lines laid. There was no effective artillery support for the crossing.

The only information about Finnish defences on the northern bank was to be gleaned from maps contained in the intelligence report of 1937. Commanders of the 461st Rifle Regiment could say nothing about the Finnish positions. Due to the morning skirmish with the Finns on the southern bank, the panic of the

461st Regiment and the delay of the pontoons, the crossing did not begin until the afternoon. The 1st Battalion, 173rd Rifle Regiment, reached the boarding area at 1530 hours. Six regimental guns and twelve 45mm guns were placed for direct fire in the same place. Five T-26 tanks and twelve amphibious T-37s also drove up. The lead trucks of the 5th Pontoon Battalion arrived and immediately started launching pontoons into the river.

Three pontoons were ready at 1600 hours, in the fading daylight of 7 December. Three rifle platoons and one machine-gun platoon boarded the pontoons. Out of twelve T-37 tanks only eight were ready to cross. These tiny amphibious vehicles immediately ran into trouble. One tank got caught in barbed wire and four got stuck on the rocks of the southern bank, so only three tanks escorted the pontoons. It was almost completely dark and the small landing party disappeared in the gloom.

As soon as the pontoons and tanks reached the middle of the river, a current of overwhelming power drove them towards the rapids and blown bridges. At the same moment the Finns illuminated the rapids with searchlights and opened devastating machine-gun fire at the pontoons and the crossing point on the southern bank. Finnish mortars and artillery joined the barrage as well. No signal flares were fired from the northern bank. The 2nd Company began boarding the pontoons in complete darkness under Finnish fire, before making for the northern bank. The result was the same: Finnish searchlights, machine-gun fire and complete silence on the northern bank.

However, several dozen soldiers from the first landing party made it ashore in darkness and charged the Finnish positions. Some men from the Finnish 3rd Battalion, 24th Infantry Regiment, left their positions, and troops of the Soviet 173rd Rifle Regiment made it into the basements and buildings of Kiviniemi village on the northern bank. In the darkness, confusion reigned supreme. The 1st Battalion, 24th Infantry Regiment, was replaced with the 3rd Battalion of the same regiment in the evening of 7 December.

A Soviet platoon leader made it back across the rapids via the wrecked bridge and told the tragic story. The current was so strong that all the pontoons were carried downstream into the rapids towards the blown bridges. His own pontoon reached the northern bank but casualties from Finnish fire were very heavy. The company commander went missing so the platoon leader suggested getting the 4th Company across the rapids over the blown bridge. The attempt was made but the Finns spotted the movement and opened concentrated machine-gun fire. The company returned to the southern bank, marched to the old crossing point, boarded the last three pontoons and left for the north – with obvious results. Three crews of the amphibious tanks and several riflemen made it back to the southern bank in the morning. The commander of the

1st Company was among them. The full extent of the disaster became apparent from their reports.

Hit by Finnish machine-gun fire, the pontoons started to sink, were carried downstream and thrown ashore at the southern end of the bridges. Out of nine pontoons sent across the river, only four made it to the opposite bank, with most of the men killed and wounded midstream. Nevertheless, the survivors managed to get a foothold on the northern bank, break into the village and take up defensive positions in the basements. There was no communication with them. The company commander could not fire signal flares as he accidentally dropped them into the river in the chaos of the crossing. One of the amphibious tanks hit a large rock in the rapids, capsized and sank. The two remaining tanks made it across but could not get ashore due to large boulders and thick ice. They were also carried downstream and sank in the rapids.

The crossing was called off in the morning of 8 December. The 173rd Rifle Regiment was withdrawn from the crossing point, to be replaced by the 268th Rifle Regiment. The 173rd Rifle Regiment reported 144 men missing after the fateful night crossing. Some thirty men of the regiment still held on in the basements on the opposite bank, completely isolated from the main Soviet force.

Despite this complete disaster, Yakovlev reported to Meretskov that two battalions were holding a bridgehead on the other side of the rapids. Such lies were typical for the early days of the Winter War and caused a lot of frustration and anger at High Command (Stavka) in Moscow. When it turned out that the report was untrue, both Meretskov and Yakovlev received serious warnings.

After the failure of the night crossing, the L Rifle Corps demanded that the commanders of the 142nd and 90th Divisions should continue the crossing on the remaining three pontoons, while 250 civilian rowing boats were brought from Leningrad in great haste. The crossing was to take place during the daylight hours of 8 December. However, when the new crossing was discussed, all the regimental and divisional commanders decisively protested and refused to continue sending men to slaughter. All the commanders demanded at least twenty-four hours' preparation for the crossing, as well as adequate artillery support and crossing equipment. The commander of the L Rifle Corps had to take heed of the protests and agreed to meet the demands of the divisional commanders.

The 90th Rifle Division was to cross the river in several places. The new orders were as follows:

● The crossing was to take place during the night of 9/10 December.
● The crossing was to take place along a wide front in several places.

- The crossing could only take place after proper preparation, reconnaissance and with proper support.

A sapper party was sent across the ice from Cape Lehti-kylä in order to investigate the thickness of the ice. Plans for artillery preparation and the support of advancing troops via a creeping barrage were drawn up. The sappers reported that men could cross the river on foot – the ice was over 5 centimetres thick. The 90th Rifle Division was to cross the river in two places: in the old place with boats and pontoons, and across the ice from Cape Lehti-kylä on foot. The distance between these two places was about 2 kilometres.

The Scout Company of the 588th Rifle Regiment was sent across the frozen lake on the evening of 9 December. The 2nd Battalion of the regiment stood ready on the southern bank. Late at night the scouts reported that they had crossed Vuoksi unnoticed by the Finns, taking up defensive positions on the northern bank. Everything was set and ready for the crossing, but the L Rifle Corps cancelled it.

Zaitzev and his regimental commanders did not know that Yakovlev, Commander of the Seventh Army, had lost interest in the Eastern Isthmus by 8 December. He proposed that Stavka should return to the original plan, with the main emphasis on the Vyborg strategic axis. Moscow approved Yakovlev's proposal while, at the same moment, removing him from command on the grounds of poor performance. Kirill Meretskov – leader of the entire military campaign against Finland – was demoted and put in Yakovlev's place. This shows how unhappy Stavka was with the Leningrad Military District and the Seventh Army in the first week of the war.

Nevertheless, as stated, Yakovlev's plan was approved, and a huge mass of troops marched off across the Isthmus to the west. The staffs of the L Rifle Corps, X Tank Corps, 90th Rifle Division, 35th Light Tank Brigade and 24th Corps Artillery Regiment were to relocate to the Western Isthmus within forty-eight hours. The arrival of troops at the new area of operations was set for 12 December, and they were to spend three more days in preparation for the assault on the main defence line south of Vyborg.

But the march was badly organized, especially with regard to traffic control. Apparently, the question of how such a mass of men and matériel would make it to the Western Isthmus on just two roads was not considered. The result was a gigantic traffic jam. The 24th Corps Artillery Regiment could not even begin its march, as the road was completely blocked by the 35th Light Tank Brigade. The regiment's chief of staff described the chaos:

> Due to lack of traffic controllers in the tank brigade, some supply vehicles turned towards Martikka, instead of continuing to Martikkala.

After driving some 3 kilometres in the wrong direction, these supply vehicles drove back towards the crossing at Latva-lampi. The Scout Battalion of the 90th Rifle Division had already occupied the road at the crossing. All this created a traffic jam of cars, tanks, trucks and tractors, standing in three or four rows at a length of 8–10 kilometres.

This traffic jam not only forbade our regiment from starting the march at the scheduled time, but even from leaving the firing positions. The entire mass of vehicles on the road was not protected from air attacks at all. Only the absence of Finnish heavy artillery and air assets saved us from heavy losses.

Despite the fact that a huge mass of troops was moving along the road towards Perk-järvi, for example, the 35th Light Tank Brigade, the 24th Corps Artillery Regiment, 302nd Howitzer Artillery Regiment, 1st and 2nd Battalions of the 116th Howitzer Artillery Regiment, 21st Heavy Corps Artillery Regiment and a Detached Air Defence Battalion, the road was not prepared. The L Rifle Corps could not take care of this as the 90th, 142nd and 43rd Divisions of the corps were sent into the other corps and the new divisions that the corps was supposed to receive were on the other sectors of the front. Thus, the responsibility for the march lay with the staff of the Seventh Army. Nevertheless, the landmines were not properly removed, bridges had been blown up and not repaired, and there was no cover against possible air attack. As a result of all this, the 35th Light Tank Brigade advanced very slowly, delaying the troops behind. Lack of discipline among the tank crews only aggravated the situation. Broken tanks were not removed from the road but were repaired right in the middle of it. This created additional traffic jams. For example, two broken tanks delayed the 24th Corps Artillery Regiment at Kylläetilä for four hours. It was not possible to bypass the tanks due to deep snow and there were no other roads. Due to situations like this, our march was extremely slow. We spent the night of 11/12 December on the road, expecting the 35th Light Tank Brigade to free up the road at Kylläetilä.

The disaster at Kiviniemi and the hectic shifting of troops back and forth from one strategic axis to another had far-reaching consequences. First, the Soviet offensive halted for a while, as transferring troops from the Käkisalmi axis to the Viipuri axis took a long time. Secondly, the Kiviniemi area became a quiet sector until peace was signed on 13 March 1940. This gave the Finns freedom of manoeuvre. Units of the 8th Infantry Division could be transferred from

Kiviniemi to more critical sectors of the front, such as Taipale (in December 1939) and Äyräpää (in March 1940). Thirdly, it became obvious that Meretskov's plan of defeating Finland in three weeks was failing. This caused more hectic and nervous activity among Soviet planners, and the first assault on the Mannerheim Line south of Viipuri began without proper reconnaissance and preparation. The result was heavy casualties, the complete failure of Meretskov's plans, and a month-long break in the Soviet offensive on the Karelian Isthmus.

The handful of men from the 173rd Rifles who had crossed the rapids during the night of 7 December held the basements north of the rapids until 13 December, repelling several Finnish attacks. Finnish officers had been sure that no one got across the river in the night, but on the morning of 8 December Finns came under fire from the basement of Mustonen's car repair shop, a local drug store and a local food shop. Soviet riflemen were defending several basements stubbornly, and assaulting them was a hard task. Soviet artillery also harassed the Finnish assault parties. The Finns had to bring up field guns to fire at the buildings over open sights. This assisted them in burning the drug store, but the car repair shop was too strong for field guns.

Major Sahlgren, Chief of Staff of the 8th Infantry Division, arrived in the village to inspect the situation on 11 December. When crossing the road, he was hit in the leg by a bullet from the car repair shop's basement. He fell down and a moment later a second bullet hit his head, killing him instantly, at around 1130 hours.

The next Finnish assault against the car repair shop started on the morning of 12 December. The Finns again opened fire at the Russian weapons emplacements in the basements. This led to nothing, but the Soviet riflemen returned fire, killing the six artillery horses that drew the field gun. Finally, at 1600 hours the Finns captured the local food shop, killing thirteen Soviet riflemen and taking one prisoner. The car repair shop was captured at 2300 hours. The Finns managed to approach the repair shop unnoticed and threw hand grenades and petrol bombs into the building. The petrol bombs did not ignite, but the Finns occupied the building, coming across three dead Soviet men, weapons and plenty of ammunition. The Finns did not go into the basement because, in the darkness, they could not find the door. The Finns heard conversations in Russian from the basement and stormed it the next morning, on 13 December. The Finns threw several hand grenades through the door, and pleas of surrender in Finnish were heard from the basement. Twenty-eight starving and exhausted men were taken prisoner. Two more were found dead in the basement. During the day the Finns took seven more prisoners, found hiding next to the railway bridge. The northern bank was now free from Soviet troops. Finnish casualties in the skirmishes were seventeen killed and wounded.

The Grand Soviet Offensive

The 150th and 49th Rifle Divisions had a firm bridgehead on Cape Koukkuniemi by 13 December and prepared for a breakthrough offensive against the Finnish main defence line. Meretskov issued orders for the offensive the same day. The grand offensive was planned to start on 15 December.

The divisions on the bridgehead were almost at their official strength. The 49th Rifle Division had 13,882 men, while the 150th Rifle Division had 14,764 men before the offensive. The armour of the 39th Light Tank Brigade, under Colonel Lelyushenko, and fifty flame-thrower tanks of the 204th Detached Tank Battalion, were transferred to the bridgehead and made ready to take part in the offensive.

In addition to the division's own artillery, howitzers and guns of the 116th Howitzer Regiment, the 311th Cannon Regiment and the 2nd Artillery Battalion of the 402nd Heavy Howitzer Regiment were deployed for the artillery preparation. However, the artillerymen had no time to study the Finnish defences and fired at vast areas without aiming at specific targets. Attempts to locate Finnish defences by observation from land and air failed. Finnish positions were well camouflaged; machine-gun nests were placed for flanking fire and were hard to spot from the Soviet side. Air observation did not yield results because the Finns only used sleds and ski troops to supply the front-line units. This made it impossible to trace the Finnish front line from the location of supply roads. In fact, the Finns had carried out a series of flights before the war, in order to test the visibility of prepared positions from the air: if pilots spotted any front-line troops, steps were taken to rectify their deployment.

The Soviet commanders realized that they were about to storm the main defence line and ordered the formation of assault parties comprising armour, riflemen and sappers. The entire Soviet force on the bridgehead was to take part in the offensive – all six rifle regiments. They were supported by fifty-nine T-26 tanks from the 39th Light Tank Brigade and about thirty flame-thrower tanks from the 204th Detached Tank Battalion. Each rifle regiment was given a tank company as support.

Rifle units with supporting armour moved into jump-off positions between 1100–1120 hours. The artillery barrage lasted for three hours. It looked (and sounded) impressive from the Soviet side, but did little harm to the Finnish defences. When the assault began, the Finns hit the advancing rifle units, easily pinning the Soviets down and cutting riflemen off from tanks. The tanks had to turn around, urging the men to move on, so the Soviet assault-party tactic failed from the start. The Finnish defensive tactic, by contrast, worked perfectly.

Finnish anti-tank gun crews had a great chance to fire at Soviet tanks obliged to drive back and forth across the battlefield, trying to keep the assault parties together. The Finns fired anti-tank guns from the flanks at short range, then immediately changed the gun's position. In many cases the Soviet tank crews did not even have time to notice where a shell came from. As tank commanders bitterly reflected later:

> The enemy pinned down our riflemen on numerous occasions in battle on 15 and 16 December, thus separating riflemen from tanks. Tanks drove forward without infantry support, crossed the anti-tank ditch and were executed by Finnish anti-tank guns while returning to own infantry at close range (100–150 metres).

Greeted by a wall of fire, the Soviet units advanced some 100 metres to the Finnish anti-tank ditch. Most riflemen preferred to stay there, while some tanks got stuck in the ditch. The tanks that managed to negotiate the anti-tank ditch drove forward and engaged the Finnish machine-gun crews and anti-tank gun crews alone, without infantry support. When the tanks could not find targets on the battlefield, they used their tracks to destroy Finnish barbed-wire obstacles.

The offensive was called off at 1700 hours. Only four tanks of the 39th Light Tank Brigade had returned to the rallying point at that time. Thirty-one tanks had arrived, or were towed back, by 0600 hours next morning.

Indeed, 15 December was the worst day for that brigade in the whole war: it lost twenty-five men killed, twenty-seven wounded and six missing in action. Tank losses were also extremely high: out of fifty-nine tanks that took part in the offensive only sixteen came back undamaged; sixteen had hits from Finnish AT guns, while twenty-eight were left on the battlefield, destroyed or badly damaged.

The Soviet offensive continued on 16 December but was repelled again. On that day the 39th Light Tank Brigade sent seventeen tanks into battle, losing ten during the course of the day. Seven tank men were killed, seven were wounded.

On 17 December Soviet units stormed the Finnish positions again, with no result. Losses in rifle regiments were high but registration of casualties was not arranged in December 1939, so exact information about casualties is missing. The Soviet offensive ran out of steam. Success was minimal and losses heavy. The Finns managed to destroy all Soviet penetrations with local counter-attacks and firmly held on to the main defence line. On 19 December the Chief of the General Staff of the Red Army, Komandarm 1st Class Shaposhnikov, agreed to allow the Right Group to rest.

Units of the 49th Rifle Division stormed the main defence line on 24 December for the last time that year (1939). The purpose of the offensive was to support the 4th Rifle Division, which was crossing Lake Suvanto at Kelja. This offensive was also repelled by the Finns.

According to the plan of the Seventh Army, the 142nd Rifle Division was to support the offensive in Taipale by a local attack at Kiviniemi on 15 December. The 461st Regiment tried to cross Lake Suvanto at Haitermaa but was stopped by machine-gun fire at the barbed-wire fence and had to fall back. The Soviet offensive failed and Meretskov received permission to take a pause for several days to regroup and prepare a new offensive.

The morale of the men on the bridgehead plummeted after the failure of the offensive and the high losses that followed. The Soviet military police and the surviving regimental political workers carefully tracked the morale of the Red Army men. The most common methods involved planting informers among the soldiers and reading letters bound for home. The men of the 49th and 150th Rifle Divisions were responsible for most of the critical remarks found in soldiers' correspondence. They were shocked by high casualties, lack of efficiency in the Soviet Air Force, and the scale of Finnish fortifications and resistance. For example, a soldier named Churkin, of the 150th Rifle Division, wrote to his sister, Yefimova, in Moscow:

> Sister! Starting from 6 December we have been trying to drive the enemy away and failed. I had a lot of dear friends near me, now they are no more. It was a battle. I guess you heard something about hell? The same happens here: some men cry, some complain, others shout and beg to be finished off after being wounded. The Devil himself would not understand what is going on around here.

And Sporkov, of the 222nd Rifle Regiment, wrote to Polyakova in Leningrad:

> Nyusha! The enemy is well camouflaged and delivers sure blows on us. Don't believe the newspapers – they lie. See the truth. We only advanced 3 kilometres in seven days. We lost a lot of men when crossing the river and storming the enemy's fortified line.

Borisov of the 469th Rifle Regiment wrote to his wife in Ideshkovo village, in Smolensk area:

> My wife Nastya! Our regiment suffered heavy casualties in battle against the White Finns on 6 December. About 70 per cent of men and commanders are killed or wounded. The Finns have good

fortifications here, they slow us down. We don't know about Finnish losses. Your husband.

Tarasov of the 150th Rifle Division wrote to his father in the Kursk area:

> Father! We await death every moment. Three times it was very near: one time a Finnish airplane attacked and two times we were under very heavy artillery fire. Many of my comrades were killed or wounded. There were days when 600 and 700 men were killed and wounded. Trucks are evacuating the wounded day and night. By now the artillery had been firing for sixteen days, but nothing helps to drive the Finns out of there. Their fortifications are of eleven layers of soil, then 3 metres of concrete and then more soil on top. If you end up there, you don't notice anything, until you come under fire. Gun ports open automatically and then they start pouring at our infantry and tanks. When our artillery fires at their fortifications, grenades just bounce back. Many men were killed here, many wounded also by friendly fire. We were ordered to withdraw into a forest and at this moment we are digging in against a possible Finnish air raid.

Vereshak of the 9th Battery, 328th Artillery Regiment, 150th Rifle Division, wrote to his family in the Ukraine:

> My beloved ones. There are no achievements here. We fire 100,000 rounds per day and all is in vain. There are many killed and wounded.

And Koplov of the 49th Rifle Division wrote to his family in Leningrad:

> My dear family! The Finns fire shrapnel salvos at us and very few will make it back home. One more thing – it looks like Italy and Germany are helping the Finns. We went into battle at 0800 on 30 November, and have not seen a single Soviet aircraft, just the Finnish ones. We were told that our air force is grounded due to poor visibility, but apparently the visibility is good for the Finns. If we continue fighting like this, we will not finish the war against Finland in six months, not to mention the six days as we had planned before. After twelve days of fighting we do not make it to evacuate our dead and wounded from the front line. What's next? I have no idea. We had three regiments in our 49th Rifle Division, after twelve days we have only two regiments left.

Despite the pessimistic and desperate tone of these letters, most men preferred not to disturb their loved ones at home with descriptions of the horrors

of war. Only a small percentage of letters from the front were negative or
critical. A study of men's opinions, conducted by the NKVD, is summarized in
the table below:

Date	Letters scanned	Positive	Negative
15 December 1939	4,500	4,363	147
16 December 1939	10,600	10,329	271
16 December 1939	4,550	4,421	121
19 December 1939	5,200	5,028	178
20 December 1939	4,860	4,707	153

The Final Attempt: Christmas Battle at Kelja

Meretskov, demoted to Commander of the Seventh Army, was not happy
with the results of the offensive in Taipale. Although the 49th and 150th
Divisions managed to get across the river and establish a bridgehead, there was
no decisive breakthrough. The price paid for this initial limited success was
high. A bypassing manoeuvre over the frozen Lake Suvanto, combined with a
simultaneous attack from the bridgehead, looked like a logical solution for
a quick, decisive breakthrough in the east of the isthmus.

The first units of the fresh 4th Rifle Division, transferred to the Karelian
Isthmus from Byelorussia, arrived at the Eastern Isthmus on 16 December.
According to Grendal's plan, by 20 December the units of the Right Group
were to resume the offensive towards Käkisalmi after a short rest. Soviet
divisions were to attack on a wide front from Kiviniemi to Taipale.

The 142nd Rifle Division's mission was to start the offensive east of Sakkola,
in order to distract Finnish attention and tie down Finnish reserves. The fresh
4th Rifle Division was to launch the offensive over Lake Suvanto with two
regiments (the 220th and 39th Rifle Regiments), with one regiment in reserve.
The main thrust of the division was along the Kelja–Vilakkala axis of advance,
with distractive strikes at Patoniemi and Volossula. The 150th and 49th Rifle
Divisions were to hit the Finns simultaneously from the Taipale bridgehead
with all six regiments, or whatever was left of them.

According to this plan, the units on the bridgehead started a two-hour
artillery preparation at 1400 hours on 24 December and attacked along the
entire front. Rifle units made small, local, penetrations but were thrown back
by Finnish counter-attacks. Soviet units resumed the offensive on the bridgehead on 25 and 26 December, but failed to achieve a breakthrough. The Military
Council of the Seventh Army ordered the units of the Right Group to dig in

and halt all offensives on 27 December 1939. On that day it was obvious that the offensive had failed on the entire front from Kiviniemi to Lake Ladoga.

The 4th Rifle Division began its offensive in the early hours of 25 December. The front on Lake Suvanto had been quiet all December – the Soviets had only sent a few scout parties across the ice. Finnish officers and soldiers were in a relaxed mood and the Soviet offensive caught them almost completely offguard.

The 39th Rifle Regiment crossed the ice of the lake at Volossula and Patoniemi and established tiny bridgeheads, but was driven back across the ice by the afternoon of 25 December. Finnish artillery and the Patoniemi cannon fort forbade any movement of Soviet reserves from the southern bank. The 1st Battalion of the 30th Infantry Regiment succeeded in the very first counter-attack, although Battalion Commander Major Jaakko Sohlo was killed in the battle. Total losses for the Finnish battalion on 25 December were forty-six men, with nineteen of them killed.

The Soviet assault at Kelja created a much more complicated situation for the Finns. The 2nd Battalion, 220th Rifle Regiment, and a scout company of the 101st Rifle Regiment crossed the ice unnoticed in the early hours of 25 December. The offensive was supported by the 80th Anti-tank Artillery Battalion and the entire artillery of the 4th Rifle Division.

Finnish officers in the sector ignored intelligence reports about the coming Soviet offensive time and again. A Finnish scout party reached the southern bank of the lake in the evening of 24 December and saw that the whole forest on the southern bank was swarming with Soviet riflemen. The scout party reported this to their battalion commander, but Captain Mueller, Commander of the 3rd Battalion, 29th Infantry Regiment, did not take any measures to strengthen his defences on the northern bank of the lake. According to some sources, the battalion's staff had already celebrated Christmas at a table with plenty of food and alcohol. Lauri Keskinen, a signals operator with the 3rd Battalion, 29th Infantry Regiment, recalled:

> It was all quiet on Christmas Eve, and all hell broke loose on Christmas Day. I am still amazed – in the first hours of Christmas Day, at 2 or 4 a.m., we received a message that a Russian attack could start any time soon. The battalion commander did not react to this message at all! At that moment the battalion commander had the situation completely out of control. Luckily, we managed to stop the offensive in the end.

Forward Soviet platoons reached the northern bank and easily forced the Finnish outposts to withdraw. The first report from the lake informed Mueller

about one platoon of Red Army men on the northern bank. Mueller decided
that this was a small scout party and remained idle. A bit later a report
concerning a Soviet company came in. Two squads, under the command of a
chemical defence officer, were sent into a counter-attack. The latter returned
to the battalion HQ at 1400 hours and reported that the Russian bridgehead
was destroyed. Mueller reported this to the regimental HQ and went to rest.
His report bore little resemblance to reality: the 2nd Battalion, 220th Rifle
Regiment, and the scout company of the 101st Rifle Regiment still held on to a
bridgehead some 700 metres wide and 700 metres deep on the fields of Kelja
village. The 6th Company, 30th Infantry Regiment, arrived from Taipale to
Kelja by forced march and started their assault at 0830 hours, still in darkness.
The assault failed immediately, and the company lost a quarter of its men in a
matter of minutes: seven men were killed and thirty wounded. The 6th Company
was ordered to attack again but the company commander asked for rest and
replenishment. The men were too exhausted.

Captain Mueller realized the scale of the threat as late as the morning of
26 December. Both his counter-attacks failed and reinforcements were brought
along from Kirvesmäki area. Two companies from the 3rd Battalion of the
28th Infantry Regiment arrived at Kelja. According to the Finnish plan, the two
companies were to start the attack at 1715 hours, after a short artillery barrage,
with suppressing fire from Finnish machine-guns. One minute before the
offensive, the Finnish machine-guns opened fire, and although the Finnish guns
remained silent, the companies went forward. It turned out that the Finnish
artillery battalion that was supposed to support the attack did not receive the
order to open fire. Nevertheless, the Finns managed to close with the Soviet
defenders. Soviet commanders fired three red flares and Finnish companies
were hit by all seventy-two guns and howitzers of the 4th Rifle Division. The
Finns had to withdraw in the twilight of evening, after taking casualties. Both
companies disengaged and then marched back to Kirvesmäki.

Although the Finns did not manage to destroy the Soviet bridgehead on
25 and 26 December, Finnish artillery fire, along with fire from the Kekkiniemi
Fort, completely stopped any movement across the lake by Soviet troops. The
Finns also managed to silence the greater part of the Soviet guns firing over
open sights from the ice of the lake and its southern bank.

The commander of the 4th Rifle Division lost his great chance to crush the
Finns in his sector. The Chief of the General Staff, Komandarm 1st Class
Shaposhnikov, harshly criticized the 4th Division for taking too long sending
the rest of the division across the lake. A reinforced rifle battalion was definitely
not enough to continue the offensive from the bridgehead and was barely
holding out against the Finnish counter-attacks. In fact, the reinforced battalion

of the 220th Rifle Regiment was seen as a scout party, not as the main striking unit of the regiment and the division.

The Finns were alerted by the events at Kelja and no other Soviet unit made it across the ice of the lake. Let's take the example of the 101st Rifle Regiment, which tried to make it across the lake to the bridgehead. The 7th Company of the regiment, with a machine-gun platoon and a platoon of 45mm anti-tank guns, started a reconnaissance in force on the lake. When the company was some 80 metres from the northern bank, the Finns opened a devastating fire from the Kekkiniemi Fort. Nine men were killed, thirteen were left abandoned on the battlefield.

Late in the evening of 26 December the 101st Rifle Regiment attacked across the lake in order to assist the men on the bridgehead. The 2nd Battalion marched off across the ice at 2330 hours, the 3rd Battalion at midnight, and the 1st Battalion joined the battle at 0400. The regiment was trying to make it to the eastern part of the bridgehead at Kelja. The 2nd Battalion reached the northern bank but was pinned down by Finnish machine-gun fire, taking heavy casualties and falling back on the southern bank. The 1st and the 3rd Battalions fared little better. The regiment lost fifty-seven men killed and 367 men wounded. Some 318 men did not make it back from the ice field and no one knew whether they were dead, alive or taken prisoner. The regiment's commissar, Bezborodov, was wounded; the political worker of the 2nd Battalion, Vorobyev, was killed; and the commander of the 2nd Battalion, Captain Lukyanenko, was wounded. Several company commanders were lost as well. The chief of staff of the 1st Battalion did not make it back from the ice field. He carried all the commanders' codes and decoding tables with him.

The Finnish 6th Detached Battalion under Major Saarelainen (a unit dubbed 'The Hounds of Saarelainen') arrived to take care of the Soviet bridgehead. The new assault was to begin at 0900 hours next morning. However, the battalion was not ready in time, so the assault was postponed until 1030. Again, Finnish officers forgot to inform the artillery of the delay. Consequently, the Finnish artillery fired at 0900 hours, one and a half hours before the actual infantry assault. The battalion encountered even more problems with fire support: only two machine-guns of the battalion managed to find good positions to support the assault. The machine-gun crews of Captain Mueller bluntly refused to provide suppressing fire, having hit their own troops by mistake the night before. The mortar platoon of the battalion was in position already in the evening of 26 December, but one mortar base had been left forgotten in Rautu, on the other bank of Suvanto, before the war. This meant the battalion only had one mortar to support the assault.

The 1st and the 3rd Companies charged across the open field at 1030 hours. They had to fall back one hour later, after taking heavy casualties. Signals operator Lauri Keskinen saw how the battle progressed: 'I was a couple of hundred metres from the jump-off position of the 6th Detached Battalion and I saw them charging forward. It was insane, many men died in vain. This all looked useless to me.'

Despite the first failure, the assault was repeated at 1145 hours and the Finns managed to reach the Soviet positions, advancing along the bank of Suvanto. The battle immediately became a hand-to-hand fight.

Meretskov had lost interest in the entire offensive of the Right Group even before the first difficulties at Kelja. One more time his troops failed to reach a quick, decisive victory. The entire offensive was called off and the few brave defenders of the bridgehead were ordered to fall back during the night of 26/27 December. Apparently, the Finns engaged those who failed to withdraw, and those who remained at the bridgehead to cover the withdrawal of their comrades. After a long and fierce hand-to-hand fight, the Finns pushed the last defenders of the bridgehead onto the ice. The entire Finnish main defence line was again intact. After the battle was over, the Finns witnessed the stoicism of the last defenders: a Soviet machine-gunner remained standing at his weapon in a trench – the man was stone-dead but did not fall, as his body was almost completely buried in empty cartridges.

Individual Red Army men continued to resist on the northern bank of Suvanto, firing from the barns and hay stacks during 28 December. Most of them were taken prisoner. The men that ran across the ice towards the southern bank were almost completely wiped out. As the Finns calmly observed, only eleven men made it across the lake. Junior Lieutenant Kuzmenkov, who withdrew from the bridgehead in the night and survived, recalled:

> We held out in the ditch for forty-eight hours, without food and water. Finally we received an order to fall back. We started to with-draw during the night. We could not take the body of our Senior Lieutenant Kuksov with us. We had to leave him on the spot. Twenty-two men were left alive from our battalion, the rest were killed or wounded.

Losses of the 6th Detached Battalion in battle on 27 December were also heavy: forty-nine killed and 101 wounded. Officers of the battalion had extremely heavy casualties. The Finns collected 140 machine-guns, 1,700 rifles, twelve anti-tank guns and other equipment from the battlefield and the ice of the lake. When local Finnish peasants returned to Kelja village in 1942, they saw a

Russian mass grave on a field by their village. The text on the grave stated that this was the final resting place of 850 men and commanders from the 4th Rifle Division.

This failure was the last assault on the Mannerheim Line in the Eastern Isthmus. A static warfare began. Soviet units were sending scout parties, preparing for the new assault, taking stock and studying the mistakes of the first month of the war. The Finns remained idle, watching the enemy's lines and building additional fortifications in the rear. Both sides knew all too well that the second round would follow and the Red Army would try its best to take revenge and restore its reputation. The December battles on the Eastern Isthmus were over.

Central Isthmus: the New Axis of Advance

The Stavka agreed to shift the main strike from Käkisalmi to the Viipuri strategic axis as early as 8 December. The plan was to march the X Tank Corps, the 90th Rifle Division, the 35th Light Tank Brigade and supporting artillery to the Western Isthmus in three days, from 9–12 December. The newly arrived units would then spend five days preparing a new offensive and spotting Finnish fortifications. The grand offensive was to start on 17 December – almost simultaneously with the offensive in Taipale sector.

In reality, the march from the Eastern Isthmus took much longer. The last units arrived in their positions on the evening of 16 December – just a few hours before the beginning of the scheduled grand offensive (the result would be a complete failure of the entire offensive). The main blow was to fall along the highway in the Summa village sector. Distracting strikes were to be delivered in Lähde, Merkki, Tassiolammet, Suurniemi, Oinala and Muolaa Church village sectors.

Merkki Sector – Swamps at the Railway

The 24th Rifle Division, supported by the 40th Light Tank Brigade, reached the area of Perk-järvi Station village on 6 December and continued the offensive along the railway. The commander of the 24th Rifle Division, Kombrig Veshev, was killed in action on the same day. He was replaced by Kombrig Galitski. Before the arrival of the 90th Rifle Division, the 24th attacked the Finnish main defence line on a wide front of 9 kilometres, from Munasuo Swamp in the west to the western bank of Muolaanjärvi in the east. The division had no connection with its neighbour on the left, the 123rd Rifle Division. Due to the wide front of attack, the division had to assault with all three regiments abreast, with the 168th Regiment attacking along the railway, the 274th Regiment attacking Tassiolammet in the middle, and the 7th Regiment attacking along the western bank of Muolaanjärvi. The 175th Tank Battalion of the 40th Light Tank Brigade was attached to the division. Rifle regiments assaulted the Finnish positions on 8 December but failed to penetrate the line. The 40th Light Tank Brigade lost twelve tanks on that day as a result of Finnish anti-tank fire. The 168th Regiment failed even to drive away the Finnish outposts on the River Kosenjoki, at the railway. All attacks after 8 December were called off and the 24th Rifle Division waited for the arrival of the 90th Rifle Division, which was still fighting its way through traffic jams on the roads from Kiviniemi.

The 24th Division resumed the offensive after the arrival of the 90th Division but failed to achieve any significant results. On 18 December the 7th Regiment, supported by the 2nd Company, 157th Tank Battalion, attacked towards Väisänen, a small farm on the western bank of Muolaanjärvi. Tanks were stopped by anti-tank obstacles and came under Finnish anti-tank fire. One tank was knocked out and left on the battlefield, another took two hits but managed to drive away from the battlefield.

The 7th Rifle Regiment repeated the attack on the next days, supported by the 1st and 3rd Companies of the 155th Tank Battalion. The result of the battle was six knocked-out tanks. Four tanks were left on the battlefield, one of them burnt out. Five tank men were killed, six were wounded. Riflemen of the 7th Regiment could not go forward at all. Such fruitless attacks continued in the sector of the 24th Division until the end of December. The Finns held their positions without any difficulties.

In the meantime, the 90th Rifle Division finally arrived from Kiviniemi and took up half of the sector from the 24th Rifle Division on its left flank. The 90th Rifle Division attacked the Finnish main defence line with two regiments: the 588th Regiment, under Major Bogdanov, attacked Finnish positions on the tall banks of Musta-oja Brook, while the 173rd Regiment, under Major Bondarev, attacked Hill 44.8 at Lampestenoja Brook. The 3rd Company, 160th Tank Battalion, supported the 173rd Regiment. The 286th Rifle Regiment was in reserve behind the 173rd Regiment, ready to go into battle and build on its sister regiment's success after the breakthrough. The 339th Tank Battalion of the division, with a company of eight T-26 tanks and twelve T-37 tanks, was in reserve at Perkjärvi Station village. The Sapper and Scout battalions of the division were also stationed there. The 45mm anti-tank guns from the division's 66th Anti-tank Battalion also reinforced the 173rd and 588th Rifle Regiments. The sister regiments at the front lacked communications. The 173rd Regiment also had no contact with its neighbour on the left, the 123rd Rifle Division, which was storming Finnish positions at Lähde.

The 90th Rifle Division arrived at the new sector without fuel, fodder or large stocks of food. Supply units of the division were still stuck in traffic jams.

This immediately had a negative impact on the division's horses. The supply situation of the division improved only one week later. The situation with supply was critical: while commanders could tell their men to survive without food for a day or two, horses accepted no explanations and could not work without proper nutrition. The report: 'men are all right and can hold on for a day or two, but horses are starving and cannot work' is often seen in Soviet documents from the Winter War.

On 16 December the T-26 Tank Company was attached to the 1st Battalion of the 588th Regiment in order to support the attack of the battalion towards Musta-oja Brook. The assault was to begin immediately after minefields and barricades were cleared. Again, just as at Kiviniemi, the division was not given enough time to prepare the offensive or carry out reconnaissance of the Finnish defences.

The 3rd Battalion, 13th Infantry Regiment, and detached battalions of the 1st Brigade were holding the sector in front of the 90th Rifle Division. The Finns had vast minefields, barricades and barbed-wire fences built in front of their positions. Sectors of fire were cleared in front of Finnish positions, as the entire sector was almost completely covered with forest. In the sector of the 3rd Battalion, 13th Infantry Regiment, the fortified line had to be built on a swamp, with a trench built of soil and logs. It was not possible to dig in the wet ground. According to the accounts of Finnish veterans, the field fortifications were in rather weak shape. Lack of time and the swampy terrain deprived the Finns of the chance to construct a strong defence line. Anti-tank defences of the Finnish battalions were also in a pitiful state. Toivo Ahtimo, a soldier from the 3rd Battalion, 13th Infantry Regiment, recalled:

> Anti-tank defence skills that we were taught in peacetime were of little use. The manuals told us that one could stop a tank by putting a crowbar or a log into its tracks! One man from the 7th Company, Vieno Loimu from Loimaa, tried to stop a Russian tank in this way at Lampestenoja. His crowbar flew out of the tank's tracks with a horrible sound, inflicting no damage on the tank. Loimu grabbed a thick log and pushed it into the tank's track. The log turned into a pile of tooth sticks that would be enough for a whole company. The tank drove on until it was destroyed by a satchel charge.
>
> The second recommendation to stop a tank was to fire a shotgun at point-blank range at the tank's observation slits! Some men brought shotguns along from home to the front, but I never heard of anyone using them like this in the war.

After the outbreak of war we received a new anti-tank manual. In general, the message of the manual was that tanks were not something to be afraid of. We were also recommended to remove road signs in the rear, so that the enemy's tanks would get lost in our rear after a breakthrough.

Snow was just 30–40 centimetres deep in the central parts of the Karelian Isthmus. Cold weather was yet to arrive, so it was just minus 4 degrees Celsius on the morning of 17 December 1939.

The 90th Rifle Division went over to the offensive with two regiments on that day. The 588th Rifle Regiment, attacking in the direction of Musta-oja, came across booby-trapped barricades of logs and barbed-wire obstacles. The tank company of eight T-26 tanks remained at the jump-off positions, supporting the assaulting riflemen with fire. The tanks could not move forward as sappers had failed to make passages for them in the barricade line. The Finns managed to knock out one tank. Major Bogdanov, commander of the 588th Rifle Regiment, ordered the regimental 76mm guns to be moved into positions to fire over open sights.

The 1st and 2nd Battalions of the regiment assaulted the Finnish defences without tank support and were stopped by Finnish fire at the barbed-wire fence. All attempts to move forward failed. Twenty-three commanders and eighty-eight junior commanders and men were wounded in the battle. It was not possible to count the dead due to the continuing fighting. Two regimental guns were hit by Finnish mortars and knocked out.

The 173rd Rifle Regiment assaulted Hill 44.8 supported by the 1st Company, 160 Tank Battalion, but failed to capture it. The Finns managed to pin down the Soviet riflemen. When tanks approached the Finnish trenches, they were hit by Finnish anti-tank guns at a distance of about 50 metres. Four tanks were knocked out and remained on the battlefield. Two tanks managed to break through the Finnish line and were later destroyed in the Finnish rear.

The offensive continued on 18 December. Major Bogdanov formed assault parties in his regiment with the task of making passages in the barricades and minefields. His assault parties failed. Again the regiment's battalions stood up and charged against the Finnish line with the support of regimental guns, 45mm guns and mortars. Two regimental guns were knocked out, after firing some ninety rounds at the Finnish fortifications. The 45mm guns fired half their daily ammunition ration. The tank company lost three more tanks and was withdrawn from the front to HQ of the 588th Regiment by order of the division's chief of staff. Total losses of the 1st Battalion of the 588th Regiment had reached 377 men since the beginning of the campaign.

The 173rd Regiment lost commanders of the 1st, 2nd, 4th and 8th Companies wounded on 18 December. The 1st and 2nd Companies had only one commander left per company. The 286th Regiment was deployed on the left flank of the 173rd Regiment, bypassing Hill 44.8 from the left, but was stopped by Finnish fire.

All three regiments of the division continued their assaults on 19 December and suffered heavy casualties, especially in commanders. The 173rd Regiment lost almost all company commanders; the Chief of Staff of the 3rd Battalion was also wounded, as was the Chief of Staff of the 173rd Regiment.

The 286th Regiment continued the offensive on the left flank of the division. The regiment's artillerymen carried their guns into position on their shoulders – horses and gun tractors were of no use in the swamps of the Merkki sector. The mortar platoon of the 2nd Battalion got too close to the front line, was spotted by the Finns, and was immediately exterminated in a hail of Finnish machine-gun fire. The 286th Regiment lost fifteen men killed and forty-one wounded, including five commanders, on that day.

The 588th Regiment lost about eighty men killed in the 1st and 2nd Battalions. The chief of staff of the 1st Battalion was wounded, his deputy killed. The Chief of Chemical Defence of the regiment, Major Nechaev, was killed, and the commander of the 3rd Battalion was wounded. In addition to this, the regimental artillery battery lost three section leaders wounded.

The 173rd Regiment was withdrawn from the front line on 20 December and replaced by the 286th Regiment. The 286th lost twenty-three men killed and 170 wounded during the day. The only achievement for this price was that the regiment's outposts could now dig in at the third row of Finnish barbed wire. Major Nikiforov, Commander of the 2nd Battalion, and Senior Lieutenant Kuchin, Chief of Staff of the 2nd Battalion, were wounded. The commissar of the regiment Vorobyev was also wounded.

The 588th Regiment again stormed the Finnish positions at Musta-oja after a two-hour artillery bombardment. The 1st and 2nd Battalions of the regiment went into battle. The 2nd and 3rd Companies fled the battlefield in panic immediately after coming under Finnish fire. Despite this disaster, Major Kuzmin, commander of the 1st Battalion, reported to the regiment that his companies had crossed the brook. The lie was soon revealed. Major Bogdanov, commander of the 588th Regiment, lost his patience and went to the front line to lead the assault of the 2nd Battalion in person. There was almost no one left to lead, as the battalion had shrunk to about 100 riflemen. The 3rd Battalion had lost almost all members of its machine-gun company. Men dug in, and it was almost impossible to make them stand up and charge forward. Despite this, the regimental commander ordered the assaults to continue until the mission was completed. The 2nd Battalion attacked the Finnish lines three times, and three times its assault was repelled. The commander of the 2nd Battalion, Lieutenant Lazarev, was wounded in the final assault and only after this was the battalion withdrawn.

Major Bogdanov was planning to assault Finnish positions at Musta–oja again on 21 December with armour and artillery support, but the assault had to be cancelled. Regimental mortar crews forgot to bring enough ammunition to the front line, while the commander of the tank company, Lieutenant Shartanov, was apparently unwilling to drive across the swamp again under the fire of Finnish anti-tank guns. He used all sorts of excuses to delay the departure of his company to the front. As darkness set in, Shartanov called Major Bogdanov and informed him that it was too late to go to the front line as it was already dark. Bogdanov was outraged but the attack had to be postponed until the next day. Bogdanov scolded the mortar crews of his regiment and filed an official complaint about Shartanov to the division commander.

Only 561 men were left in the 588th Regiment by the morning of 22 December 1939. The 1st Battalion had 325, the 2nd 125, and the 3rd just 111. Despite these staggering losses, Major Bogdanov insisted on a continuation of the attack. Regimental assault parties tried to set Finnish log barricades on fire, in order to detonate any booby-traps, but the logs would not burn. The 2nd Battalion, supported by the T-26 company (two cannon tanks and four machine-gun tanks), which had finally arrived, charged the Finnish lines again. The 45mm guns and regimental guns supported the assault. The regiment's artillerymen managed to suppress one Finnish MG bunker and scored five direct hits on a second, but the Finnish system of fire remained intact. The battalion was pinned down at the approaches to the brook. Men refused to stand up and charge forward, despite all the efforts of their commanders. Tank men decided to assist the infantry commanders in rallying the men: the political worker of the tank company plus a platoon leader climbed out of the tanks and tried to get the riflemen to attack. They also failed. Both brave tank men were wounded. Two tanks threw tracks in the swamp. Two more tankers were wounded while trying to repair the tanks. By 1700 hours the remains of the battalion had dug in before the Finnish barbed-wire fence and were engaged in a firefight with the Finns.

The regiments of the division successfully repelled the Finnish counter-offensive on 23 December. The 588th Regiment captured three heavy machine-guns, one Suomi submachine-gun, ten sleds, eighty-six ammo boxes, six tripods and thirteen rifles. Fifty-nine Finnish corpses were counted on the battlefield. Three Finns were taken prisoner; one of them had been wounded and abandoned on the battlefield during the Finnish retreat. The losses of the 588th Regiment were eighteen killed, twenty-six wounded, and nine missing in action. On the same day the regiment received the order to cease attacks due to heavy losses.

It turned out after the battle that Finnish troops attacked through an unguarded gap between the 173rd and 588th Regiments. The distance between the two regiments was about 1 kilometre of unguarded forest and bog. Lieutenant Levin, commander of the 3rd Battalion, 588th Regiment, was ordered to establish contact with his sister regiment. Levin personally led a ski patrol, which set out for the 173rd Regiment. The patrol got lost and spent the whole night circling around the forest. On the morning of 25 December Levin returned and reported his failure to Major Bogdanov. Levin was immediately dismissed as a battalion commander. Lieutenant Paluhin was tasked to take over the battalion, but even after the third order to comply, Paluhin openly refused to take command. Consequently, both lieutenants were immediately sent to divisional HQ. As a final gesture, Major Bogdanov sent an extremely negative description of Lieutenant Levin, writing to divisional HQ: 'I am sending him to you, as he is unable to lead a unit of any size.'

Despite the failure of the Finnish counter-attack, measures to strengthen discipline and defensive lines were taken in the 90th Division. Political workers and commanders held talks with the men about holding the ground, the consequences of panic, and the meaning of the 'not a step back' order. The regiments dug in properly, while sentry and guard services were improved.

For three more days – on 27, 28 and 29 December – the 286th and the 588th Regiments attacked the Finnish main defence line, only to be beaten back with casualties. On 28 December the 286th Regiment lost 100 men wounded and seventeen killed; the 588th Regiment forty-one men killed, thirty-two wounded, and twenty-three missing in action. The offensive of the 90th Division had run out of steam.

Total losses for the 588th Regiment in December 1939, since the beginning of the campaign, were 227 killed, 611 wounded, four missing in action, and 788 men frostbitten. The 286th Regiment lost 101 men killed, 662 men wounded, and four frostbitten. The 173rd Regiment lost 156 men killed, 665 men wounded, 245 men missing in action (due to the fateful crossing at Kiviniemi), and 133 men frostbitten.

Morale in the division's units was ebbing away, largely due to the high casualties sustained in fruitless assaults. Tank man Ustinov, fighting in the division's 339th Tank Battalion, wrote to his parents:

> Dear parents! By this day about one-half of our battalion's men and commanders have been killed. Tanks have drowned [Author's Note: during the failed crossing at Kiviniemi.]. The surviving men are

missing a foot or a hand or a leg or something else. We have very few
tanks and men left. Our artillery fires day and night, but we cannot
drive them away from their fortified line.

Replacements started arriving in the division on 30 December. Some replacements that arrived at the 286th Regiment had no military training at all. A quiet
period began in the Merkki sector, during which battle training and careful
reconnaissance of the Finnish main defence line were initiated.

Lieutenant Vasily Skvortsov, a 26-year-old career officer, fought in the ranks
of the 90th Rifle Division in December 1939. He commanded a gun section in
the 66th Anti-tank Battalion. Here is an extract from the first and last letter he
wrote to his older brother, Captain Yevgeny Skvortsov, Chief of Staff of the
3rd Battalion, CCLXVII Corps Heavy Artillery Regiment:

> Their fortifications are strong – made from stone and concrete. Your
> guns would be of great help, brother [the regiment of Yevgeny
> Skvortsov had 152mm and 203mm guns]. I guess we are getting the
> heavy artillery here later, but now we approach their fortifications as
> close as we can and fire at them almost at point-blank range.

On 28 December 1939, as the 588th Rifle Regiment tried in vain to break into
the Finnish positions at Musta-oja, Vasily Skvortsov was supporting them
with his guns over open sights. A splinter from a Finnish mortar round struck
his breast, killing him immediately. This was the first loss in the Skvortsov
family in the Second World War. His older brother, Captain Yevgeny
Skvortsov, arrived at the Karelian Isthmus with his regiment in late February
1940. His regiment went into battle against the Finnish main defence line some
20 kilometres east from the place where his younger brother died. Photos taken
by Captain Skvortsov are included in this book.

The Finns easily repelled all assaults by Red Army units in the other
sectors of defence on the Central Isthmus. Cooperation between different
arms of the Red Army did not work properly and the Finnish tactic of rigid
defence worked perfectly in December 1939.

For example, the 1st and 2nd Companies of the 161st Tank Battalion
stormed Muolaa village five times and penetrated the Finnish lines, but
the riflemen of the 43rd Rifle Division did not arrive and the tanks had to fall
back. As a result, four tanks were knocked out; five tanks were hit but could
still move. One tank drove into the Finnish rear and vanished there. The
43rd Rifle Division attacked on a very wide front from the eastern bank of Lake
Muolaanjärvi to Valkjärvi but the men were spread too thinly and the result
was nothing but heavy casualties.

Finnish machine-gun bunker No. 7 in the Inkilä sector, spring 1940. Note the small size of the gun ports in the armoured wall.
(*St Petersburg State Photo Archive*)

Red Army men study a Finnish anti-tank rock fence.
(*Natalia Filippova collection*)

Soviet men study bunker No. 4 'Poppius' after the assault.
(*Author's collection*)

A Finnish machine-gun
bunker in Muolaa,
spring 1940.
(*Colonel Skvortsov's collection*)

Finnish barbed-wire fence
and T-shaped markers for
aiming from bunkers,
Muolaa sector.
(*Colonel Skvortsov's collection*)

The reinforced banks of
the River Muolaanjoki.
(*Colonel Skvortsov's collection*)

Finnish soldiers in improvised snow camouflage, early in the Winter War, Karelian Isthmus. (*Author's collection*)

Finnish soldiers in working overalls during the construction of fortifications. They had a sign reading: '30 November 1939, the first day of war between Finland and Russia, shore of the Gulf of Finland. The "Exam" of our engineer course. Our course ended just in time.' (*Author's collection*)

On the first day of the war Finnish farms were set on fire by Finnish delaying troops. Note the light spread of snow on the ground. (*St Petersburg State Photo Archive*)

Evacuation of wounded, 462nd Mobile Surgery Unit, Red Army, Western Isthmus.
(*Author's collection*)

Soviet riflemen attack.
(*Author's collection*)

A female journalist lieutenant, interviewing the men of an automobile battalion.
(*St Petersburg State Photo Archive*)

Soviet commanders examine war booty, early in the Winter War.
(*St Petersburg State Photo Archive*)

Finnish tree barricades in forest.
(*Author's collection*)

Captain Laakso (commander of the 3rd Battalion, 13th Infantry Regiment) and his men posing with a T-26 of the 40th Light Tank Brigade, Lampestenoja Brook area, December 1939. The tank was knocked out by a direct hit from a 37mm round on the side, under the turret.
(*Author's collection*)

Finnish machine-gun bunker No. 7 in the Inkilä sector, spring 1940. Note the small size of the gun ports in the armoured wall. (*St Petersburg State Photo Archive*)

Red Army men study a Finnish anti-tank rock fence. (*Natalia Filippova collection*)

Soviet men study bunker No. 4 'Poppius' after the assault. (*Author's collection*)

Equipment of the
34th Light Tank Brigade
captured by the Finns in
Lemetti.
(*Author's collection*)

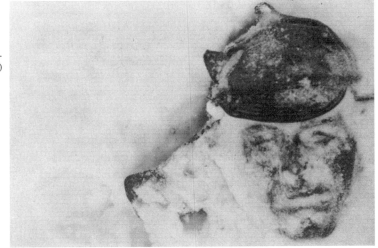

A dead Red Army man.
(*Author's collection*)

In the tundra at Pechenga.
(*St Petersburg State Photo Archive*)

Finnish ski troops in
Suomussalmi.
(*Author's collection*)

Soviet prisoners of war i
Suomussalmi.
(*Author's collection*)

A Finnish war booty
collection area.
(*Author's collection*)

ad Soviet ski troopers,
ihmo area.
Author's collection)

A Soviet M-4 anti-aircraft
machine-gun mounted on
a truck, Lemetti area.
(*Author's collection*)

Soviet prisoners of war.
(*Author's collection*)

Finnish front-line soldiers in Löytövaara at the end of the war. The second man from the right has war booty AVS-36 automatic rifle that he took from Soviet ski troops. (*Author's collection*)

Soviet armour commanders planning the Mannerheim Line breakthrough: Deputy Commander 20th Tank Brigade, Military Engineer 2nd Class Oleinikov; commander of the armoured units of the Seventh Army, Kombrig Vershinin; and Colonel Dementiev. (*Author's collection*)

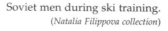

Soviet men during ski training. (*Natalia Filippova collection*)

(*Left*) A Soviet scout captured by the Finns, January 1940, Lähde area. (*Author's collection*)

(*Right*) Lieutenant Stepan Komlev, Company Commander, 91st Tank Battalion, 20th Tank Brigade. Awarded the Gold Star of the Hero of the Soviet Union for the action on the Mannerheim Line, he was killed in action in Lithuania as commander of a tank battalion holding the rank of captain on 10 October 1944. (*St Petersburg State Photo Archive*)

Red Army men study captured guns of the 2nd Detached Artillery Battalion. (*St Petersburg State Photo Archive*)

A Soviet commander
examines the captured
bunker No. 2 'Terttu'.
(*St Petersburg State Photo Archive*)

A piece of bunker No. 11
'Peltola', thrown off the
bunker by an explosion.
(*St Petersburg State Photo Archive*)

A Soviet heavy Maxim
machine-gun on skis.
(*Author's collection*)

The ruins of the Church of
Muolaa.
(*Colonel Skvortsov's collection*)

A general view of
Kirka-Muolaa Church Hill.
(*Colonel Skvortsov's collection*)

A destroyed Finnish
anti-tank gun.
(*Colonel Skvortsov's collection*)

Men of the 306th Rifle Regiment go on the assault.
(*St Petersburg State Photo Archive*)

A dead Finnish soldier.
(*Colonel Skvortsov's collection*)

The body of a Finnish soldier burnt by a flame-thrower. The location is Muolaa, probably bunker No. 14.
(*Colonel Skvortsov's collection*)

(*Left*) A Finnish bunker destroyed by artillery in Ilves village, April 1940. (*Colonel Skvortsov's collection*)
(*Right*) Senior Lieutenant Vasily Moiseev, Company Commander, 232nd Tank Battalion. (*Moiseev's family archive*)

Soviet machine-gun crew in action. (*Author's collection*)

A Finnish coastal cannon captured on Ravansaari.
(*St Petersburg State Photo Archive*)

Finnish prisoners of war.
(*St Petersburg State Photo Archive*)

The crew of a Soviet 82mm mortar getting into position. Note the special equipment of Soviet ski troopers.
(*St Petersburg State Photo Archive*)

The Main Strike: Lähde and Summa Village

Two battalions of the 15th Infantry Regiment from Häme province of Finland defended the sectors in Summa village and Lähde. The 1st Battalion of the regiment, under the command of energetic Jaeger Captain Auno Kuiri, was defending the Lähde sector. The battalion arrived at the Lähde sector in October 1939 and had spent the two last months before the war in intensive training and construction of fortifications.

In addition to the concrete bunkers in the area, some eighteen wood-and-soil machine-gun bunkers were constructed along the whole length of the sector, from Munasuo Swamp to Lake Summajärvi. An anti-tank ditch was dug at Munasuo Swamp. Platoon strongpoints were built for all-round defence, which could provide covering fire for each other. The directions of counter-attacks, in case of a Soviet breakthrough, were rehearsed time and again. In October firing exercises with live ammunition began.

The Soviet 123rd Rifle Division, under Colonel Stenshinski, made first contact with the Finnish main defence line on 11–12 December. First, Soviet scout parties emerged in front of the Finnish outposts and began digging in 300 metres from the Finnish obstacle lines. The Finns withdrew their outposts behind the main defence line on the same day. Soviet armour arrived on 13 December, inspecting the Finnish obstacle lines and firing at the anti-tank rocks (these were granite boulders, some 70–100 cm high, placed in four rows). Finnish artillery tried to knock out the tanks with indirect fire but failed. The 1st Battalion of the 245th Rifle Regiment received an order to capture Hill 65.5 and advanced along the road but was stopped immediately by crossfire from all the bunkers of the defence sector. At twilight the battalion withdrew to the edge of a forest and dug in. Small units of the 245th Regiment carried out reconnaissance-in-force on 14, 15 and 16 December, supported by a light tank company. On 15 December the Finns managed to knock out three T-26 tanks at Poppius bunker, with two tanks burnt out and abandoned by their crews on the battlefield. Rifle companies of the 255th and 245th Regiments of the 123rd Rifle Division began making passages through the Finnish barbed-wire obstacles.

Three days of reconnaissance-in-force did not reveal the Finnish defence works, and the largest bunkers had not been spotted as they remained silent. Rifle units were more or less acquainted with the terrain but knew little about the Finnish positions before them. Artillery and armour had no time to prepare for battle. Only one battalion of the 20th Heavy Tank Brigade had a one-day training session with the theme of 'cooperation with rifle units in battle' and 'crew's action during emergency situation'. Some tanks were fitted with mine-clearing rollers. Artillery units of the division had not yet built positions and observation posts, or laid phone lines. Most of the artillery commanders had not managed to make any arrangements before the offensive began.

Regiments of the division failed to prepare for the offensive by the scheduled time. Colonel Stenshinski postponed the beginning of the offensive in his next order. The afternoon of 16 December was spent in a low-intensity exchange of fire and harassing salvos from Soviet artillery. Soviet artillerymen failed to carry out proper reconnaissance of the Finnish line. Artillery observation aircraft were grounded due to poor weather; forward artillery observers were still on the march in traffic jams. Artillerymen did not have time to lay phone lines between their artillery battalions and the rifle regiments they were supposed to support.

It was 0200 hours on the morning of 17 December when all firing died out. Soviet divisional and regimental staffs were working around the clock preparing the offensive. Colonel Stenshinski issued a new order at 0645 hours, scheduling the artillery preparation to start at 0900 hours and the general offensive to start at 1100.

Soviet artillery opened fire on the Finnish defence line as early as 0840 hours. The artillery fired deep into the Finnish defences, and Finnish officers calmly observed 'grenades are falling everywhere'. Although the artillery barrage looked like a hurricane of fire to the Finns, the Soviet artillery could only fire at 30–40 per cent of its capacity. Only two battalions of the 323rd Artillery Regiment and two battalions of the 24th Corps Artillery Regiment could open fire on the morning of 17 December. All the other units – the remaining battalions of the 323rd Artillery Regiment and 24th Corps Artillery Regiment, and the entire 302nd Howitzer Artillery Regiment – were still on the march. The four battalions were low on ammunition, having only 50 per cent of the daily ammo ration with them.

Out of the entire IL Corps Heavy Artillery Regiment, only Colonel Tsvetov made it to the front on time. The Chief of Artillery of the 123rd Rifle Division, Major Vakulenko, failed to coordinate the action of the divisional artillery group. The Chief of Staff of the 24th Corps Artillery Regiment, Major Koziev, reflected later:

> Artillery staff of the 123rd Rifle Division, Chief of Artillery Major Vakulenko, and his Chief of Staff, Major Grigoriev, in fact did not command the divisional artillery group. During the entire battle we did not receive a single battle order from the 123rd Rifle Division that would state specific objectives for infantry or artillery. The only thing that Vakulenko did was summon the Commander of the divisional artillery group, Colonel Tsvetov, and the Commander or

Chief of Staff of the 24th Corps Artillery Regiment, and repeated the same sentence: 'Tomorrow's mission is the same as today.'

The barrage was over at 1100 hours and the offensive began. The 4th Company, 245th Rifle Regiment, followed the tanks closely and managed to get across the barbed wire into the Finnish trenches. They captured about 70–100 metres of Finnish trench in the Harkkila strongpoint. Second Lieutenant Harkkila was mortally wounded at the very beginning of the battle and his platoon failed to repel the Soviet assault. Soviet tanks easily negotiated the Finnish anti-tank obstacle line, which was a very unpleasant surprise for the Finns. It turned out that the Finnish anti-tank rock barrier had several fatal flaws. First, the rock barrier was not camouflaged and was clearly visible. This gave the Soviets a chance to destroy the barrier with direct or indirect artillery fire from a safe distance. Secondly, the rocks were too small to stop a T-28 tank handled by an experienced driver. Thirdly, tank crews of the 20th Tank Brigade and the 35th Light Tank Brigade could destroy the rocks with fire from their main guns or pull the rocks apart with chains.

After negotiating the obstacle line, two tanks turned towards Millionaire bunker, crushing the barbed-wire obstacles. The 37mm anti-tank gun in a wooden bunker next to Millionaire bunker almost immediately knocked them out. One flame-thrower tank started to shoot burning liquid into the trenches at Harkkila strongpoint; the second flame-thrower tank drove towards Finnish dugouts, burning everything in its way. Two Soviet tank men jumped out of their vehicle with pistols in hand at Harkkila dugout and opened fire at its doors, urging the Finns to surrender. Other tanks (the Finns counted about fifteen of them) drove into the Finnish rear. The Finns tried to counter-attack and recapture the trenches but in daylight this was suicide. The trenches were in the sights of the main guns and machine-guns of the Soviet armour. Second Lieutenant Myllylä, a platoon commander from the 3rd Company, was killed by a burst from a Soviet tank in one such assault.

The men of the 245th Rifle Regiment managed to drive away the Finnish outpost at the southern end of 'Tongue' Hill and occupied the southern tip of the hill by the swamp. Then they moved forward and took up defensive positions in the anti-tank ditch at the southern end of the hill. The Finns tried to recapture the outpost, bypassing the Soviet riflemen by moving through the swamp, but all the Finns fell through the thin ice covering the swamp (after the flood dam on the River Majajoki had been opened by the the Finns themselves).

Events unfolded in the same way in the centre of Finnish defences, at Poppius bunker. Riflemen of the 255th Rifle Regiment followed the tanks closely, crossed the barbed wire and captured the Finnish trenches in Louhi strongpoint. Second Lieutenant Louhi was mortally wounded, and the remains of his platoon withdrew along the trenches to the east. Some men took cover in the Poppius bunker. Over 100 men found refuge there – machine-gunners, anti-tank gun crews, phone operators, artillery observers. The bunker was so crowded that men started to run out of oxygen during the night. Luckily, the phone line from Poppius bunker to the rear was still intact and the besieged men could be briefed on the course of events. Some Soviet tanks drove into the Finnish rear, others remained at the front line with the infantry, mopping up the trenches with fire from main guns and machine-guns. The Finnish commander of the 2nd Company, 15th Infantry Regiment, Lieutenant Oiva Porras, described the daytime battle on 17 December:

> On the morning of the battle we all stood in our trenches and MG nests, waiting for a possible enemy assault. Enemy artillery was firing intensively. Heavy grenades were flying over our heads and judging from the sound, exploding somewhere next to the battalion CP and the second line of our defences. Smaller grenades were falling on our positions. From the sound one could easily tell where the grenade was about to fall. Judging from the sound of the incoming grenade we would press ourselves against the frozen bottom of the trench. The enemy was firing on wide areas. We could hear grenade explosions to our left, in the positions of the company under Lieutenant Jukka Korpinen and to the right from Summa village.
>
> In our positions the first were the strongpoints of Second Lieutenant Harkkila and Lieutenant Kölli. In the middle of our defensive sector was bunker Sj5 or Millionaire bunker, a concrete machine-gun bunker and shelter combined. In front of it was Finger Hill, which was held by Second Lieutenant Puosi. On our right flank was the platoon under Lieutenant Kettunen.
>
> The Harkkila and Kölli strongpoints were located on a sandy field, which was the best possible terrain for armour. This is why a rock obstacle was built in front of them. The only anti-tank gun allocated to our company was set next to the wall of Millionaire bunker and was capable of covering the area with flanking fire. The areas in front of other strongpoints were not so tank-friendly, being partially swampy.
>
> We observed no-man's-land. It was still so dark that we could not even clearly see the obstacle line in front of us. Here and there we illuminated the area with flares from signal pistols. We could see the flashes of enemy artillery fire in the distance. Grenades started to fall

on our positions more intensively than before. Bitter explosion fumes filled the air. The terrain around our positions was all ploughed up into a dirty mass of sand and snow. Snow remained white only in the area near the enemy.

I met Harkkila in his strongpoint. He told me that the noise of engines and clashing of tracks from the enemy's side could be heard all night long. They were most likely keeping the engines warm and ready during the night.

It seemed that the situation was unfolding in complete accordance with Soviet field manuals. The night before they made a reconnaissance-in-force in many places. The firefight in Puosi's forward position on Finger Hill lasted all through the night. Now they were softening our positions with artillery. One can be sure that after it gets light they will start an offensive with armour support. The mission of the enemy was to wipe us out of their way and continue their march into Finland. Waiting in trenches became a well-known feeling on the eve of the battle.

I continued my inspection, together with my runner, and went into Kölli's strongpoint. I saw Lieutenant Kölli standing and sadly watching the smoke pillars looming over the burning houses of Summa village. 'It will be a hard day for us,' he predicted. I could not but agree with him. Today our positions would be under the steamroller of enemy armour – their trump card. Even if we were lucky, we would not be able to repel a massive tank assault with just one anti-tank gun. It would be hard and risky to use satchel charges and petrol bombs in open terrain during daylight. Our only way to hold out is to repel the infantry assault. Without infantry support armour would not be able to consolidate its gains and control the terrain.

I also went into Millionaire bunker in order to meet the commander of the machine-gun company, Lieutenant Keinänen, and the artillery observer of the fortification, Lieutenant Aarne Sipilä. Machine-guns in the bunker were ready for action. Men were filling more ammunition belts for the battle.

As morning grew light, the offensive started. Two heavy tanks drove out of the forest in front of us, followed by three more – there were more and more tanks coming, forming an assault line. They were slowly approaching our positions, roaring their engines and clashing their tracks. Fifteen tanks were approaching Harkkila's strongpoint, firing their main guns. Infantry followed, protected by tanks. We could see assaulting lines of infantry spreading out in front of our entire sector. In lines and groups, often following one another, enemy infantry marched into battle sinking knee deep in snow. We could see machine-gun crews and ammunition bearers carrying ammo boxes among the riflemen. There were more tanks coming out of the forest following the infantry.

A thought flashed through my brain that the decisive battle would take place within hours and many of us would not live to see its end.

Intensive fire opened from all our positions. Machine-guns from Millionaire bunker joined our fire. Our own artillery also opened fire. We could see grenades exploding in the assaulting lines of infantry. Some men started to duck for cover in folds of the terrain, the rest just continued to move forward with a loud battle cry. In a couple of hundred metres, enemy infantry entered the sector of fire of our machine-guns. The assault stopped. We could see many men taking cover in the snow, the rest were trying to dig into the frozen ground.

The lead tanks and the infantry that followed them reached the anti-tank barrier. The tanks easily drove over it. They turned to left and right and started to crush the barbed-wire obstacles. Many tanks crossed our trenches and continued their journey into our rear. Then a surprise came. Two tanks started to mop up the trenches of Harkkila strongpoint with flame-throwers. They were driving along the trench, raining burning liquid and thick clouds of black smoke on men in the trenches. I went to the firing position of our anti-tank gun, under Junior Sergeant Rintala, and saw that the flame-thrower tanks were out of range. But other tanks that were crushing the obstacles were entering the sector of fire.

The anti-tank gun fired. A hit on the turret of one of the tanks could be seen clearly. The tank turned to the left and stopped. Load, aim, fire! The second tank also took a hit and stopped. In a second the turret hatch of the tank opened. I saw the hands and head of a man in a leather helmet coming out of the hatch, but at the same moment the tank was consumed by flame – its ammo blew up inside and the tank burnt out.

The flame-thrower tanks were still in action. One of them followed the communication trench and drove up to Harkkila's dugout, while the second was wiping trenches out in the Kölli strongpoint. Sometimes the liquid that it threw did not ignite and merely left the target dirty and covered with oil. In a moment, the second flame-thrower tank also moved towards the dugout. At the same time two more tanks were destroyed in front of Kölli strongpoint.

Machine-guns from Millionaire bunker fired without respite; we were also firing from the trenches. Enemy infantry tried to continue the assault regardless of cost. There were already many silent, dead, corpses littering the terrain in front of our positions. The enemy tried to support the assaulting infantry by bringing field guns to firing positions over open sights. Their shells started to explode all over. The shell exploded simultaneously with the sound of a shot. A shell from such guns killed runners Jaakkola and Sisto. I think they did not even have time to realize what happened.

Some time around noon I got a message that Harkkila was badly wounded and his assistant-platoon-leader was killed. The runner also told me there were many dead and wounded already. We could not evacuate our wounded because of the tanks. One of them was standing on the roof of Harkkila dugout and many more were driving back and forth in the rear and at the supply road. The enemy captured part of our trench.

The situation quickly deteriorated. We could not recapture the enemy-occupied part of the trench, despite many attempts. Second Lieutenant Myllylä was killed in one such counter-attack – he only managed to advance some 20 metres. Tanks repelled any assault at its very beginning. However, we managed to contain the breakthrough, as the enemy did not have sufficient power to extend it. Kölli had time to organize Harkkila's platoon and man the flanking positions.

During the whole day the machine-guns in Poppius and Millionaire bunkers fired without respite. The two machine-guns in Poppius fired 20,000 rounds, the two machine-guns in the eastern casemate of Millionaire fired 40,000 rounds. Corporal Toivo Ahola, of the 3rd Company, 15th Infantry Regiment, recalled:

Sunday, 17 December came. At seven o'clock, enemy artillery fire intensified to a degree we have not seen before. Their assault was to start along an almost forest-free sand field on both sides of the road from Kaukjärvi. Visibility from our side was good, at least 500 metres in depth. We had a barbed-wire fence in front of our position, as well as anti-tank rocks. They were the weakest and the most modest anti-tank obstacles I have ever seen. The reason for their weakness was the absence of natural stones in the area. To make things worse, the stones were of reddish granite, which disintegrated after a single hit from the main gun of a Russian tank.

The artillery barrage shifted into our rear (exactly according to the manuals!) and our positions were hit with all the might of the armed forces of the Soviet Union. The games were over: everything was serious. We were also ready to welcome the uninvited guests. About fifty tanks were driving at us on a front of 500 metres; the largest tanks were 8 metres long, 3 metres wide and 3 metres tall. They quickly drove over open terrain and fired their main guns and machine-guns non-stop, although their fire was inaccurate. A huge mass of infantry advanced behind the tanks in several waves. Although the ground was covered with snow, the Russians did not yet have snow-camouflage suits. This was a clear advantage for us, as we could see our targets. Our artillery fired several salvos at the assaulting enemy, but they should have fired ten times more shells in order to achieve at least something!

Our anti-tank teams managed to neutralize several tanks in no-man's-land; one tank hit a mine, but there were still plenty of them coming. The bravest crews drove over our trenches and into our rear. Other tanks started driving back and forth, levelling our barbed wire fence, and a third group of tanks stopped in order to clear passages through anti-tank obstacles. The tanks that drove into our rear were in a vulnerable position – they immediately came under attack from our tank busters. A tank has rather poor visibility and a brave man in a trench with a satchel charge or a petrol bomb is a dangerous opponent for a tank.

The fire of our automatic weapons stopped the infantry assault, which lasted for several hours. Small dark hillocks – the bodies of our opponents – littered the wide battlefield. There was a terrible number of casualties in front of us. As darkness fell, we could hear the screaming of the wounded, and among other cries we could clearly hear: 'Comrade medic!' Two or three enemy tanks that had broken into our rear made it back to their lines.

The leader of the 3rd Platoon, Second Lieutenant Myllylä, was killed in the battle. Out of the men that I knew, Junior Sergeants Eskola and Honkala were killed, as well as Privates Turve, Vahermo, Kaurimo and Järvinen. About fifteen men in the company were wounded. That day was quite special for me, as my job was to destroy as many living creatures called Homo Sapiens as possible.

Jaeger Captain Auno Kuiri left his command bunker immediately when he heard the news of the Soviet breakthrough. He had walked just 50 metres towards the front line when he encountered five Soviet tanks. The captain had to take cover in a nearby dugout and hide there until darkness fell. And so the battalion commander was out of the game for the whole day and no one in the battalion knew where he was. Rumours about the death of Kuiri immediately spread among the battalion officers. Soviet tanks surrounded the battalion's command bunker and the command bunker of the 3rd Company, keeping the doors in their sights. Second Lieutenant Ihaniemi, from the 3rd Company, tried to slip out of the bunker and destroy the Soviet tanks with satchel charges, but he was immediately killed. Officers of the battalion staff burnt secret papers and prepared for the worst.

The situation changed in the late afternoon with the arrival of darkness. The 255th Rifle Regiment had suffered heavy losses during the day; the chain of command was broken, and the regiment's battalions did not advance further than the trenches around Poppius bunker. This was a mistake that doomed the entire offensive. By nightfall the Finns had recovered and prepared for a counter-attack.

Soviet tanks remained in the Finnish rear until the arrival of darkness, firing signal flares into the air and blowing their horns, urging riflemen to follow. When they realized that riflemen would not arrive, the tanks drove back to their initial positions. Most of them were knocked out on the way back. The Finns claimed twenty-two or twenty-three tanks destroyed out of thirty-five that broke into Finnish positions during the day. One T–28 tank got stuck in a trench at Ketola strongpoint and was abandoned by its crew. Apparently the tank had picked up the crew of another vehicle, as there were nine men in the tank. One tank man was killed as he baled out, three made it to the barbed wire and were killed there, one man was killed on the roof of a nearby dugout and four men were taken prisoner. The Finns did not search the prisoners thoroughly in the darkness, and one Soviet tanker shot himself on the way to the Finnish rear. The abandoned T–28, which was completely intact, was towed to the rear by the end of December.

In an evening counter-attack the Finns managed to recapture the trenches at Harkkila strongpoint. Soviet archive documents laconically describe the loss of trenches at the Harkkila strongpoint like this: 'the 4th Company withdrew to its initial positions under heavy pressure from the enemy and suffered heavy losses'.

Despite the stabilization of the front line for the day, the 1st and 2nd Battalions of the 255th Rifle Regiment held Louhi strongpoint and the larger part of Äijälä strongpoint. Poppius bunker was still under siege. During the night of 17/18 December the 3rd Company of the 15th Infantry Regiment counter-attacked in vain, trying to regain the lost strongpoints.

On the same day, 17 December 1939, the 35th Light Tank Brigade lost its commander, Colonel Kashuba, a veteran of the Russian Civil War. He lost his foot when trying to arrange the combined assault of his armour and riflemen. Kashuba described the battle later:

> The battle was especially fierce – for the first time our tanks engaged the concrete bunkers. It was a duel of tanks and artillery. It is very difficult to describe it. I saw artillery duels in the Civil War, but I had never seen anything as spectacular as a battle of tanks against a fortified line. This was an utterly fantastic view: powerful fire, roar of guns, artillery and tanks firing salvos. It looked as if our tanks fired at the same time; the bunkers were returning fire in the same way. The battlefield seemed to be a breathing living creature, engulfed in fire. Pink flames of explosions illuminated the battlefield. Machine-guns could be heard along with the roar of guns. When you observe the battle from the side, all tanks stood in a row in front of the stone fence and were returning fire.
>
> I got out of my tank and ordered the tank company commander to pull anti-tank rocks away with chains, making way for our tanks. The Company Commander was Senior Lieutenant Kulabuhov, now a Hero of the Soviet Union. After giving this order, I went to ask the infantry to support us. The battle went on. Enemy mortars were pouring fire on us. One explosion followed another. I came to the infantrymen and asked for support. Then I saw that two of my tanks had already passed the obstacle line. I shouted: 'Forward! For Motherland! For Stalin!' and rushed forward. The infantry followed. Then something hit me. I felt a push and fell down. However, I did not pass out. I saw the battle continuing as one more tank negotiated the obstacle line and several tanks drove into the Finnish rear. Then I took care of my wound. I bandaged myself and shouted for help. An infantryman ran up. I saw one of my tanks driving up. I asked the infantryman to call for the tank, so that my men could pick me up. The tank drove up. Military Technician First Class Razin came out of the vehicle and when he saw me in this condition, he almost burst into tears. The driver also got out of the vehicle. They tried to lift me and failed, as I weighed around 100 kilograms then. I helped the guys myself, grabbing the tank by its track and climbing the tank myself.
>
> We drove back under constant enemy fire. Any pine tree at a fortified line was a marker. I knew that if we drove slowly, the tank

would be knocked out. I hurried the crew: 'Drive faster!' We made it anyway. Razin got me out of there.

The 123rd Rifle Division and supporting armour continued the offensive on 18 December. Finnish artillery observers counted sixty-eight Soviet tanks lined up in the open for the attack. The Finns immediately used this mistake of the Soviet tank crews and hit the concentration of Soviet armour with indirect fire from all available artillery. The artillery strike dispersed the Soviet attack formation even before the tanks started moving. According to the Finnish count, the artillery hit twelve Soviet tanks. Eight tanks caught fire and burnt out 1.5 kilometres south of the Finnish main defence line. Finnish artillery continued to deliver strikes at concentrations of Soviet armour, prohibiting any assault. The Finns claimed a total of sixteen tanks destroyed on 18 December. The Soviet artillery fire was quite weak on that day, as all artillery regiments were low on ammunition and the roads were still jammed with traffic. The 24th Corps Artillery Regiment had just 200 rounds left by 1600 hours on 18 December. Regimental ammo trucks sent to pick up ammo replenishments were not back by the evening of 18 December. There was no communication between the regiment and the ammo depot, as Soviet tanks accidentally destroyed all phone lines, even though most of the cables were attached to poles. Only on 18 December did the artillery battalions finally establish communication with the 245th and 255th Rifle Regiments, opening fire on the request of rifle units.

The offensive resumed on 19 December. Twelve Soviet tanks broke through the Finnish infantry at Louhi and Äijälä strongpoints and drove into the Finnish rear. However, the 255th Rifle Regiment failed to follow the armour again and the tanks had to return to their initial positions. The Finns lost the Rosenberg 37mm field gun that they deployed in the sector. The gun was wrecked by two Soviet tanks, which were later destroyed by a Finnish anti-tank gun. The Finns claimed the destruction of nine Soviet tanks that day. A Soviet assault party blew up the eastern entrance to Poppius bunker in the evening of 19 December, but the damage was insignificant.

On 20 December Soviet armour attacked again: tanks first blocked the exits from Poppius bunker and then opened fire at its gun ports at point-blank range. Still the bunker held out. In the evening the Finns counter-attacked and tried to recapture the two strongpoints. The counter-attack led to only partial success – Finns joined hands with the right casemate of Poppius bunker and recaptured part of Äijälä strongpoint. They could not go further as the Soviet tanks standing at Louhi strongpoint could fire along the trenches of Äijälä strongpoint.

Colonel Stenshinski pointed out the serious mistakes made by his subordinates during the offensive on 17–19 December 1939. In his next order for
the offensive he tried to adjust the tactic.

However, there was almost no one left to lead the new assaults. The 255th
Regiment had lost all three battalion commanders: the commander of the 1st
Battalion, Captain Golovin, was badly wounded; the commander of the
2nd Battalion, Captain Zuev, was wounded; the commander of the 3rd Battalion,
Captain Vasiliev, was killed. The Chief of Staff of the 1st Battalion, Captain
Lyasov, was also wounded. The surviving commanders were losing their grip
on the situation: 'we have unconfirmed reports that some men were taken
prisoner. The 2nd Battalion is holding the positions with one platoon of the
5th Company, we do not know where everyone else is.'

Tank battalions had suffered even more serious losses. Captain Yakovlev,
who took over the 91st Tank Battalion, reported to Brigade Commander Borzilov
after the battle of 17 December:

> The battalion lost its combat value after the battle of 17 December.
> Seven men are killed, twenty-two are wounded, including the battalion
> Commander, Major Drozdov, sixteen men are missing, among them
> the battalion Commissar, Dubrovski. Out of twenty-one tanks that
> made it back from the battle, five were sent into a new assault on
> your orders, and two tanks are sent to the repair workshop. Other
> tanks need repairs, which are under way. Four tanks burnt out on
> the battlefield, one tank is trapped, and one is missing [this was the
> vehicle abandoned on the evening of 17 December and later used
> by the Finns]. The remaining vehicles are loaded with fuel and
> ammunition. During the assault we destroyed five anti-tank guns, up
> to three bunkers, and many machine-gun nests. We made it to the
> area 1 kilometre south of Hill 63.4. But as the infantry did not
> advance further than the anti-tank rocks on Hill 65.5, this area is not
> under our control.
>
> I am awaiting your orders. I am taking over the battalion; Alekseev
> is taking over as battalion Commissar. We have summoned Udodov
> from the rear repair workshop.
>
> Commander of the 91st Tank Battalion Captain Yakovlev.
> Commissar of the 91st Tank Battalion Military Technician 1st Class
> Alekseev.

The Acting Commissar of the battalion, Military Technician First Class Alekseev,
sent a more emotional and dramatic report to the Commissar of the brigade:

To the Commissar of the 20th Tank Brigade Regimental Commissar Comrade Kulik:

A short report from Military Technician First Class, secretary of the brigade's Bolshevik Party Commission Alekseev:

I am reporting that, as a result of the assault and the battle of 17 December, the battalion has twenty-seven tanks, which returned from the battle (twenty-five T-28 tanks and two BT tanks).

(1) Two T-28 tanks are knocked out, burnt out and exploded on the battlefield. Out of the crews of these two tanks, Company Commander Reshetov, his driver Yefimov and ... [name unclear], both badly burnt, were sent to the aid station in the rear. I have no information about the rest of the crews.

(2) We do not have precise information about the two tanks with crews, most likely they are on the battlefield, knocked out. One tank platoon, under Technician First Class Dudko, is sent to the battlefield for their evacuation. Dudko knows where these tanks are.

(3) One tank capsized in the anti-tank ditch, it was impossible to evacuate it from the battlefield due to intense machine-gun fire. The crew, equipment [of the tank] and weapons are evacuated.

(4) Six men were killed inside the tanks that arrived at the gathering point, among them: political worker of the 1st Company Novikov; three military technicians, Rezanov, Orlov, Lysov; Junior Commanders Manturov and Gorkunov. Twelve men are wounded, most of them heavily, among them Battalion Commander Major Drozdov, wounded in his hand and neck. Military Technician First Class Kravchuk is wounded in the head. All wounded received medical treatment and were sent away to a hospital. Until now we have no information about the Battalion's Commissar, Dubrovski, and the political worker of the 3rd Company, Borodin. Both have not returned from the battlefield.

(5) We have no more than five battleworthy tanks left. Ten to twelve vehicles need minor repairs and some ten vehicles cannot be repaired in the battalion (armour penetrations and major damage), not counting the vehicles that remained on the battlefield.

We are refuelling the vehicles and loading ammo now. I am lightly wounded in my head, now I am very much amazed how I have

[Author's Note: the original document is handwritten and this phrase is crossed out by the writer] by some miracle I survived. I was the last one to leave the battlefield, bringing two tanks and three crews to the gathering point.

I have temporarily taken over as the battalion's commissar. I held a short session for the communists, then a short meeting of the battalion, rallying men to fix the tanks into a battleworthy condition. I appointed deputy political workers in the companies; they will replace the ones that are out of action. Deputy commanders of the 1st and the 3rd Companies are appointed.

In general, the battalion is not battleworthy; it needs replacements of vehicles and men. The men are not depressed; after the tanks are repaired they are ready to go into battle again.

I have not yet made a list of recommendations for decorations, but I witnessed myself that the men of the 91st Battalion acted as true heroes: for example, Military Technician 1st Class Dudko, radio operator Potapov and others.

I am sending a more detailed and precise report from the 91st Tank Battalion later.

Secretary of the Bolshevik Party Commission of the 20th Tank Brigade Military Technician 1st Class Alekseev, 0230 hours, 18 December 1939.

In addition to the above, X Mechanized Corps gets five T-28 tanks with crews, we have no more battleworthy tanks left.

Among the Soviet tankers taken prisoner on 17 December was driver Sergey Larionov, 91st Tank Battalion. His parents were told he went missing in action. His fate was hard. After an exchange of prisoners in April 1940, Sergey Larionov was put into a detention camp in the Ivanovo area and then sent to Norilsk with other former prisoners of war. Official sentencing came as late as February 1941: 'The special commission of the NKVD of the USSR sentences Sergey Larionov to five years in a labour camp for surrendering to the enemy.' Fifteen years later the military department of the Supreme Court of the USSR re-examined his case and cancelled the NKVD's sentence. Larionov was fully vindicated and managed to return to his family in Leningrad in 1962.

The Commander of the Mortar Company, 15th Infantry Regiment, Lieutenant Paavo Kairinen, described the capture of a Soviet commander from the 91st Tank Battalion. This incident gave birth to one of the legends of the Winter War:

My orderly, Corporal Reino Syrjänen, was a brave and independent soldier. During the Battle of Summa on 17–19 December I sent him to Summa village to establish communication with Captain Frans-Julius Jansson, as the phone lines were down. Syrjänen made it to Jansson's command bunker but it was harder to leave. The door of the bunker was in the sights of a Russian tank. Syrjänen spent the night in Jansson's bunker, slipped out in the morning and set off back to our place. He ran into another Russian tank in the forest. The tank stood still, its main gun was blown up. Syrjänen wondered why this monster stood still in our rear. As the tank was silent, Syrjänen decided to knock on the tank's hatch with a stone. Just in case, he held his pistol ready, loaded with a cartridge in the barrel. When he knocked on the tank's armour, the upper hatch of the turret opened and hands emerged in a gesture of surrender. As Syrjänen did not speak Russian, he ordered the tank man to get down with signs. The latter obeyed and again lifted his hands. Syrjänen ordered the prisoner to walk forward.

A sentry stopped Syrjänen and the older prisoner that was dragging behind. After reporting to me, he invited the prisoner and Syrjänen into my dugout. I greeted the Russian prisoner in his mother tongue. He looked scared and tired. When I invited him to sit down and take off his sheepskin coat, he seemed to calm down. I offered him a cigarette, which I lit and tried myself first. It seemed that the Russian was wondering at the good taste and flavour of Työmies tobacco.

I took a map of Finland and a small Russian phrasebook out of my map case and started the interrogation: 'To which corps or division does your unit belong?' After I received answers to all the standard questions, I found out why the tank stood in such a strange place. The prisoner told me that he drove forward until he ran out of fuel. After that his crew abandoned the tank and returned to their own lines.

I interrogated the enemy officer in greater detail. He told me that their offensive failed due to strong artillery fire and he ordered a retreat. He acknowledged that he was afraid of returning to his unit and stayed with his vehicle, so that a Finnish soldier could kill him. I interrupted the interrogation and ordered Syrjänen to go back to the tank and pick up all papers from it.

The company driver arrived at my dugout and called on us to pick up food from his sled. I ate and also gave some food to the prisoner. He thanked me with a bow. I continued my conversation with the prisoner, using my dictionary. I have really forgotten the Russian language since my studies in Cadet Academy! The prisoner offered me tobacco for a pipe, but I refused immediately after I smelled it.

As I have already mentioned, the prisoner was afraid of going back to his unit without his tank. According to the laws of the Soviet Union this was a serious crime. When I asked him: 'What would happen to you if you returned without your tank?' he showed me a sign as if to cut his throat.

At that moment the captain pulled out *roubles* from his pockets and map case and offered them to me. When my orderly also started to pull out roubles from his pockets, the prisoner explained. He had a large amount of money in his tank because he was carrying the whole battalion's monthly salary. It was a payday in the battalion and yet he had been ordered to take part in the assault. He was not able to issue the money to anyone. What sort of system was that?

Syrjänen ran to the tank again on my orders and brought a whole bag pack of roubles in different bills. I took a bill of each type as a souvenir and ordered Syrjänen to visit our rear positions, get sleds there, and take the prisoner to the regimental HQ. When Syrjänen and the prisoner left, I called the liaison officer of the regiment, Second Lieutenant Välimaa, and informed him that I had sent off a prisoner with a large amount of money in roubles.

I wrote down on the front page of the Russian–Finnish phrase-book I took from the prisoner's map case: 'I took this as a souvenir from the Commander of a heavy tank battalion, Captain Vasilevich, in Summa 19–20 December 1939.'

According to some reports, Syrjänen also brought a whole bag of letters for the 91st Tank Battalion. It was after this incident that all T-28 tanks were dubbed mail coaches or 'post trains' by Finnish soldiers. The Finns well knew American Western movies, in which post trains carried mail and money, and referred to the T-28 tanks in the same way.

The Soviet tank commander could not have been a commander of a tank battalion as there were no battalion commanders among the killed or missing in action in the first Battle of Summa. Apparently, the Soviet prisoner called himself by a fake name. Most likely, he was a political worker. Distribution of salaries and post could have been one of his duties. One cannot exclude the possibility that this was the Commissar of the 91st Tank Battalion, Dubrovski, who went missing in action on 17 December 1939.

The story of a Soviet battalion commander who surrendered to the Finns due to high casualties in his battalion persisted. This story is still often seen in many Finnish and other Western books on the Winter War. The incident is depicted as a defection, and the rank is often described as a brigade commander.

Paavo Kairinen, who served in the US Army after the Second World War, attached a map showing the location of the tank to his memoirs. His information is confirmed by the map of Military Technician 1st Class Oleinik, Chief of the Technical Department of the 20th Tank Brigade. In March 1940 he went through the battlefield of Summa and Lähde and marked all knocked out and abandoned tanks of his brigade on the map. Three tanks were left on the battlefield in the area pointed out by Kairinen – the tanks got stuck in boggy ground near River Majajoki. The Finns did not have tractors powerful enough to evacuate such heavy tanks as the T–28, and most of these tanks remained on the battlefield. All the Finns could do was dismantle the radios, machine-guns, sights and all possible spare parts from the knocked-out tanks in their rear.

The 20th Tank Brigade also deployed teletanks in the battle. Radio-controlled vehicles equipped with flame-throwers drove into battle but failed to negotiate the anti-tank rock fence. The operators directing the vehicles with remote control could not see clearly how to negotiate the fence. As a result, all the hi-tech tanks simply got stuck in the obstacle line.

The renewed Soviet offensive on 21 December failed to impress the Finns. All assaults were easily stopped in the sector of the 1st Company.

At the same time, the Finns continued their assaults towards Louhi strong-point, still held by two battalions of the 255th Rifle Regiment. Auno Kuiri's plan was to assault the trenches from both flanks, from east and west, along the trenches.

The first attempt to recapture the trenches started at 0230 hours on 22 December but failed – the Finns ran out of hand grenades, and the assault was called off. The second assault began at 0430 hours but was stopped by machine-gun fire from the Soviet side. The battle reports of the 255th Regiment describe how the battalions were gradually losing men and the ability to resist:

> At 0300 hours on 22 December the White Finns surrounded the 1st and the 2nd Battalions from all sides and started an energetic attack, throwing hand grenades, The battalions returned fire and called in artillery strikes, but still the 2nd Battalion suffered heavy losses: the Commander of the 1st Battalion, Golovin, is badly wounded; the Chief of Staff of the Battalion, Lyasov, is wounded, and we do not

know whether the Commander of the 2nd Battalion is killed or wounded. We take all measures to hold the line, but we are running out of resources; we need replacements and more firepower.

The third Finnish assault began at 0615 hours, when most of the Russian machine-guns were suppressed or destroyed. The Finns managed to get the upper hand in the battle. At the same time, apparently, the remains of the battalions of the 255th Rifle Regiment received an order to fall back.

By the morning of 22 December, after five days of fighting that lasted day and night, the Finns drove the 255th Rifle Regiment from the trenches. The entire Finnish main defence line was again secure. The first assault on the main defence line in Lähde was over. The Finns estimated Soviet casualties in the trench battle around Poppius bunker as 300 men killed, including one major (apparently the Finns found the body of Captain Vasiliev, Commander of the 3rd Battalion, 255th Rifle Regiment). Thirty-four men and one lieutenant were taken prisoner. Finnish estimates of Soviet losses look exaggerated, as the total losses of the 255th Regiment during the whole of December 1939 were twenty-three killed. The regiment also lost 236 men missing in action during all four months of the war. At the same time the Finnish 15th Infantry Regiment, which defended the Summa village and Lähde sectors, lost only around ninety men killed. The highest casualty rate was among the men of the Gun Company of the regiment – eleven men killed. The Gun Company was armed with 37mm anti-tank and field guns and had to engage superior Soviet armour. The men of the company went through the battle in the Lähde sector with relatively light losses – only one 37mm field gun was destroyed – but all the guns and almost all the men in Summa village were lost. There is a large gap in the war diary of the Gun Company after 17 December 1939, as there was no one left to write the diary. Toivo Ahola of the 3rd Company, 15th Infantry Regiment, wrote:

> After four hours of intensive night combat we finally recaptured the trenches. Luckily, we managed to avoid high losses. Dead Red Army men littered the bottom of the trenches – we stumbled over them all the time. It was strange to step on human bodies that had not stiffened yet. We were ordered to clear the trenches of dead. It was not a problem, as there were deep shell craters in front of our positions. The Red Army men found their last refuge there.

On 23 December the 1st Battalion, 15th Infantry Regiment, undertook a counter-attack, which was part of the general counter-offensive of the II Army Corps in the Western Isthmus. The Finns were pinned down before they could walk 100 metres towards the Soviet lines. The commander of the 3rd Company was wounded. It turned out that the outposts of the 123rd Division were just several dozen metres from the Finnish obstacle lines.

The days of 24 and 25 December went by in an exchange of fire between the Soviet outposts and the Finns at the main defence line. Soviet artillery delivered several strikes on the Finnish positions, and artillery observation balloons were flown. A dugout at Urnberg strongpoint took two direct hits at 1545 hours on 25 December. Seven men were killed, five wounded.

A Finnish sniper killed the Chief of Artillery of the 123rd Rifle Division, Major Vakulenko, as he inspected the front line. He was buried with full military honours next to Perkjärvi Railway Station on an area of high ground, together with other commanders of the division. As his coffin descended into the grave, all Soviet artillery regiments fired a salvo at the Finnish positions as a final salute to their commander.

In the evening of 26 December two exhausted and starving Red Army men surrendered to the Finns. They had hidden in a knocked-out tank during the Finnish counter-attack in the first hours of 22 December and spent four days in the tank, waiting for the arrival of their own troops. Both had bad frostbite.

One more dugout was hit on 27 December. Three men were killed and seven wounded. One more assault started against Poppius bunker. The Finns estimated the attacking unit as two companies supported by a light tank platoon. The Finns managed to pin down the Soviet riflemen but the tanks broke into the strongpoint, stopped and then opened fire in all directions. The lead tank had mine-clearing rollers. The Finns knocked out three tanks out of four – one tank burnt out, two more were immobilized. The battle was over by 1800 hours.

The Soviet outposts carried out several attacks from their positions and they were all repelled by the Finns. Louhi and Äijälä strongpoints were the primary targets for the assaults. The sectors of fire for Poppius bunker were already well known and Red Army men moved outside the bunker's range. The Finns had to repel the assaults with mortar fire.

On 30 December a Soviet battery fired at Poppius bunker over open sights but was quickly suppressed by Finnish artillery. The exchange of fire, sniper duels, scout missions and propaganda leaflets were becoming a routine for the Finns and the Soviets at the front. Static warfare came to Lähde sector.

Summa Village in December

In early December 1939, as the Finnish delaying troops were still carrying out delaying actions in front of the main defence line, the 2nd Battalion of the 15th Infantry Regiment, under Captain Frans-Julius Jansson, had already taken up positions in Summa village and started fortification works. The battalion built anti-tank obstacles and spare positions for machine-guns, and deepened the main trench and communication trenches. Teenagers from Summa village assisted them in this. Some young men in the village were left behind after evacuation in order to take care of the village's cattle and watch over the property. The rest of the village had been evacuated even before the breakout of the war.

The 4th and 6th Companies took up defensive positions at the front. The 2nd Machine-gun Company manned the bunkers of the defence sector. The 5th Company manned the supporting line in the rear and continued fortification works. The 6th Company defended the crucial platoon strongpoints of Tuomola, Mikkola, Bäcklund and Rantala from the highway to bunker No. 2; the 4th Company defended the strongpoints Mäkipää, Lehtonen, Koskinen and Porras from the highway to Lake Summajärvi. The platoon strongpoints were named after the platoon leaders.

The last Finnish units had withdrawn behind the main defence line by 5 December 1939. They told the men of the 15th Regiment that there were no Finns behind them. The battalion blocked the highway with anti-tank rocks and prepared for battle, organising sentries and outposts. Captain Jansson laconically wrote in the battalion's war diary: 'now it is our turn'.

The order to burn the village down came on 6 December, Finland's Day of Independence. Men of the battalion set the village on fire in the sight of local teenagers who were completing the fortification works. Vilho Turta, one of these young men, described the tragic day:

> We heard the distant sound of guns all the time. Sometimes we clearly heard machine-gun bursts. It took us a long time to load all instruments and belongings on our carriage. Liimatainen said that the neighbouring village was on fire. I thought it was Repokorpi. We continued loading and were ready to leave when it was already five o'clock in the evening. I stayed in the village and saw fire consuming it, one house after another. We saw the soldiers walking around Evesti Farm and breaking windows. They took some straw from the barn, brought it into the farm and set it on fire. They did the same with our school. The house of Ville Turta – the house in which I was born – and Lipponen's house were already in flames. I cannot describe the feelings that engulfed me at that moment. Mikko Liimatainen, from Karjalainen village, walked up to me. We were classmates from Elementary School. He said that his house was probably no more. I was of the same opinion. Such was our sad conversation. We spoke with short phrases, with trembling voices. We left. Summa village was left behind us in the past.

The Red Army units did not make contact with Finnish troops in the sector between 5 and 11 December. Finnish scout parties sent south along the highway reported to Captain Jansson that they had not encountered the enemy. The first Soviet shells started to rain down on Finnish positions at Summa on 12 December. The lead elements of the Soviet 138th Rifle Division emerged in front of the Finnish positions in the evening of 13 December. The reconnaissance-in-force continued on the next day: around sixty Red Army men with two tanks approached Finnish positions at Korpela Farm. The Finns repelled the tanks and riflemen with mortar fire.

A group of journalists visited Jansson's battalion on 13 and 14 December. After a cup of coffee in command bunker No. 16, they went to the front line, where they took photos of the battalion preparing for battle. The famous photo of Finnish men in a trench ready to fire was taken then, and became a symbol of the Mannerheim Line in post-war years; it was published in almost all books on the Winter War. This is no wonder, as it well illustrated the statement of Mannerheim himself:

> As I have already mentioned, the fortification line was of course there, but it was formed of rare machine-gun nests and two new bunkers that were built on my proposal, between which were trenches. Yes, the fortified line existed but it lacked depth. This line was named the 'Mannerheim Line' by the people. Its strength was in the stoicism and bravery of our soldiers, but not strength of the fortifications.

The seventeen concrete bunkers of Summa village did not fit into this photo. Neither did they fit into the memories of Mannerheim.

The regiments of the 138th Division prepared for the grand offensive after the reconnaissance-in-force. Soviet artillery delivered three strikes on the Finnish positions in the village on 15 and 16 December, without causing any damage to the Finnish fortifications. The 138th Rifle Division was marched to Summa village from the nearest Karhula sector.

The division's battle order No. 10, issued on 16 December 1939, set the following missions for the division's units:

- The 768th Rifle Regiment, with the 2nd and 3rd Companies of the 108th Tank Battalion, 1st Company of the 179th Detached Sapper Battalion, and two platoons of sappers from the 45th Engineer Battalion, was to assault the Finnish lines at the front from Lake Summajärvi to the highway. The objective was to take the hills to the north-east from the lake and then continue the offensive towards Hill 52.5. The supporting artillery for the regiment comprised the 3rd Battalion, 295th Artillery Regiment, and the 1st Battalion, 24th Corps Artillery Regiment.

- The 650th Rifle Regiment, with the 1st Company of the 108th Tank Battalion, two platoons of flame-thrower tanks from the 210th Chemical Tank Battalion, the 2nd Company of the 45th Engineer Battalion, and two platoons from the 179th Sapper Battalion, was to storm the front between Sepänmäki Farm and Turta Farm, and continue the assault in the direction of the highway. The 1st Battalion, 295th Artillery Regiment, and the 3rd Battalion, 302nd Howitzer Artillery Regiment, supported the rifle regiment.
- The 544th Rifle Regiment (minus one rifle battalion), with the 436th Tank Battalion, was to assault the second line behind the 768th Rifle Regiment.

The artillery barrage was planned for two hours, from 0900–1100 hours on 17 December 1939.

Just as in the other offensives in December, most of the division's artillery was still on the way to the battlefield. Only the 136th Howitzer Artillery Regiment and the 1st and 3rd Battalions of the 295th Artillery Regiment were ready to open fire at 0900 hours on 17 December. However, all these artillery battalions arrived at their firing positions in the evening of 16 December but were not ready to provide adequate artillery support. The reconnaissance-in-force that had taken place one day earlier revealed only an anti-tank rock fence, an intricate labyrinth of barbed-wire fences and an anti-tank ditch. Finnish weapon emplacements, trenches and bunkers had not been spotted. The division's staff knew the Finns had six bunkers at the highway in the village, but their precise location remained unknown.

The morning of 17 December was foggy; the temperature was around minus 3 degrees Celsius. Finnish sentries reported two explosions at the highway at 0615 hours. The 6th Company was alerted and manned the trenches. In the opinion of the Finnish officers, the explosions meant that a Soviet scout or sapper party had run into the minefield. In reality, a sapper party under Junior Lieutenant Drozdov, from the 1st Company, 179th Sapper Battalion, had triggered the explosions. Their task was to clear passages for tanks through the obstacle lines. A rifle company from the 650th Rifle Regiment covered their work. At 0800 hours an intensive firefight erupted between the Finns and the scout party of the 650th Rifle Regiment, which, along with the sappers, was pinned down north of the anti-tank obstacles. The commander of the 138th Division was afraid of hitting his own men with artillery fire, so he cancelled the artillery barrage at 0900 hours. He gave regimental commanders a free hand in deciding when to start the artillery preparation of the assault in their sectors.

Soviet artillery finally opened fire at 0925 hours. The artillery barrage ended only at 1700 hours. Artillery battalion commanders did not know where the rifle units where; there were no forward observers at the front and artillery fire was chaotic, doing little harm to the Finnish defences. 'In fact, our artillery barrage was a complete failure,' reflected the staff of the 138th Division.

The main Soviet blow was delivered on the 6th Company on the highway and west from it. Three Soviet tanks emerged in front of the Finnish positions at 1100 hours and the general assault began. More tanks arrived. At 1150 hours the 6th Company reported knocking out two tanks; another tank hit a landmine. The Gun Company of the 15th Regiment suffered the first losses: the company commander, Second Lieutenant Saloranta, was killed along with one gun leader. Two more men were wounded. Soviet tanks gave up their attempts to break into the heart of the Finnish defences at 1340 hours. Fifteen tanks formed a line at the anti-tank rock fence and opened fire at the Finnish positions. The loss of three tanks and the retreat of others, plus well-aimed concentrated fire from bunkers, demoralized the riflemen of the 650th Regiment. The men were pinned down and could not move forward.

The 2nd Machine-gun Company that manned the bunkers reported at 1530 hours: 'all quiet at bunker No. 10; one machine-gun fired half of an ammo belt. Machine-guns from Mäkipää strongpoint did not fire. Bunker No. 6 did not fire. Bunker No. 5 destroyed enemy machine-gun with its fire. Bunker No. 3 fired at the enemy machine-guns, the result is unknown. Bunker No. 2 fired in the direction of the highway.'

Soviet artillery began a renewed barrage on the Finnish lines at 1540 hours. The Finns noted that 'The enemy's artillery is firing at vast areas, both the forward positions and the rear of the company.' At 1800 hours the Soviet artillery switched to harassing fire.

The Soviet offensive in the sector of the 4th Company was less dramatic. The Finns noted a strong artillery barrage and infantry assault on the morning of 17 December: 'The enemy started an assault against Lehtonen and Mäkipää strongpoints. They marched in close formation, just like on parade. We opened fire and the enemy retreated under cover of forest, leaving 20–30 men on the ground.' The Soviet riflemen assaulted with a single company on 18 December. As the Finns observed: 'Enemy soldiers use folds of terrain better than the previous day.' After a forty-five-minute firefight the Soviets retreated into the forest again. Several tanks penetrated the Finnish defences and circled around bunker No. 12, but drove away as darkness set in. The next assault against the 4th Company only took place on 22 December. There were just sixty men in the assaulting group: 'Enemy soldiers advance in a very skilled manner, fully utilising the terrain.' This small Red Army unit made it to the barbed-wire fence but was again stopped there and obliged to fall back.

The main battle unfolded at the highway. The 138th Rifle Division concentrated all its efforts at this narrow spot. During the night of 17 December the Finns smartly planted mines in the passages made by the Soviet sappers the day before. The 768th Rifle Regiment disengaged and was replaced with the 544th Rifle Regiment.

Soviet artillery opened fire at 0945 hours on 18 December and the artillery barrage grew into a hurricane of fire at 1515 hours. During that day the Finns only spotted five Soviet tanks. The Soviet assault began at 1600 hours and was over by 1625 hours. A small Soviet rifle unit with tanks launched a renewed assault against Tuomola strongpoint at 1715 hours but also failed. Finnish officers noted the intensity of Soviet fire: during the period from 1600–1800 hours the intensity was some thirty shells per minute. Later, the intensity decreased to some fifteen to twenty shells per minute. Many shells did not explode. Soviet artillery switched to harassing fire at 1800 hours.

The 90th Tank Battalion of the 20th Heavy Tank Brigade was attached to the 138th Rifle Division on 18 December. The battalion had about thirty medium T-28 tanks. The Special Tank Company, which fielded three top-secret experimental tanks, was also attached to the division. These three tanks were the models T-100, SMK and KV. One of these tanks was supposed to become the next generation of Soviet heavy tank, with armour of 5–6 centimetres, which could not be penetrated by anti-tank guns of the 1930s. The T-100 and SMK were gigantic vehicles, each equipped with two turrets with main guns and numerous machine-guns. Each vehicle had a crew of eleven men. The KV was a smaller single-turret tank, with a crew of five men. The experimental tanks drove to the front line straight from the Kirov Works in Leningrad. The tanks were to be tried in battle and one of the three designs had to be chosen to replace the T-35 and T-28 tanks.

The day of 19 December 1939 was the culmination of the Soviet offensive at Summa village. Soviet artillery opened fire at 0900 hours and half an hour later ten tanks negotiated the anti-tank fence at Mikkola strongpoint. At 0915 hours Mäkipää strongpoint reported:

> a large formation of tanks spotted at the highway. Part of the formation crossed the anti-tank fence and is driving back and forth between the 4th and 6th Companies, destroying the barbed-wire fence.

The Soviet Air Force dropped bombs on the forward Finnish positions at 1100 hours and more tanks joined the battle at 1130 hours. At least seven tanks were moving in the area of Peltola bunker at 1118 hours. Part of the Soviet tank force drove back from the Finnish rear at 1240 hours, and at 1355 all the tanks attacked the Finnish trenches, firing their main guns, machine-guns and flame-throwers.

The arrival of masses of armour on the battlefield did not demoralize the Finnish infantry. Even under the fire of flame-throwers, the Finns held on to their positions and once again pinned down the riflemen of the 138th Division.

The Finnish Gun Company was completely destroyed in an uneven battle against the two Soviet tank battalions. After the anti-tank guns were destroyed, the Soviet tanks drove over the trench line into the Finnish rear. Captain Jansson was sending repeated requests for more anti-tank guns. As the Soviet tank assault progressed, these requests grew more and more panicky in tone. There was good reason to panic: a group of eight T-28 tanks had stopped right outside Jansson's bunker No. 16. They had been obliged to stop after the experimental top-secret vehicle SMK hit a mine and halted just 50 metres from the Finnish command bunker. T-28 tanks formed a defensive perimeter around the damaged giant and fired their main guns and machine-guns in all directions. The crew of the SMK tried to repair the immobilized vehicle. Jansson could only send radio and phone messages to the regiment and noted in the war diary: '1630: Already eight enemy tanks are standing outside our bunker, firing at us.' In the afternoon, the SMK crew gave up the attempt to repair their tank and all the Soviet armour retreated. The SMK tank stood outside bunker No. 16 for the whole war and was photographed by the Finns on several occasions. It is mistaken for a T-35 in most of the Finnish books.

Bunker No. 10 took ten direct hits at 1345 hours but the damage was insignificant. Apparently, the Soviet tanks spotted bunker No. 5 and opened fire on the bunker's gun port at point-blank range. A direct hit killed the machine-gunner and destroyed the machine-gun at 1430 hours. The 6th Company reported at 1800 hours: 'at least eighty tanks are between bunkers No. 5 and 3 (observed from Peltola bunker)'.

Soviet tanks began driving back to their lines at 1900 hours. Some tanks decided to spend the night in the Finnish rear and await the arrival of their infantry. Most of these tanks stood in the forests north of Summa village, and as darkness fell the Finnish infantry had a perfect chance to attack the Soviet tanks with close-range weapons – satchel charges and petrol bombs. The 3rd Detached Battalion was sent to the front line to deal with the situation.

Two Soviet tanks drove around the battalion's CP all night, firing their main guns and machine-guns. One of them was destroyed around midnight. The battalion of Captain Jansson reported the destruction of eighteen tanks during three days of fighting from 17 to 19 December 1939. This number did not include tanks knocked out but later evacuated by the crews from the battlefield. Jansson estimated that there were about ten such tanks.

All Finnish reports noted powerful attacks by Soviet armour and artillery strikes, but they said very little about Soviet infantry. This is one more proof of the weak cooperation between the armour and riflemen of the 138th Rifle Division. Captain Jansson recorded in the battalion's war diary on 18 December: 'companies report from the front line about artillery fire and armour assault; enemy infantry assaults are rather weak'.

The Soviet units halted all assaults on the next day, 20 December. There was only one small task force sent into the Finnish rear, in order to evacuate the top-secret SMK tank, but the task force only made it to the anti-tank fence and could not advance further. On the other hand the Soviet artillery continued pounding the Finnish positions. Thus, the entire battle for Summa lasted just three days. The cliché about the Battle of Summa being 'a week of bloody infantry assaults, when Red Army men charged against the bunker line holding hands and singing the Soviet national anthem' does not describe the battle correctly. There are no records in the Finnish or Soviet archives that would point to Red Army men assaulting while singing and holding hands. Certainly, two companies of the 768th Rifle Regiment assaulted Mäkipää strongpoint in close formation on 17 December, but switched to a looser attack formation next day. However, assaulting in close formation while singing patriotic songs did take place in another battle of the Mannerheim Line, and its story will be told in one of the following chapters.

The record for 20 December 1939, in the war diary of the 6th Company, was: 'strong artillery barrage, all lines are down'. Soon this became a routine entry in Finnish reports.

Although the first Soviet assault in the Summa village sector failed, the Soviet command still held the sector crucial for the next offensive. More heavy artillery was brought into position in order to soften up Finnish defences in the sector.

A Soviet artillery observation balloon appeared in the air on 21 December. Captain Jansson requested fighter planes be sent to deal with it, as the balloon was out of range of the battalion's weapons. The air balloon was launched in the Soviet rear, some 5 kilometres from the front line. An artillery observer with good binoculars and a phone line to the artillery control centre was in the balloon's basket. The Finnish defences in Summa village could be clearly seen from the balloon in fine weather. The first Soviet artillery observation planes emerged in the air as well. Due to the weakness of the Finnish Air Force and its air defences, these Soviet biplanes circled over Finnish positions at a speed of 40–50 kilometres per hour. An artillery observer in the plane maintained radio contact with the batteries and orchestrated Soviet artillery fire in the area. The Finns dubbed these aircraft 'Lazy Guys' or 'Bats'.

Soviet heavy artillery concentrated fire at the bunkers along the highway on 21 and 22 December. As the Finnish defence line ran straight across Summa village, there were also a lot of cellars, basements of destroyed buildings and other ruins in the area. To the Soviets they all seemed to be bunkers or weapon emplacements, and the Soviet artillery fired at any suspicious hillock near the highway. Out of all the targets marked on the Soviet maps, only half were real bunkers.

In addition to air observation, Soviet artillerymen used other ways to observe the Finnish lines and orchestrate artillery fire. For example, forward artillery observers often used knocked-out tanks on the battlefield as observation posts. The Finns managed to spot one of these posts and destroyed it. The report read:

> Two of our men burnt a tank that stood at a cellar in the village. The tank looked intact from the outside, the hatches were locked from the inside. There were phone cables running in the direction of the enemy's lines from the tank, and there were antennas on the roof.

However, it might be that the Finns had destroyed one of the remote-controlled teletanks. The artillery barrage on Summa village continued every day.

The heaviest loss for the 2nd Battalion was the result of a direct hit of a heavy shell on the dugout of the 5th Company. A high-explosive shell apparently penetrated the roof and exploded inside, completely destroying the dugout. All nineteen men inside were killed. Only a sentry (who stood outside) and a man at the exit of the dugout survived. Finnish Army units were formed from men from the same locality before the war, just like the British 'Pals' battalions in the First World War. Almost all the men of the 5th Company were from the small village of Kalvola, near Hämeenlinna. It was impossible to excavate the bunker in December 1939, when the front was just 1 kilometre from the dugout. A regimental chaplain arrived at the ruins of the dugout on the evening of 21 December and read a funeral prayer for the dead men inside. The dugout was officially declared a war grave. The Finns installed a simple wooden cross of two birch branches on top of it. Excavation of the bodies and their interment in Kalvola took place three years later, in 1942. A Russian search party reopened the ruins of the dugout in the 1990s. They found rifles and other field equipment of the men of the 5th Company. The rifles inside the dugout were twisted like question marks by the explosion.

The Soviet Air Force dropped bombs on the Finnish lines in the village on 21 and 23 December, but the air bombardment did little harm to the Finns. Bunker No. 5 took a direct hit on 24 December, and the old part, constructed in the 1920s, collapsed. Second Lieutenant Tuomola reported in the evening of the same day that around 200 heavy rounds had rained down on his platoon during the day, with one-third of them not exploding. Trenches were almost completely destroyed and Tuomola's men too few to dig them open again during the night. The soil and stone layer on bunker No. 6 was destroyed and the frontal wall of the bunker was clearly visible from the Soviet side. Men of the 6th Company and the 2nd Machine-gun Company did their best to repair the fortifications themselves; the work continued until three o'clock in the morning. The scale of damage in this defence sector grew to such an extent that specialized units had to be summoned for repair works. The 28th Sapper Company was responsible for maintenance of the bunkers, obstacle lines and trench work in Summa village sector. Finnish sappers worked non-stop when darkness fell. Luckily for the Finns, in the first weeks of their work the Soviet artillery did not disturb them with harassing fire during the night. When the sappers were overwhelmed with the amount of work, infantry units had to be called up from the rear.

Soviet artillery opened fire at 1000 hours on the morning of Christmas Day and ceased fire as late as 2030 hours. The result of the Christmas barrage was the destruction of all the trenches in the Tuomola, Mikkola and Perttula strongpoints (Rantala strongpoint's name was changed to Perttula in December). The 6th Company reported that bunker No. 5 was completely destroyed. All lines within the battalion were down for the whole day. Soviet riflemen did not show up, and some scout parties were only spotted late at night.

The barrage continued on 26 December and lasted from 1000 hours till 1700 hours. This became a joke among the Finns, who claimed that the Russian artillery had an eight-hour working day. Bunker No. 3 took a direct hit at 1500 hours and the old part of the bunker collapsed immediately. One soldier in the garrison was lightly wounded, others got off with light shock. The casemate of the bunker with the machine-gun was not damaged.

Bunker No. 11 ('Peltola') took several direct hits next day, 27 December. The bunker was still missing its protective layer of stones and soil, and heavy shells penetrated its roof. The explosions killed two men inside and destroyed the central heating system of the bunker. The underground gallery was full of water. The casemates with machine-guns were not damaged, but the bunker's garrison had to move into dugouts of the 5th Company further away from the front. Finnish sappers completed the repair works in the bunker as late as 6 January 1940. In addition to this, the Soviet batteries fired around 200–300 heavy rounds at Tuomola strongpoint and bunker No. 6. There were no direct hits, but all the trenches were again destroyed.

The situation was repeated on 28 December. The only bright event on that day was the arrival of Finnish fighter planes at 1545 hours. This forced the

Soviet artillerymen to ground their observation balloons immediately. However, that was the only time during the entire Battle of Summa when Finnish fighters attacked the air balloons.

Artillery fire continued on 29 December. Two observation balloons were again in the air. At the same time Finnish officers spotted troop activity on the Soviet side. Second Lieutenant Tuomola reported that bunker No. 4 was under fire the entire morning and its walls were starting to crack. Although the Finnish defenders did not have to fight off Soviet attacks, fatigue was growing. During the day the men on the front line had to lie in trenches or dugouts under artillery fire; during the night they had to repair the damage. The men were exhausted and had no chance to sleep. Soviet sappers blew up an anti-tank fence in front of the 4th Company, but the damage was insignificant.

The next day, 30 December, was relatively quiet. On 31 December Soviet artillery opened fire at 0930 hours. Two Soviet tanks drove up to the anti-tank obstacle and cleared a passage with fire from their main guns. Finnish officers again spotted more activity on the Soviet side than usual – infantry movement could be seen all day long, and the roar of tank engines was more intensive than usual. Underscoring the battle for Summa village in 1939, the commander of the 6th Company wrote in his war diary: 'I estimate enemy casualties in our sector as 10–15 officers and 300 men killed.' A heavy round hit a corner of bunker No. 6: the walls cracked and a stove had to be replaced, but the bunker was still fit for action and habitation.

On New Year's Eve there were celebrations in all Soviet staffs. Despite the disastrous end of the first offensive against the Mannerheim Line in the Summa and Lähde sectors, morale was not as low as one might expect. At midnight on 31 December, when the New Year of 1940 arrived, the entire 24th Corps Artillery Regiment fired a salvo at the Finnish positions, sending a New Year's greeting to their opponents.

The pounding of the Finnish positions continued and became a daily routine in the Summa village sector. Bunker No. 4 took more direct hits and collapsed on 1 January 1940, burying Sergeant Ernest Pohjola inside. Bunker No. 7, which served as ammunition storage, was destroyed in the second week of January. The Finnish bunkers crumbled one by one. The same was happening with the trench work and obstacle lines. Soviet preparations for the next offensive were under way during the whole of January.

West of the Isthmus: Karhula and Inkilä

The 4th Infantry Division defended the western part of the Isthmus with attached units. The Karhula sector and the northern bank of Lake Hatjalahdenjärvi were held by the 10th Infantry Regiment and the 11th 'Ace' Regiment from

Helsinki. The 7th Detached Battalion from Kuolemajärvi defended the Inkilä sector. Men of the battalion came from the Western Isthmus and were literally defending their home ground.

Soviet units in the sector were quite weak, as this was a secondary theatre of operations. The 113th Rifle Division stormed the Karhula sector, the 70th Division was fighting against the 11th 'Ace' Regiment, while a task force from the Karelian Fortified Sector faced the 7th Detached Battalion. ('Fortified Sector' was the official name for battalions that manned Soviet fortified lines with concrete bunkers.) The task force was regiment-strong and fielded several detached machine-gun and artillery battalions, but it was spread too thinly and lacked supporting armour and artillery units. Colonel Lazarenko, commander of the task force, sent daily requests for supporting units and replacements.

The only day in December when Lazarenko received some help was 13 December, when a platoon of three T-28 tanks from the 91st Tank Battalion of the 20th Heavy Tank Brigade arrived from the Summa area. The three tanks attacked the Finnish lines with the support of infantry along the Terijoki–Koivisto highway. They were assaulting towards bunkers 6 and 7 on the northern side of Ahven-oja Brook. The terrain at the highway was very unfavourable for tanks and they had to drive on the highway in column. On the left side of the highway was a dense forest, and on the right side a steep ridge that ran along the highway.

The only Finnish anti-tank gun crew in the area knew the terrain well and expected the Soviet armour to act in exactly this way. The two lead tanks were immediately knocked out. The third tank tried to turn around, drove off the highway and hit a landmine – an improvised charge based on a First World War Russian sea mine with 200 kilograms of explosives. The blast was so strong that the tank's main turret was blown off and flew some 200 metres from the tank. It landed in the garden of a local Finnish farmer, who found it in 1942 when he returned home. Soviet riflemen were stopped by machine-gun fire from the bunkers and trenches.

Industrious Finnish artillerymen from the Humaljoki coastal fort heard about the battle and arrived to inspect the battlefield on the evening of 13 December 1939. They dismantled the main guns from the two knocked-out Soviet tanks and took them to their fort, planning to use them for close defence of the fort. However, a war booty party that arrived from Viipuri confiscated these guns next day.

A lull descended on the sector after these events. Bunkers 6 and 7 came under heavy artillery fire in early February 1940. Bunker No. 7 took a direct hit on its roof and had to be repaired. Bunker No. 6 took several direct hits from a

6-inch Soviet cannon that fired at the bunkers over open sights. As a result, the armoured plates of the casemates cracked and had to be reinforced with concrete blocks. The Finnish defences at the highway and at the coast came under coordinated attack from Colonel Lazarenko's freshly formed 42nd Rifle Division on land, and Marines of the Baltic Fleet on the ice of the Gulf of Finland. Nevertheless, the Finns still held the sector on 15 February 1940, when the order to fall back to the Intermediary line came.

Leonid Sobolev, a writer and war correspondent attached to the Marines of the Baltic Fleet, described bunker No. 6 in the Inkilä sector after the Finns finally left:

> The thick armoured plate is dotted with cracks, holes and scars. The blown concrete that surrounds the armour plate has steel reinforcements sticking out. The reinforcement rods are twisted and mingled like intestines. The corner of the gun port has been blown off by a direct hit. Deformed armour gleams with the fresh sheen of metal; a crack goes from the gun port to the edge of the armoured plate. The armour did not stand and cracked under direct fire from the sailors of the Baltic Fleet.
>
> This monstrous construction of 1½-metre-thick concrete and ½-metre-thick armour, this armoured turret, as if taken from a battleship and buried in the ground, was considered invincible by the Finns.
>
> This powerful position of two armoured bunkers, or, more accurately, forts, was built over several years. The art and skill of the best European engineers were invested into this ensemble of fortifications, which even the first-class European defence sector would envy. All forts, bunkers, trenches and snipers' nests protect each other. Then the best trained Finnish Home Guards were brought here, they were shown this concrete and steel, anti-tank rocks, underground galleries and mines, camouflaged anti-tank gun positions, sniper nests in trees, ten rows of barbed wire and full ammunition storages. They were told: 'This is the fortress that will wear down any army, repel any assault, withstand any artillery round. It is indestructible. You are safe from bombs and artillery, shells and hand grenades here. Your job is to choose your targets carefully and kill the attackers from these gun ports calmly, like at a firing range.'
>
> One could, indeed, hold out here as long as one had to. The splinters of our heaviest shells, which exploded next to the bunker, ricocheted from the armour and did no harm. Even a direct hit from

a heavy round could only shake this monstrous shell; bite off a chunk of concrete, but not more. A direct hit from artillery at long range is a matter of pure luck, one chance in a thousand.

The attacks of the 70th and 113th Rifle Divisions against the 10th and 11th Regiments failed to impress the Finns at all. The only achievement of the 113th Rifle Division was capturing the Finnish forward strongpoint with the poetic name 'Bird's Song' at the foot of Marjanpellonmäki Hill, where the main positions of the 10th Regiment were. Other strongpoints in the sector of the 10th Regiment had even odder names related to nature: 'Wolf's Lair', 'Hamster's Hole' and 'Bear'.

The Finnish Counter-offensive on the Karelian Isthmus

By 20 December 1939 it was obvious to the Finnish High Command that the Soviet offensive on the isthmus was failing. It was also clear that the Seventh Army units had suffered high casualties. Almost the entire Finnish main defence line was in Finnish hands. In the Lähde sector the weakened battalions of the 255th Rifle Regiment still held Poppius bunker under siege, but the Finnish battalion commander, Captain Kuiri, managed to deal with the situation by 23 December, without even requesting regimental or divisional reserves. Inspired by this success in the defensive battle, and probably driven by personal ambition, Harald Ökvist ordered his corps to launch a counter-offensive. Mannerheim also sent the 6th Division from his reserves to take part in the operation. The objective of the counter-offensive was extremely ambitious. It was to encircle the Soviet divisions in the central isthmus.

At this point it is important to see the larger picture of operations on the other fronts of the Winter War in late December. At Tolvajärvi Colonel Talvela managed to defeat the 139th and 75th Rifle Divisions of the Soviet Eighth Army. Talvela's units were preparing for an assault on Äglä-järvi village, despite Mannerheim's personal request to Talvela to halt the attacks in order to spare Finnish blood. Talvela and Pajari, the two architects of the Finnish victory at Tolvajärvi, were promoted and immediately became national heroes. The IV Army Corps, on the northern bank of Lake Ladoga, had already launched a successful counter-offensive and was delivering serious blows to the supply lines of the 18th Rifle Division. The Army of the Isthmus repelled the series of grand Soviet offensives in the east and the centre of the isthmus. Probably a desire not to be left behind by the other generals of the Finnish Army caused Ökvist to take this risky step. However, he grossly overestimated Soviet casualties and supply problems on the Karelian Isthmus.

According to Ökvist's plan, Finnish units were to deliver strikes from Hatjalahdenjärvi with the 6th and 4th Divisions, and from the Väisänen–Leipäsuo area with units of the 1st Division. The two pincers of the Finnish offensive were to meet at the southern tip of Lake Kaukjärvi. This would have meant the encirclement of the Soviet 113th, 138th, 123rd and 90th Rifle Divisions, as well as the 35th and 40th Light Tank Brigades, the entire X Tank Corps and the 20th Heavy Tank Brigade. This would have also meant the destruction of the 24th Rifle Division at Väisänen and the 70th Rifle Division at Hatjalahdenjärvi. The 11th Division delivered a distracting strike in the Oinala–Parikkala area.

The plan of the offensive was approved on 20 December and passed on to the commanders of the divisions by phone in the evening of the same day. The next day the order was sent to the divisions in writing. The 6th Division marched off to the front from Säiniö and Näykki on the evening of 21 December and arrived at Karhula on the evening of 22 December, just a few hours before the offensive. The 25 kilometre march in freezing cold had seriously exhausted the regiments.

General-Lieutenant Ökvist moved his command post and staff to the CP of the 10th Infantry Regiment in Kolmikesälä for closer command and control of the operation.

The 6th Division was to strike from the Karhula area, reach the northern tip of Lake Kaukjärvi and cut the Summa–Uusikirkko highway in cooperation with the 4th Division, and then be ready to attack to the east and south-east.

The Finns started the counter-offensive without artillery preparation, as it was planned to exploit the element of surprise. According to the Finnish plan, the artillery had to open supporting fire immediately after the beginning of the infantry attack. Due to poor communication equipment and lack of proper organization, in most cases the Finnish artillery remained silent for the whole battle. This is why the Soviet units that came under attack perceived the counter-offensive of the entire Finnish II Army Corps as a 'raid of White Finnish gangs to destroy our supply units and staffs'. Due to poor communication, the Finns could not carry out organized attacks with larger infantry units. In some places they even failed to feed the reserves into battle, as there was no communication available. As a result, small company- and battalion-sized task forces stormed the Soviet positions. To the Soviets this indeed looked like small local raids or a reconnaissance-in-force.

The offensive of the 6th Division had to be called off by 1530 hours – all three regiments of the division returned to their old line after taking casualties. It became obvious at the very beginning of the assault that the Finns were storming with company-sized task forces against well prepared, dug-in Soviet regiments.

The offensive of the 1st Division began two hours later than planned. The time of march of the troops was miscalculated and, to make things worse, Finnish sappers had not cleared passages through the barbed wire. As a result, the battalions of the 2nd and 3rd Brigades spent ages negotiating their own obstacle lines. The 14th Infantry Regiment was ready at 0730 hours but decided to wait for its neighbours, attacking as late as 0930 hours. Finnish units easily penetrated the unguarded gaps between the regiments of the 90th and 24th Divisions and attacked the Soviet supply areas and artillery positions. Some Soviet 6-inch batteries had to turn their guns and fire shrapnel at the attacking Finns at distances of 100 and 200 metres. The staff of the 286th Rifle Regiment came under Finnish attack in the sector of the 90th Rifle Division. The arrival of Soviet armour saved the day. The Finns had to quit the battlefield. At Väisänen the Finns managed to push back the 7th Rifle Regiment, enter gaps between the 274th and the 168th Rifle Regiments, and reach the River Peronjoki. Here Soviet units had prepared positions on the southern bank of the river. Tanks of the 40th Light Tank Brigade were urgently summoned from Perkjärvi and soon arrived on the battlefield. This sealed the fate of the Finnish attackers, as they had no anti-tank guns with them. Leaving equipment and dead behind, the Finns had to fall back.

Colonel Lazarenko's battalions of the Karelian Fortified Sector easily repelled the offensive of the Finnish 4th Division, reporting only several wounded. The 5th Bicycle Battalion, on the contrary, managed to surprise and shock the 70th Rifle Division, pushing it some 2–3 kilometres to the east.

Ökvist received the first reports on the course of the offensive from the 4th and 6th Divisions at 0900 hours. Reports from the 1st Division only came at 1400 hours, when it was obvious that the offensive of the 6th Division had failed completely. Ökvist called off the offensive at 1500 hours and ordered all troops to return to their start positions. Finnish units lost 1,328 men on 23 December, of whom 361 were killed, 777 wounded and 190 missing in action.

On 28 December Ökvist wrote a report giving his reasons for the disaster:

> I would like to list the reasons for failure in order of their importance:
>
> The enemy turned out to be much stronger, especially in the River Summajoki–River Työppölänjoki area, the sector which was crucial for the offensive.
>
> Contact with artillery was non-existent, which means that even the most important targets had not been destroyed and our infantry

did not receive any support from artillery. It is also important to mention here that some of the mortar rounds had faulty fuses (in the 1st Division) and some mortar rounds had the wrong calibre. This was especially noticeable in the 6th Division. We had spotted this problem in the units of the II Army Corps long ago and corrected it, but the 6th Division was attached to us too late and we did not have time to check this matter. I consider these two points to be crucial reasons for our failure. It is obvious that if our artillery and infantry are not equipped with decent radios we will run into serious problems in any future offensives. In addition to these, the following factors also played their role in our disaster:

Unfavourable weather conditions. Contrary to all our expectations, the weather was clear. This gave the enemy the possibility to orchestrate the fire of their superior heavy artillery from air observation balloons. The enemy air force actively harassed front-line units and supply lines in the rear.

Lack of front-line experience in the 6th Division. The result was panic in the division's units when enemy artillery and armour joined the game.

Poor organization of the offensive in the 1st Division, which caused a two-hour delay of the offensive.

Other factors contributed to the Finnish failure. Finnish counter-attacks worked in areas where the Finns were numerically equal to, or superior to, the opposing force. Finnish units were especially good in wood-covered terrain with a low density of units. The Karelian Isthmus was packed with Red Army units compared to the other theatres of operations of the Winter War. Despite all the Soviet mistakes, with unguarded gaps between the regiments and divisions, the Finns could not carry out deep outflanking manoeuvres on the isthmus.

To make matters worse for the Finns, the Seventh Army did not have such serious supply problems as pertained on the other fronts. Supplies and reinforcements arrived at the front by three railways and three highways. The main supply depot of the Seventh Army, Leningrad, was just 70 kilometres away from the front. The Finns could not cut the supply roads due to the large number of Red Army units on the isthmus. All the supply routes were heavily guarded. Finnish rangers sent into the Soviet rear failed to blow up railway bridges that might have interrupted the supply of troops to the front.

Finnish battalions went into battle light, taking only machine-guns with them. As a result, as soon as the Soviet armour arrived, the attacks had to be called off and the Finns had to withdraw into the woods.

Finally, Ökvist gave his officers only about twenty-four hours to prepare and plan the offensive. Ökvist himself had served on the isthmus during the 1930s and knew almost every bush and stone in the area. It could be that, based on his superior knowledge of the terrain, he expected all other officers to find their bearings in the forests of the isthmus as easily as he did.

After the Finnish counter-offensive failed, the Seventh Army assaulted the Mannerheim Line again on 28 and 29 December, but the fighting spirit of the units had been broken by the failures of mid-December. Meretskov sent a report to the People's Commissar of Defence, Marshal Voroshilov, describing the situation of his troops. The report stated that the Seventh Army had run into a well-fortified line and resources were insufficient to break through. Meretskov requested reinforcements and time to prepare the next assault on the Mannerheim Line. Stavka, the Soviet Supreme Command in Moscow, approved Meretskov's plan. A lull fell on the Karelian Isthmus. More troops were on the move to the front. Intensive battle training of the Seventh Army began. The Finns remained passive for January 1940, only building new fortifications in the rear.

In early January 1940 the Finnish divisions changed their numbers, in order to confuse Soviet intelligence.

Old unit number	New unit number
6th Infantry Division	3rd Infantry Division
17th Infantry Regiment	7th Infantry Regiment
18th Infantry Regiment	8th Infantry Regiment
22nd Infantry Regiment	9th Infantry Regiment
6th Artillery Regiment	3rd Artillery Regiment
6th Light Unit	3rd Light Unit
11th Infantry Division	2nd Infantry Division
31st Infantry Regiment	4th Infantry Regiment
32nd Infantry Regiment	5th Infantry Regiment
33rd Infantry Regiment	6th Infantry Regiment
11th Artillery Regiment	2nd Artillery Regiment
11th Light Unit	2nd Light Unit

All fighting on the Karelian Isthmus died out by the end of December 1939. Large-scale battles resumed in the area one month later, on 1 February 1940.

CHAPTER 3

North of Ladoga

The Soviet Eighth Army, under Khabarov, launched its offensive across the border on 30 November 1939, with the mission of destroying the Finnish IV Army Corps north of Lake Ladoga. Then Khabarov was to advance west and north-west towards Sortavala and Joensuu. Later, the Eighth Army had to continue its advance along the northern bank of Lake Ladoga and attack the Finnish main defence line on the Karelian Isthmus from the rear. Thus, the mission of the Eighth Army was to support the offensive of the Seventh Army on the Finnish main defence line.

Army Commander Khabarov had six rifle divisions – five on the front, one in reserve (the 75th Rifle Division) – and the 34th Light Tank Brigade, which was to build on the success of the rifle units and carry out a deep raid into the Finnish rear. The divisions were divided between two rifle corps: the I Army Corps in the north under Komdiv Panin (the 155th, 139th and 56th Rifle Divisions), and the LVI Army Corps under Komdiv Cherepanov (the 18th and 168th Rifle Divisions). All divisions of the army advanced into Finland along different roads. Gaps between the divisions were from 10–50 kilometres, so the Soviet offensive disintegrated into smaller operations from the very start.

The 155th Rifle Division attacked on the right flank along the Porajärvi–Liusvaara–Ilomantsi–Joensuu road. The division had 14,128 men, twenty-two tanks and 100 guns, including regimental guns and anti-tank guns. The division was stopped by energetic Finnish counter-attacks in the Möhkö–Oinassalmi area and the front line there stabilized until the end of hostilities.

The 139th Rifle Division attacked towards the Suojärvi–Aittajoki–Tolvajärvi–Korpiselkä road. At the beginning of hostilities the division had 15,362 men, ninety guns and twenty light tanks. The 56th Rifle Division attacked in the direction of Suojärvi–Loimola–Suistamo–Ruskeala, along the highway and the railway. The 56th Rifle Division had 15,876 men, 138 guns with attached artillery and around 100 tanks. The 410th Tank Battalion of the division had twenty T-37 tanks and fourteen T-26 tanks. The division also had the 112th Detached Tank Battalion with fifty-four T-26 tanks.

Cherepanov's corps attacked along the eastern bank of Lake Ladoga. The 18th Rifle Division attacked along the Lemetti–Koirinoja–Impilahti–Sortavala road. The 168th Rifle Division attacked along the Salmi–Pitkäranta–Impilahti–Sortavala road.

The 18th Rifle Division's supplies came along the only road through Uomaa and Lemetti. The commanders of the 18th Rifle Division well understood the vulnerability of the situation. As a result, the entire 97th Rifle Regiment was earmarked for protection of the supply route.

The IV Army Corps of the Finnish Army stopped the offensive of Cherepanov's corps and launched its own counter-attack in mid-December. The Finns managed to cut the supply lines of the 18th Rifle Division. At Ruhtinaanmäki and Syskyjärvi the 168th and 18th Rifle Divisions managed to repel the Finnish counter-attacks but were forced to withdraw 2 kilometres to the south of Syskyjärvi village. The Finnish offensive resumed on 6 January 1940 and resulted in the encirclement of the 18th Rifle Division, 168th Rifle Division and the 34th Light Tank Brigade in the Lemetti, Uomaa and Kitilä areas. The 168th Rifle Division managed to maintain its integrity and proved too hard a unit for the Finns to crack.

The largest tragedy for the encircled 18th Rifle Division and the 34th Light Tank Brigade was that they spent too long in encirclement with very limited supplies. The Soviet Air Force dropped food to the trapped units, but used light biplanes with limited cargo capacity. To make matters worse, the drops were inaccurate and the supplies often ended up in Finnish hands. The Eighth Army did little to assist the encircled troops.

Reports and radio messages from the trapped troops were getting more desperate every day. On 18 January 1940 the Commander of the 18th Rifle Division, Kondrashov, reported:

All units of the division are in an extremely difficult situation. A lot of deaths from starvation. Men have stomach cramps and night blindness. Horses are dying. We are waiting for your help every day.

And on 29 January 1940:

We have been encircled for sixteen days. We have 500 wounded. No ammo left, no bread. Around 600 men are sick. Hunger, sickness, death are here.

On 9 February, a radio message from the Head of the Special Department of the 34th Light Tank Brigade, Doronkin, ran as follows:

Men have been without proper food for forty days. Most men are starved and have frostbite. We have difficulties in holding our positions. The Air Force is dropping too little food. We have about 4,000 men in our garrison. On 7 February the Air Force delivered only 350 kilograms of dry tack, 60 kilograms of fat, 44 kilograms of sugar, 160 kilograms of preserves, 30 kilograms of bread and eighteen survival food packages, which is obviously an insufficient amount.

On 13 February 1940 Doronkin's message was: 'We are dying of hunger. Please get us more food, don't let us die here in vain.'

And on 18 February 1940: 'Why don't you drop food to us?'

And on 23 February 1940: 'Forty days of encirclement, we do not believe that the enemy is so strong here. Save us or we will die in vain.'

And on 25 February 1940: 'Save us, assault the enemy, get us food and tobacco by airplanes. Come to help us or we will all die here.'

Sergeant Arkadi Tverskoi of the 224th Detached Scout Battalion, 34th Light Tank Brigade, recalled:

Before the war the brigade was stationed in Naro-Fominsk, near Moscow. We were very well equipped, well dressed and well trained. We had the best uniforms. On 1 May 1939 my battalion paraded on Red Square in Moscow. We were allowed to have a longer haircut than the rifle units and had much nicer uniforms. It was great, as Naro-Fominsk is a town of light industry, where most workers in the factories were young women. We were very popular with them.

Our Brigade Commander, Kondratiev, had just come back from the Spanish Civil War with an Order of the Red Banner. All commanders who had taken part in that campaign were treated like heroes and we were proud that our brigade commander was one of these heroes. He was a very cheerful and friendly person.

Our Air Force did not impress us in Lemetti. They did not assist us at all. They dropped supplies from high altitude, and the supplies often ended up in Finnish hands. We were all in a difficult supply situation, both the Finns and us. Airplanes normally dropped canned meat, butter and dry bread. When an airdrop was happening, all fighting stopped. Hungry Red Army men and Finns ran around the forest, trying to snatch the supplies. As soon as the last box of food was picked up, all grabbed their rifles and opened fire on each other.

The whole campaign was badly prepared and badly planned. I have no idea who sent our brigade into the woods. What could we do with our tanks in the forests? We only dug the tanks in and used them as bunkers. We were well dressed for winter, but the riflemen of the 18th Division had light autumn uniforms! They lost about 70 per cent of men to frostbite. It was terrible.

There was very little food anyway. We ate all the horses from the rifle and artillery units. Then we started boiling their skins, leather belts and so on. It was a terrible situation.

The Finns were furious and merciless in that war. They did not take prisoners at all. In Lemetti they destroyed all the dugouts full of our wounded. I think they were even more ruthless than the Germans when they invaded the USSR in 1941.

The breakout from our pocket started on 17 February. Our battalion was covering the withdrawal of the riflemen from the pocket. I think only thirty riflemen broke out. I was wounded but could still move. We were seven men from the Scout Battalion in the same condition: wounded, but able to walk. We decided to disengage and slip away from the pocket during the night. We knew where to go, as we were scouts. After some days of wandering in the forest we reached our troops at Lake Ladoga. The NKVD received us rather coldly and we had to spend one week in interrogation. One of our men ate too much and died as his stomach could not digest all the food after one month of starvation.

In 2006 Arkadi Tverskoi visited the Russian Military Archives, where he was given a certificate showing that, according to the battalion list of casualties, he was killed in battle on 17 February 1940, during the breakout. All Russian and Finnish books mention the 224th Battalion as being destroyed to the last man.

There was no large-scale assistance from the LVI Rifle Corps and the Eighth Army to the encircled troops. The army and the corps were only sending promises of help and orders to hold on. As a result, when the breakout finally began, the men were starved and weak.

Extreme cold inflicted casualties on both armies at Lemetti. For example, the 4th Jaeger Battalion of the Finnish Army, an elite unit, lost around 70 per cent of men to frostbite. Jaeger soldiers were elite ski troops and had only thin leather ski boots. The 1st Company of the battalion fared a little better because before departure to Lemetti the company sergeant major helped himself to 100 pairs of felt boots from a wool factory in Äyräpää. Other Finnish units also suffered from the severe cold. Mauno Laaksonen, Häme Cavalry Regiment:

Our uniforms were such that I am still wondering why we all did not have frostbite. Men who brought warm clothes from home were in a better situation. The uniform pattern 1936 was not warm enough when temperatures dropped to minus forty degrees Celsius.

The lightly dressed men of the Soviet 18th Rifle Division were in an even more desperate situation. Arkadi Tverskoi again:

> Those men in the 18th Rifles were extremely badly dressed. They only had overcoats and leather boots with putties. Their casualties were 70 per cent, mostly from frostbite. Men lost their hands and feet. It was a terrible sight.

The Finns destroyed the bulk of the 18th Rifle Division and the 34th Light Tank Brigade in one month of fighting in February. The encircled troops decided to break out in late February, after they realized that help from the Fifteenth and Eighth Armies was coming too late. During the breakout the commander of the 18th Rifle Division, Kondrashov, made the shameful decision to split the force into two parts, one under his personal command and one under the command of the division's Chief of Staff, Colonel Alekseev. Alekseev was ordered to take care of all the wounded and sick men, while the best troops were in Kondrashov's group. However, Alekseev managed to slip past the Finnish outposts and safely arrived at the Soviet positions. The bulk of Kondrashov's group was destroyed during the breakout. However, Kondrashov himself made it to the Soviet lines, being only lightly wounded. According to some reports, he put on a soldier's uniform in order to disguise himself among his own troops.

The commander of the 34th Light Tank Brigade, Kombrig Kondratiev, was killed during the breakout together with his entire staff. According to some accounts, Kondratiev, his Commissar Gapanyuk and the Chief of the NKVD Special Department, Doronkin, committed suicide when they saw that the situation was hopeless. The once-proud brigade that paraded on Red Square before the Winter War lost over 90 per cent of its tanks. Losses of personnel were well over 50 per cent. Out of 3,787 men of the brigade, 902 were killed, 414 were wounded, ninety-four were sick or frostbitten, and 291 men were missing. All the battalion commanders were lost.

The commander of the 18th Rifle Division, Kombrig Kondrashov, was arrested and executed in March 1940, after the breakout from the encirclement. The division's Chief of Staff, Colonel Alekseev, was appointed commander of the division, or what was left of it. The 18th Rifle Division lost a total of 8,754 men, which is the highest casualty rate of a Soviet rifle division in the Winter War.

In March 1940 Soviet units broke through the ring encircling the 168th Rifle Division after several failed attempts. The whole new Fifteenth Army was formed south of Pitkäranta for this task. The strikes were delivered both on land and over the ice of Lake Ladoga at those islands the Finns held with small forces.

Loimola: Deadlock at the Railway

The 56th and 139th Rifle Divisions captured Suojärvi in a joint assault and then split. The 56th Division continued its march west along the highway and railway along the line Suojärvi–Loimola–Värtsilä–Joensuu.

The Finnish 34th Infantry Regiment was ordered to withdraw to the River Kollaanjoki and take up positions on its western bank and hold them at all costs. The Finnish front of defence was only about 3 kilometres wide. Taiga forests were to the south and the north of the defences. The 2nd and 3rd Battalions of the regiment, with support from the 1st Battalion, 12th Artillery Regiment and Armoured Train No. 1 held the front at the River Kollaanjoki. Other units of the 12th Division were in reserve, ready to move out to a threatened sector.

The 56th Rifle Division began its offensive against the new Finnish defence line on 7 December. The 37th Rifle Regiment, with a tank company from the 204th Detached Tank Battalion and a sapper company from the 79th Detached Sapper Battalion, were in the first line. Behind them was the sister 213th Regiment with a tank company from the 111th Detached Tank Battalion and a sapper company from the 245th Detached Sapper Battalion. One howitzer and two cannon battalions supported the offensive. The frontal assault on 7 December did not yield any results. After three days of fighting the 37th Rifle Regiment lost its battle value. When the Finns counter-attacked on 9 December, two battalions of the regiment retreated without orders. The 213th Rifle Regiment was sent to the front line to replace the exhausted 37th Regiment. The new regiment continued the frontal assaults on the Finnish line. They all failed. Then the Soviet commanders decided to launch flanking manoeuvres. The 184th Rifle Regiment was earmarked for a deep bypassing manoeuvre into the Finnish rear. The 2nd Battalion of the regiment was to cut the railway line at Loimola station, some 10 kilometres from the front line.

The Soviet battalions tried several flanking manoeuvres into the Finnish rear to the north and south of the Finnish defences during five days from 12–17 December 1939. The Finns suspected such a move and patrolled the flanks far from the front. They managed to spot the Soviet task forces well in advance and thus liquidate the danger. Finnish forces at Kollaa were significantly reinforced: one battalion of the 35th Infantry Regiment, the 3rd Battalion of the 12th Artillery Regiment and a bicycle company of the 12th Light Unit arrived at the front.

By 18 December 1939 the 56th Rifle Division had stopped all the assaults. The Finns decided to launch a counter-offensive in order to encircle the main forces of the 56th Rifle Division. The pincers of the Finnish counter-offensive were to meet at Nääntäoja, some 5 kilometres in the Soviet rear. The Finns hit the Soviet flanks on 20 December with two battalions and launched a simultaneous frontal assault at Kollaa, but failed. The repeated assault on 21 December was also repelled. As a result, the Finns also had to switch to the defence, at the same time widening their front. As a result of Finnish attacks, the Battle Group Teittinen, which was defending the Kollaa sector, had only four battalions, two artillery battalions and the armoured train left.

The 56th Rifle Division attacked Teittinen's positions again on 24 and 25 December but failed to achieve a breakthrough. The front line then stabilized and remained quiet until March 1940.

The Soviets concentrated six divisions on the Kollaa front by the end of February 1940. The grand offensive began in the first days of March. The Finns managed to repel the frontal assaults and held the flanks. The Finnish line held out until the end of hostilities, although the situation on their flanks began to deteriorate on 12 March. The battles at Kollaa became one of the symbols of the stoicism of Finnish men in the Winter War.

Tolvajärvi and Äglärjärvi: Finnish Triumph in the Land of Lakes

The 139th Rifle Division was opposed only by Battle Group Räsänen, which fielded a little more than two battalions: the 10th Detached Battalion, the 112th Detached Battalion, the 8th Company of the 37th Infantry Regiment and the 9th Battery of the 13th Artillery Regiment. After the first successful actions of the 139th Rifle Division, Battle Group Räsänen was reinforced with the 7th Bicycle Battalion. The 9th Detached Battalion arrived at Tolvajärvi to reinforce the battle group on 6 December.

The 139th Rifle Division was victorious in the first days of the campaign. The division had good battalion and regiment commanders, and used flanking manoeuvres to defeat Finnish pockets of resistance. The 139th Rifle Division, jointly with the 56th Rifle Division, captured Suojärvi on 2 December 1939. The remaining civilians in the village suffered during the assault: some were wounded or killed by hand grenades; some were detained by the Red Army men. They were suspected of opening fire at the Red Army units from cellars and house windows. Most of the detained civilians were released the same day.

On 2 December Mannerheim received Colonel Talvela. This dramatic meeting was the key to the Battle of Tolvajärvi. Colonel Talvela knew the Ladoga

Karelia very well from the two invasions into Soviet Karelia in 1919 and 1920–1921. During those years the right-wing radical officers of the Finnish Army arranged a private incursion into Soviet Karelia, in order to liberate the Karelians from the yoke of the communists. Their actions against the communists and the civilian population were so ruthless that they lost any support with the locals. Finally, the Finns were defeated and thrown back over the border by the Russian Red Guards.

Talvela was so outraged by the loss of Suojärvi and the passivity of the IV Army Corps that he insisted on a meeting with Mannerheim. Talvela wanted revenge for his defeat twenty years earlier and had carefully prepared for the second round. He graduated from the General Officer course of the Finnish Academy of General Staff in 1924–1926. He analysed plans for offensive operations in areas north of Ladoga in his thesis of 1926. Colonel Talvela retired in 1930 from the office of chief of the operations department of the general staff and was again called into service in October 1939 as the Finnish Army prepared for the war. In his memoirs, Talvela described his visit to the Commander-in-Chief of the Finnish Army, Mannerheim:

> Literally boiling with rage, I went to the reception with the Marshal. His staff was located in Hotel Helsinki at that time. I told him of my deepest beliefs and expressed all my thoughts about the importance of Suojärvi. After that I told him my view of the importance of offensive operations in war. We had to attack; no retreat. A Finnish soldier is better on the offensive; this helps his *sisu* [Author's note: a Finnish term for stoicism and stubbornness in the face of difficulties], spirit and morale. I asked the Marshal to send me to the front so that I could prove my words in action.

Talvela also asked Mannerheim to give him the 16th Infantry Regiment of Major Pajari and artillery. Major Pajari also took part in Talvela's raid into the Soviet Karelia in 1919. Pajari wrote his thesis on the capability of the Red Army to carry out offensive operations in areas north from Lake Ladoga.

Impressed by the colonel's speech, Mannerheim followed his recommendations. The Finnish Commander-in-Chief formed Group Talvela on 5 December, under his direct command. The mission of Group Talvela was to defeat Soviet troops in the area, launch a counter-offensive and reach the border, recapturing Suojärvi.

It is important to note that Mannerheim knew Talvela well and trusted the colonel. A very experienced commander, Mannerheim would not have given this task to just any colonel in the Finnish Army.

Events at the front unfolded with lightning speed, but the fortunes of war were not on the Finnish side. All attempts by Räsänen's reservists to stop the offensive of the 139th Rifle Division towards Tolvajärvi failed. The 139th Rifle Division quickly advanced into Finland, brushing off Finnish delaying parties. Räsänen's attempt to hold the offensive at the River Aittajoki failed, despite the arrival of the fresh 7th Bicycle Battalion. The 1st Battalion, 718th Rifle Regiment, engaged the Finnish defenders at Aittajoki at 1400 hours on 3 December. The Finns repelled the first attack. The entire 364th Rifle Regiment arrived at the river at 1700 hours and a joint assault began, but the Finns held the line again.

The 2nd and 3rd Companies and two machine-gun platoons from the 1st Battalion, 364th Rifle Regiment, quietly went into the forest south of the road, in order to bypass the Finnish defences. The commander of the 1st Battalion, Captain Komarinski, led the assault. The goal of the manoeuvre was the encirclement and complete destruction of the Finnish defenders at the River Aittajoki. At 0500 hours the task force made battle contact with the Finnish supply units, taking them completely by surprise. The Finns were shocked by the unexpected assault. Captain Komarinski immediately signalled the beginning of the assault on the Finnish rear by firing white signal flares. However, his two companies were not enough to completely defeat the Finns. To make things worse, the two machine-gun platoons failed to come to the battlefield and provide fire support. The reasons for this were deep snow, swamps and the cowardice of the commander of the 1st Machine-gun Company, Lieutenant Kapkanets, who tried to evade combat during the entire campaign. As a result, the men of the 2nd and 3rd Companies ran out of ammunition in the middle of the fight. The Finns saw this and launched a counter-attack. The two companies retreated into the woods in disorder, making their way with bayonets and hand grenades. Despite this, the Finns were demoralized by the surprise attack and could not put up serious resistance afterwards.

Tanks arrived at the crossing and the new frontal attack began. The Finns were still shaken by the surprise attack of Komarinski the previous night. They blew up the bridge and fell back, leaving heavy equipment behind. The retreat turned into a rout when the battalion commander, Major Juha Saarva, was wounded. He was replaced by Captain Raymond Ericsson.

The 364th and 718th Regiments took seven prisoners and captured five heavy machine-guns, an ammunition truck and a vast amount of ammunition. Soviet casualties were twenty-four killed and thirty wounded.

The lead elements of the division arrived at Äglajärvi village on 5 December. The village was 40 kilometres from the border. The village was captured by a dashing assault from two sides. Good trench work and barbed-wire fences did not help the Finns in holding the village. For the first time during the campaign, the Soviet regimental artillery supported the riflemen of the 139th Division. The 76mm and 45mm guns fired at the Finnish defences over open sights.

In the first five days of fighting, the 139th Division captured a lot of war booty: twenty heavy machine-guns, four guns, five trucks, two mortars, a lot of rifle ammunition and bicycles. It seemed that the plan of the Eighth Army was about to be accomplished. However, supply problems began in the division in the very first days of the war. These difficulties doomed many Soviet units in that war. These problems were described in the battle reports of the 139th Rifle Division in the following way:

> Roads are of frozen soil and permit movement in both directions, but in many places the roads are too narrow for two vehicles. Bridges and swampy places are blown up, which frustrates the traffic and causes traffic jams.

After capturing Ägläjärvi, the regiments of the division split. The 364th and 609th Rifle Regiments continued their advance along the only road from Ägläjärvi to Tolvajärvi. The 718th Rifle Regiment received a very hard mission – to march 20 kilometres across uncharted taiga with two battalions and reach Honkavaara on the northern edge of Lake Hirvasjärvi and strike in the rear of the Finnish units defending Tolvajärvi village. According to the plan, the march should have lasted forty-eight hours, but the terrain was so difficult the march actually took around 120 hours. To make matters worse, radio contact between the regiment and the division staff was lost at the very beginning of the march.

The 364th Rifle Regiment reached the Ristisalmi Dam on 6 December 1939 and continued its advance. Despite strict orders from Talvela to hold Ristisalmi till 8 December, the 7th Bicycle Battalion failed to hold its ground and withdrew to the Kivisalmi Dam. A fresh machine-gun company of the 9th Detached Battalion and the 9th Company of the 37th Infantry Regiment managed to stop the Soviet offensive for half a day at Kivisalmi.

The 3rd Battalion, 364th Rifle Regiment, marched off the main road to outflank the Finnish positions from the north. The battalion had the same mission as the two battalions of the 718th Regiment: bypass the lakes, cut the road from Tolvajärvi to Korpiselkä, and hold it. The battalion could not take supply vehicles and artillery with it. Men had to carry heavy machine-guns on their shoulders or in sleds. Captain Prohorov, Chief of Staff of the 364th Regiment, led the task force. The battalion ran into Finnish outposts on the northern tip of Lake Ala-Tolvajärvi but quickly drove them away and continued the advance westwards. The exhausted battalion ran into Finns on Lake Kuohajärvi and did not go any further. The battalion simply retreated to the Finnish trench line on Lake Ala-Tolvajärvi and stayed there until 11 December. The order to cut the Finnish lines of retreat from Tolvajärvi was aborted. The battalion lost two company commanders and many men in skirmishes with the Finns.

In the meantime, Finnish reinforcements arrived at the front. The 9th Detached Battalion of Captain Malkamäki arrived, and the battalions of the 16th Infantry Regiment were to arrive any moment. Talvela ordered the fresh 9th Detached Battalion to move to the Honkavaara area, in order to strike at the right flank of the 139th Rifle Division. However, events on the Ägläjärvi–Tolvajärvi road unfolded in such a way that the flanking strike was cancelled. Battle Group Paloheimo, which comprised two companies of the 112th Detached Battalion and the 2nd Company of the 10th Detached Battalion, were also sent to the northern tip of the lakes.

The 1st Battalion of the 16th Infantry Regiment arrived at Tolvajärvi village in the evening of 7 December and was immediately sent to the front to relieve the units defending Kivisalmi. The fresh battalion was under the command of Captain Herranen. The defence of Kivisalmi Dam was supposed to become the baptism of fire for the 16th Infantry Regiment. All orders were given in such a hurry that the men of the battalion were not even issued white camouflage. This cost the battalion seven men wounded by friendly fire when men of Battle Group Räsänen mistook the new Finnish troops for troops of the 139th Rifle Division. This mistake was only natural, as most of the Finns had snow camouflage, and the 139th Rifle Division had none. Any man in dark uniform was considered a Red Army man by the Finns at Tolvajärvi.

The commander of the Eighth Army, Khabarov, ordered an immediate attack by the 139th Rifle Division on the morning of 8 December. The mission of the day was to defeat the Finnish units in Tolvajärvi village and reach the important village of Korpiselkä, with roads towards Värtsilä Railway Station and Joensuu. The commander of the 139th Rifle Division, Kombrig Belyaev, asked to delay the offensive by at least twenty-four hours, in order to bring up supplies and artillery. His request was refused. As a result, units of the 139th Rifle Division attacked without artillery support. The Soviet attack across the ice shocked the newly arrived 1st Battalion of Captain Herranen, which quit its positions in the afternoon and ran back to Tolvajärvi village. Officers managed to rally the battalion only in Kokkari village, 8 kilometres from the front line. Major Pajari, commander of the 16th Infantry Regiment, coldly remarked to his men: 'You can run, but you will only die tired.'

The events of 8 December at Kivisalmi, which is one of the most beautiful places in the Republic of Karelia these days, are described in the war diary of the 1st Battalion, 16th Infantry Regiment:

> Battle units of the battalion arrived at Tolvajärvi village at 0400 hours and immediately received an order to man positions on the ridges.
>
> 0730 hours: a report came that the enemy is advancing towards Tolvajärvi village through Kotisaari Island. The 1st and 3rd Companies were ordered to strike at their flank across the lake and charged towards the island, but did not find the enemy there. The companies were hit by friendly mortar fire; two men were wounded. After that our men were hit by friendly machine-gun fire, five wounded.
>
> 1030 hours: artillery barrage against the 2nd Company. A low-intensity exchange of fire all day long.
>
> 1500 hours: the enemy is advancing towards Kotisaari with two companies.
>
> 1600 hours: enemy opened machine-gun and mortar fire at the battalion. Simultaneously – attack across the ice towards Kotisaari Island, which is held by one platoon of the 1st Company.
>
> 1630 hours [Author's Note: approximately – the handwriting is not clear]: sure symptoms of panic in the companies. The 1st Company received an order 'from somewhere' that the company was outflanked from the right and the 2nd Company on the left was defeated. An order to fall back was immediately issued.
>
> The withdrawal turned into a rout, although the enemy attacked the ridges with a small group supported by submachine-gun fire. It was hard to control the units. Soldiers left their skis and backpacks on the battlefield. We tried to assemble a counter-strike party in the rear, from men of the 2nd Company, but we failed.
>
> The rout continued. Only thirty men remained on the ridges. They held their ground and withdrew slowly. They only left their positions at 2200 hours. The 1st platoon from the 3rd Battalion was scrambled to assist them.
>
> Some 180 men from our battalion were gathered on the road in Tolvajärvi village. They were ordered to march into the rear to Kokkari village, calm down, have some rest, and put themselves in order there.

In the opinion of the Chief of Staff of the 364th Regiment, the Soviet offensive of 8 December was poorly prepared, as the division's artillery was still on the march. Only regimental artillery and anti-tank guns supported the offensive. The battle was over after a decisive assault of Finnish positions by rifle units, as noted by the War Diary of the 364th Regiment:

> This was a captivating scene of heroism by Red Army warriors. The assault looked like the assault of rebellious Kronstadt [Author's note: a naval fortress outside St Petersburg that rebelled against the Bolsheviks and was captured after a bloody assault over the frozen Gulf of Finland] in 1921. Many of the attackers, after a short cry, fell dead, or crawled back, wounded. The enemy did not withstand the decisiveness of the assault.

The commander of the 1st Battalion, Captain Herranen, believed the rumours of encirclement. Just like Second Lieutenant Luosto, he decided that Tolvajärvi village was already in Soviet hands and that they had to join the rest of their regiment at Kokkari village, some 8 kilometres west of Tolvajärvi. The men had to march through untouched taiga wilderness for the whole cold night of 8 December. This cross-country march was dubbed 'the night run to Kokkari' in Finnish military history. According to Second Lieutenant Luosto, the night march was extremely hard, even for the toughest men in the battalion.

The outcome of the battle on 8 December was the loss of the Kivisalmi area and the isolation of the 9th Detached Battalion of Captain Malkamäki and the Battle Group Paloheimo from the main Finnish forces. The two battalions were ready for a strike at the right flank of the Soviet units but ended up too deep in their rear. On 9 December Paloheimo and Malkamäki were ordered to leave their positions and join the main Finnish forces.

After Herranen's battalion fled from the front, the 364th and 609th Rifle Regiments reached the eastern bank of Lake Tolvajärvi and Lake Hirvasjärvi. They could already see Tolvajärvi village on the western bank of the lake. The 609th Rifle Regiment took a valuable prize – the new hotel of Tolvajärvi, built shortly before the war on a tall hill between the two lakes. The hotel had all the modern equipment of its time. The first floor was built of concrete and faced with beautiful granite plates. The second and third floors were built from logs. The commander of the 609th Rifle Regiment, Major Litvin, settled down in the hotel with his staff. Gun ports were made in the walls of the hotel, windows were filled with sandbags. The hotel turned into a small fort. Finnish officers could follow all these preparations and could only curse at their fate and the loss of such a strong position. Only one dam and one lake separated the Finnish defenders of Tolvajärvi village and the regiments of the 139th Rifle Division.

The 3rd Battalion of the 16th Infantry Regiment, under the command of Captain Turkka, arrived on trucks at Tolvajärvi village and was immediately set in defensive positions in the village due to the disaster at Kivisalmi.

Talvela himself arrived at the front on the evening of 8 December. He demanded immediate strikes on the Soviet units and even wanted to lead an assault of two platoons himself. After a briefing with Major Pajari, it was decided that Pajari would lead the raid of the 4th Company and Talvela would stay at the CP in Tolvajärvi village. Late at night on 8 December, Pajari left Tolvajärvi village with his company, bypassing Soviet positions on Kotisaari Island. In the meantime, the impatient Talvela planned two more strikes: the 7th Bicycle Battalion was to attack Kotisaari in the night, and the newly arrived battalion of Captain Turkka was to attack the hotel. Captain Turkka managed to talk Talvela out of this. Captain Ericsson, commander of the 7th Bicycle Battalion, replied shortly: 'My men cannot hold their ground anymore, but they could be of some use if we attack.' The 7th Bicycle Battalion attacked across the ice from Tolvajärvi village towards Kotisaari Island. The 364th Rifle Regiment repelled the assault, while Captain Ericsson was killed in the battle. The Finnish offensive failed and the battalion retreated to the jumping-off positions at 0200 hours next morning.

The troops of the 139th Rifle Division were stationed along the road for the night. The men were tired from nine days of unceasing fighting. The riflemen were unhappy about the weak presence of Soviet armour at the front and the complete absence of air support. The I Rifle Corps promised air support to the division several times but this promise was never kept. Nevertheless, the ground units impatiently waited for the Air Force. Large bonfires were lit to keep the men warm and give a clear signal to the Air Force as to the location of their own troops. At the same time this made the location of Soviet troops obvious to the Finns as well, and Pajari used this during his raid.

Major Pajari managed to slip past the Soviet outposts unnoticed. He marched deep into the rear of the 139th Rifle Division and hit the positions of the division 1.5 kilometres east of the Ristisalmi Dam. The sudden and concentrated strike caused panic and confusion among the Soviet troops. On the way back to Tolvajärvi village, Pajari collapsed. The 42-year-old major had suffered a heart attack and had to be carried back to the Finnish lines. This was the first successful flanking move against the 139th Rifle Division and boosted Finnish morale, which had been quite low. The Finnish Army had been on the retreat for over a week on the entire front, from the tundra of Petsamo to the sandy beaches of the Gulf of Finland. The Finnish Army was losing men, had surrendered one village after another, and could do little against the onslaught of the Red Army. News of a successful raid by Talvela's troops immediately spread in the Finnish Army and made the headlines in Finnish newspapers.

The 2nd Battalion of the 16th Infantry Regiment arrived at Tolvajärvi on the evening of 8 December. All units of the Talvela Group were concentrated in the Tolvajärvi area, ready to strike back at the 139th Rifle Division. Talvela had seven battalions and twelve guns against eleven weakened battalions and ninety guns. The artillery of the 139th Rifle Division, however, was scattered along the route of advance, suffering from ammunition shortage and lack of proper forward observation. Both sides calmed down and only had small skirmishes on 9 December, while preparing for the decisive battle.

The two exhausted battalions of the 718th Rifle Regiment finally reached the area of Honkavaara late in the evening of 9 December. They continued their difficult march towards Tolvajärvi village and on the night of 10 December attacked Finnish supply and artillery troops at Varolampi Pond on the Korpiselkä–Tolvajärvi road. The Finns were caught completely offguard, and it seemed the story of Aittajoki was about to repeat itself. However, this time the situation was different. The two battalions of the 718th Rifle Regiment had lost radio contact with the division in the very first days of the march, and there could be no coordinated attack from the rear and the front. The men of the 718th Rifle Regiment were on the brink of physical and psychological collapse. After a five-day march across uncharted forests with all their weapons and ammunition, sleeping in sub-zero temperatures, without hot food, the men could no longer think about fighting. When they captured the Finnish field kitchens, the battalions stopped. No one had energy left to continue the assault and strike towards Tolvajärvi village. All went for the hot sausage soup. This gave the Finns a chance to regroup and set up a counter-attack. Major Pajari was on the road from the front to Korpiselkä when he heard news of the Soviet strike. He gathered all the men at hand and personally led his scratch force into battle from the direction of Korpiselkä. The 1st and 4th Companies of the 16th Infantry Regiment attacked simultaneously from Tolvajärvi village.

The battle at Varolampi lasted through the night of 10/11 December. Men aimed at cries, at muzzle flashes. Russians and Finns bumped into each other in pitch darkness, fighting with bayonets, knives, entrenching tools – all that they had. The Finns shouted the password 'Metsä!' and the answer 'Korpi!' in the darkness in order to recognize their own men. By the morning of 11 December the Finns had won the battle. The battalions of the 718th Rifle Regiment withdrew from the road to the northern tip of Lake Hirvasjärvi. According to Finnish accounts, about 100 Red Army dead were left on the battlefield. This battle was later named 'The Sausage War', as sausages were found in the pockets and bags of some dead Red Army men. Later, the commanders of the I Rifle Corps criticized the 718th Rifle Regiment for leaving the battlefield too easily. In the opinion of the higher commanders, the two battalions could have kept the road blocked for longer, making the Finnish situation in Tolvajärvi more complicated. The 364th Rifle Regiment tried its own flanking manoeuvre on the evening of 10 December. The 2nd Battalion of the regiment marched off into the Finnish rear at 2000 hours. The battalion reached the western bank of Tolvajärvi village and stormed it from the south. Contact with the Finnish defence line was made at 0700 hours on 11 December and the battle immediately changed into a firefight. Finnish fire pinned the battalion down and the Soviet company commanders could not get their men to attack. After a while, the Soviet machine-gun company under Lieutenant Hobta ran out of ammunition. The Finns clearly heard that the Soviet machine-guns had ceased fire and counter-attacked. The Soviet battalion left the battlefield close to panic. The machine-gun company abandoned sixteen machine-guns on the battlefield, only taking the locks with them. Many rifles and light machine-guns were also left behind. The battalion suffered heavy casualties in killed and wounded and was forced to retreat back to Kotisaari.

After the 718th Rifle Regiment had already lost the night battle and withdrew from the road, the 364th and 609th Rifle Regiments attacked Tolvajärvi village. All their attacks were repelled.

Regiments of the 139th Rifle Division were in the following positions by the evening of 11 December 1939:

- The 718th Rifle Regiment was in defensive positions on the northern and north-western bank of Lake Hirvasjärvi. The regiment lacked one battalion (it was in the reserve of the I Rifle Corps) and was still recovering from its defeat in the Sausage War. The regimental HQ was stationed on the eastern bank of Lake Hirvasjärvi, separately from the battalions. This proved crucial one day later.

- The 609th Rifle Regiment held the centre of the Soviet front, on the hills between Lake Hirvasjärvi and Lake Taivaljärvi. The regimental HQ was based in the new hotel on a dominant hill between the lakes. The regiment was reinforced with a scout battalion and a company of the 218th Chemical Tank Battalion. The 3rd Battalion of the 364th Rifle Regiment was supposed to march to that area, too, but apparently lost its way in the forests and did not arrive at its positions.

- The exhausted and depressed 2nd Battalion of the 364th Rifle Regiment held the left flank of the division at Kotisaari Island. The regimental artillery was also stationed on the island. The HQ of the 364th Rifle Regiment was on the main road west of Kivisalmi Dam.

- The HQ of the 139th Rifle Division was 1.5 kilometres east of Ristisalmi Dam. The 1st, 2nd, 3rd, 4th and 5th Batteries of the 354th Artillery Regiment were also there. The 6th, 8th and 9th Batteries were closer to the front line, set in firing positions next to Kivisalmi. The 7th Battery was the closest to the front line and was in firing position to the east from the hotel. One artillery piece, under the command of Lieutenant Gromov, was set to fire over open sights at Tolvajärvi village. The 47th Corps Artillery Regiment set up in positions even further away from the battlefield, at Lake Hietajärvi, some 5 kilometres to the east. Forward observation, communication with rifle regiments, a proper phone network, and reconnaissance of targets were all lacking completely. The artillery of the 139th Rifle Division was blind and could not effectively support the riflemen.

The division had suffered heavy casualties in the eleven days of the campaign. In some battalions the casualty rate was 60–70 per cent. Casualties among company commanders were especially high – companies were led by junior lieutenants instead of captains or senior lieutenants. Constant fighting, the cold and the lack of hot food exhausted the men. They remained outdoors day and night, lacking sleep. They had fought their way into Finland and advanced 60 kilometres from the border. Morale was low. Commanders had to use more and more energy to get the men to stand up and assault the Finnish lines, and this only aggravated Soviet casualties among company commanders and platoon leaders. By 11 December around 500 men deserted from the front line and had to be detained in the rear.

The men of the division were very disappointed with the armoured units and air support. Armoured units seldom took part in the battle, and preferred to stay in the rear. This led to a heated exchange of opinions between riflemen and tank crews. Some riflemen called tank crews cowards and threatened to blow up the tanks with hand grenades if tank men did not support the assaults. All in all, Belyaev only had light T-37 tanks and three flame-thrower tanks at the front on 11 December. The remaining armour was stuck in traffic jams in the rear.

The 139th Rifle Division had not seen a single Soviet fighter or bomber plane during the entire campaign. All the men were awaiting the arrival of air support with great impatience. In order to show their location to the pilots, the men lit large bonfires. This also gave out their location to the Finns, as had happened at Pajari on 8 December. Empty promises of air support only lowered the morale of the exhausted riflemen.

The commander of the 139th Rifle Division, Kombrig Belyaev, knew the situation in the division and asked I Rifle Corps to give the division twenty-four hours for rest, organization of supply, the bringing up of artillery and provision of food to the men. He did so three times, but I Rifle Corps and the Eighth Army considered his reports exaggerated and unimportant. Belyaev, a man of noble birth and a former captain in the Tsarist Army, did not dare raise his voice too much in the Red Army. Such a background could lead to accusations of cowardice and sabotage of the Soviet offensive.

In his final report to the corps staff, Belyaev expressed doubts over the ability of his division to achieve a breakthrough on 12 December. Belyaev believed a Finnish counter-offensive very probable and estimated that it would cause the collapse of his lines. In Belyaev's opinion, his division could only continue the offensive with effective air support. Panin, commander of I Rifle Corps, did not reply to the message immediately. Belyaev summoned his regiment commanders on the evening of 11 December and made a decision to start the decisive battle on 12 December, according to the old plan. Two battalions of the 718th Rifle Regiment were to strike at the Finnish left flank from the north, the 609th Rifle Regiment with tanks and scouts was to start a frontal assault in the centre, with the 364th Rifle Regiment assaulting across the ice from Kotisaari Island. It is unclear if Belyaev was aware of the result of the Sausage War. Probably Belyaev thought that the 718th Rifle Regiment was still close to Tolvajärvi, but in fact the regiment was 5 kilometres to the north, on the northern bank of Hirvasjärvi.

The staff of I Rifle Corps reacted to Belyaev's reports slowly, but finally sent a senior officer to the division. Ponedelin, Chief of Staff of I Rifle Corps and Chief of the Political Department of the Staff Okorokov, together with the NKVD's Special Department's Chief Litvin, inspected the 139th Division on 11 December; both men were shocked by the exhaustion of the troops. The NKVD workers also reported on the catastrophic condition of the division.

During the night of 11 December Belyaev managed to bring up artillery and get his troops in some sort of order. Panin answered Belyaev's message at 0800 hours on 12 December, repeating his orders to resume the offensive immediately and report the course of the offensive by 1000 hours. Panin also promised air support. After receiving this order, Belyaev moved his CP to the position of the 609th Rifle Regiment. Panin also arrived there in order to control the course of the offensive personally. When Belyaev saw Panin at his CP, he greeted the commander with the words: 'We should not be starting this game at all.'

Other commanders were also sceptical about the success of the operation. Panin listened to their arguments and called the commander of the Eighth Army, Khabarov. The latter did not want to hear any excuses and repeated his order to launch the offensive on the morning of 12 December. When Panin tried to explain the condition of the 139th Division, Khabarov passed the receiver to Komandarm 1st Class Gregory Kulik, the envoy of Marshal Voroshilov (People's Commissar of Defence of the USSR) at the front. Kulik was visiting the Eighth Army on an inspection. He knew little about the situation at the front and simply repeated the order to attack. Panin did not dare raise his voice against the powerful Komandarm 1st Class Kulik, who was known for his bad temper and good connections at the top of the Red Army.

Belyaev began his artillery barrage at 0915 hours but the Soviet Air Force was nowhere in sight. At 1000 hours Belyaev decided to wait for air support and postponed the offensive for several hours. At the very same moment the Finnish artillery opened fire at the 609th Rifle Regiment – this was the beginning of the Finnish artillery preparation for the assault.

The Finnish offensive plan was to strike at all three Soviet regiments at once. Battle Group Malkamäki, comprising the 1st Battalion, 16th Infantry Regiment, and the 9th Detached Battalion, was to strike at the 718th Rifle Regiment. The 2nd and 3rd Battalions of the 16th Infantry Regiment were to attack the 609th Regiment in the centre. Two companies of the 112th Detached Battalion were to strike at the 364th Rifle Regiment on Kotisaari Island. They were supposed to enter the island from the south and then mop up towards the north. The 10th Detached Battalion, 7th Bicycle Battalion and 8th Company, 37th Infantry Regiment were held in reserve.

The Finnish offensive was to start at 0945 hours on the southern flank and at 1000 hours in the centre. Four batteries were allocated for artillery preparation in the centre of the battlefield (two batteries of the 3rd Battalion, 6th Artillery Regiment; 5th Battery, 12th Artillery Regiment; and 9th Battery, 13th Artillery Regiment). Due to lack of artillery, the Finns also used their heavy machine-guns before the assault in order to suppress the Soviet defences.

Battle Group Malkamäki began the offensive on the northern flank with a delay – the battalions got lost in the forest during the night and reached their start positions too late. Finnish officers had miscalculated the time needed for a cross-country ski march in untouched taiga. Joukko Luosto, a platoon leader from the 1st Battalion, 16th Infantry Regiment, recalled:

A special group marched off to make a ski track for the battalion. First we tried to make two tracks but this was too hard and we all skied on one track. We skied forward in complete darkness through dense forest. We had to wait a long time for the ski track to be ready. It was the very first ski march of our company that winter. I had never seen more difficult terrain for skiing. One had to use an axe to make one's way through the bushes. It would have been a hard task in daylight, not to mention darkness. Branches whipped our faces, we banged our heads against trees, and skis and ski poles kept getting stuck in the bushes and branches of fallen trees.

We knew nothing about the battle mission; we only knew that we had to march in a certain direction. We did not have the slightest idea of the coming offensive.

We reached Hirvasjärvi at dawn. It was only then that we were informed of the coming offensive. An older man in snow camouflage immediately attacked us with foul language:

'Why the hell are you late from the march and now delay the whole offensive?'

'Mind your own business,' replied Lieutenant Nieminen.

'And also choose your language,' I added.

He turned out to be some major (it was probably Major Malkamäki himself). Yes, we were late but it was not our fault. Someone forgot to account for the cross-country factor in calculating the march speed. We definitely could not ski in that forest with the same speed as during the Finnish national ski cup.

The 9th Battalion decided to assault directly across Hirvasjärvi in order to catch up with the schedule. According to the original plan, Battle Group Malkamäki was to go around the lake. As soon as a firefight began, Major Malkamäki ordered his troops to fall back. After that, he sent a message to Pajari about the failure of the offensive. However, Malkamäki had misinterpreted the situation. The 9th Detached Battalion reached the eastern bank of Hirvasjärvi and destroyed the HQ of the 718th Rifle Regiment, which was caught offguard and stood unprotected by its battalions. The battalions of the 718th Rifle Regiment were already on the move towards their start positions for Belyaev's offensive. They saw the 9th Detached Battalion on the ice but mistook the Finns for their own troops and did not open fire.

After the HQ of the 718th Rifle Regiment was destroyed, the battalions of the regiment retreated to the south-east in disorder and stopped at Kivisalmi Dam. Both Soviets and Finns left the battlefield, and both sides thought that they were defeated.

The Finnish artillery barrage in the centre was also delayed. After a brief artillery strike at the Soviet positions at 1000 hours, the 2nd Battalion of the 16th Infantry Regiment charged over the ice on both sides of Hevossalmi Dam. The 609th Rifle Regiment opened a hurricane of fire against the attackers. The Finns took heavy casualties on the ice (one platoon lost two-thirds of its men when crossing the field), nevertheless, they managed to cross the lake and reach the Soviet positions. The Finns crushed the defensive line of the 609th Rifle

Regiment and continued the offensive along the road east, bypassing the hotel HQ of the 609th Rifle Regiment, while units around the hotel fired at the Finns almost at point-blank range, but many weapons were set in the wrong direction, so the sector of fire was somewhat limited. The Finns charged forward at high speed and did not take serious casualties. When the leading Finnish units reached Kivisalmi, the assault on the besieged hotel began. A proposal to torch the hotel, together with its defenders, was refused and a conventional assault began. Soon the assault turned into a hand-to-hand fight. The hotel was in Finnish hands by 1630 hours. The Finnish assault was so fast that the Soviet flame-thrower tanks did not even make it to support their own riflemen. Two tanks were knocked out, the rest were captured by the Finns. The remains of the 609th Rifle Regiment ran all the way back to the old divisional CP and artillery positions 1.5 kilometres east of Ristisalmi. Belyaev and the commander of I Rifle Corps retreated with their men. They failed to stop the rout or set up any sort of defence. The commander of the 609th Rifle Regiment, Major Litvin, managed to slip out of the hotel before the Finnish assault and survived. The regiment's Commissar Balakhanov remained in the hotel with all the workers of the HQ and was killed during the final Finnish assault.

The HQ of the 609th Rifle Regiment ceased to exist in the afternoon of 12 December 1939. The entire archive of the regiment ended up in Finnish hands, but these papers have not yet been found in the Finnish National Archives. We can only hear the story of the dramatic battle from the war diary of the 2nd Battalion, 16th Infantry Regiment:

> When the battalion was ready at the jumping-off positions, the battalion commander issued an order to begin the assault at 0950 hours. The assault began on time. Our machine-guns carried out extremely effective suppressing fire before the assault.
>
> The enemy manned good positions on the other side of Hevossalmi Bridge. They had had time to dig in and set machine-guns in good positions in order to fire at the bridge and the ice field.
>
> The companies stopped for a second to catch their breath on the western bank at Hevossalmi and then simultaneously charged across the ice with the support of machine-guns. The enemy carried out a powerful counter-barrage with artillery and automatic weapons [Author's note: this was Belyaev's artillery barrage for his own offensive].
>
> The Russkies opened a hurricane of fire from machine-guns, but it was poorly aimed. Nothing helped them, as our machine-guns were also firing and aiming well. Soon our first men ran up to the opposite

bank and destroyed the first machine-gun nests. The Russkies had to
retreat to the sand quarries, where they had up to fifteen machine-
guns in position. They fought for every inch of land, but due to
pressure and heavy casualties they had to continue their retreat to the
hotel, leaving the machine-guns behind. Enemy tanks arrived on the
battlefield but were quickly destroyed one by one by our anti-tank
platoon. At that moment our men were already exhausted because of
lack of sleep and heavy fighting, so the companies stopped to catch
their breath at the quarries before continuing the assault. The enemy
retreated to the area of the hotel and the hills in front of it.

All the companies got mixed up during the battle, officers had
to attack together with men, cheering them on. The commander of
the 4th Company was wounded but remained in the ranks. Second
Lieutenant Leppänen, a platoon leader from the same 4th Company,
was killed. Lieutenant Nokkala was wounded.

The most furious battle of the day started at around 1430 hours.
The enemy had superb positions on a high hill, from which they
fired non-stop at our men below. The Russkies had a lot of automatic
weapons on a narrow isthmus between the lakes, which also fired
non-stop. Despite this, our men threw themselves at the enemy
and reached the foot of the hill, but had to fall back. The enemy's
deadly fire was too much for us. Then our machine-guns opened
fire at the defences on the hill and on the left bank of the lake. The
5th Company immediately started the assault along the right bank of
the isthmus and took a position for flanking fire at the enemy. The
6th Company and Machine-gun Company managed to suppress the
enemy's weapons on the left flank, and when we charged again,
the enemy's fire was much weaker. Our men charged fearlessly against
a numerically superior enemy, paying no attention to incoming fire.
Nothing could stop us any more, especially when our 3rd Battalion
joined the battle. The enemy had to retreat to the hotel. They had
to leave some ten to fifteen machine-guns, two tanks, two anti-tank
guns and innumerable dead on the battlefield. Our losses were also
serious. The enemy had some HQ in the hotel that did not withdraw
in time. The enemy defended the area of the hotel desperately,
fighting back tooth and nail. We also fought the best we could, in
order to finish off the whole gang. We used submachine-guns, rifles,
hand grenades, but the Russkies just held on. Lieutenant Heinivavo
was wounded in this ferocious fight, and Second Lieutenant Lehtinen
was killed in a hand-to-hand fight.

Our men on the left flank did not lose time. They hit the enemy's flank simultaneously with us across Lake Myllyjärvi. A company-strong force attacked towards the hotel. Our fire drove the enemy away from the ridge and this is how we outflanked them. This was an impressive manoeuvre. We were assaulting the hotel from two sides. The Russkies fought back as best they could from the hotel, firing from windows, doors and every possible place. The most ferocious fight raged at the hotel for an hour. We assaulted their lines again and again, but time after time the Russkies repelled our assaults. Finally, our men managed to bypass the enemy on the right as well. When the Russkies saw this, they realized that there was no point in holding their ground at the hotel. They abandoned their positions and their officers, dropped off the heavy weapons and fled the battlefield. The HQ that remained in the hotel fought bravely, but was suppressed by our hand grenades rather quickly.

Most of our units marched by the hotel in twilight, when the hotel was still in enemy hands and posed a certain danger for our flank. The 6th Company received an order to assault and capture the hotel. The enemy defended their positions with desperation, using small arms and hand grenades, but finally our hand grenades finished the job. The brand new hotel, quite badly damaged by the uninvited guests, was again in our hands. We took some thirty to forty prisoners; most of them were wounded.

When the hotel was captured, the resistance of Russkies abated. They were retreating without returning fire.

The two companies of the 112th Detached Battalion managed to get a foothold on Kotisaari Island in the very first assault and started mopping up the island towards the north. The 2nd Battalion of the 364th Rifle Regiment, demoralized by the defeat of 11 December, did not put up serious resistance. The Finns reached the battalion's HQ and the regiment's artillery. The Finns killed most of the artillery horses with knives and bayonets.

The Chief of Staff of the 364th Rifle Regiment, Captain Prohorov, the Commissar of the 2nd Battalion, Malinovski, and the commander of the 4th Company, Lieutenant Murashov, were killed in the battle. The commander of the 2nd Battalion, Timoshenko, was wounded. The Finns were about to capture the entire island when the Soviets launched a counter-attack and threw them back. The commander of the 364th Rifle Regiment, Major Dryahlov, and the Commissar of the Regiment Samohvalov, with a group of forty sappers, launched their dashing counter-attack to help the 2nd Battalion. Dryahlov had to take such a desperate step because he had no reserves left – his 3rd Battalion was engaged in the battle at the hotel and there was no contact with the 1st Battalion (apparently, it was still lost in the forests).

The Finns attempted to attack eastwards from Kotisaari Island and cut the road in the rear of the 139th Division. This attack was repelled by the artillery-men of the staff battery, the 354th Artillery Regiment, under the command of the corps Chief of Artillery and the regiment's Commissar Semenov. After defeating the 609th Rifle Regiment in the centre, Pajari directed two more companies to Kotisaari Island. Men of the 364th Regiment started to leave their positions on the island without orders at 1600 hours. Soon Dryahlov and Samohvalov saw that holding the island was useless and ordered a general retreat. The remains of the regiment left the island and gathered on the road, leaving heavy weaponry behind. The Finns captured six regimental guns, four 45mm guns, three mortars, forty-six heavy machine-guns, ninety-seven light machine-guns, ninety grenade launchers and 1,429 rifles. According to Finnish estimates, the 364th Regiment lost over 100 men killed in the fighting for the island.

Thus, the Finnish offensive succeeded in the centre and on the southern flank. After defeating the 609th Rifle Regiment, the Finns reached the area of Lake Taivaljärvi and stopped the offensive. Talvela was insisting on a continuation of the offensive, but Pajari insisted that his troops needed to rest in Tolvajärvi village. The battle that lasted all day long had exhausted the Finns and casualties were high.

Meanwhile, control over the units of the 139th Rifle Division was lost. The staff of the 609th Rifle Regiment was destroyed. The staff of the 718th Rifle Regiment did not fare any better. Belyaev asked permission from Panin to gather the defeated remains of the division at the artillery positions east of Ristisalmi. Artillerymen of the 354th Artillery Regiment fired at the advancing Finns, two guns of the 7th Battery firing shrapnel over open sights. At 1700 hours all the guns of the 354th Artillery Regiment were withdrawn to the east from Ristisalmi Dam.

During the night, the remains of the division formed some sort of defensive line: the 364th Rifle Regiment defended a narrow isthmus between Kiukkajärvi and Ala-Tolvajärvi; the Ristisalmi Dam was held by the 609th Rifle Regiment; and the 718th Rifle Regiment was in reserve east of the dam, ready to carry out counter-attacks.

The 139th Rifle Division estimated their losses in the battle of 12 December as 1,000 men killed, wounded or missing in action. According to the analysis of the battle by the 364th Rifle Regiment's new chief of staff, the main reasons for the Soviet defeat were poor reconnaissance, underestimation of the enemy's forces, exhaustion, flanking manoeuvres with too small forces, cowardice, and the lack of training for some men of the division drafted from reserve.

The division retreated some 8 kilometres to the east, so, in theory, the situation was not catastrophic. In reality, the spirit of the division was completely broken. As one NKVD report put it: 'On 12 December 1939 the division ceased to exist. They became a crowd of men that had lost the will to fight.'

Surviving Soviet commanders and political workers described their views on the reasons for the defeat. Major Litvinov, commander of the 609th Rifle Regiment, who managed to slip out of the Tolvajärvi Hotel before the final Finnish assault, commented:

> The division HQ and the division commander did not lead the units at all. There was no communication between the division HQ and the regiments. The division HQ did not have a coordinated plan of attack for 12 December. As a result, each regiment acted independently, without any common mission, which led to the defeat of the division.

Aftermath of Tolvajärvi

Worried by the condition of the 139th Rifle Division, the Eighth Army finally reacted by sending the new 75th Rifle Division to Ristisalmi, with the task of holding Ristisalmi and resuming the offensive westwards with what was left of the 139th Rifle Division. However, the deployment of the new division turned into a disaster. The new division was thrown into battle one battalion after another, without proper reconnaissance, briefing or preparations. The result was the defeat of the 75th and 139th Divisions at Ristisalmi and a retreat to Ägläjärvi village. The condition of the demoralized troops of the 139th Rifle Division also had a negative impact on the new men. The commander of the 28th Rifle Regiment (75th Rifle Division), Major Gladyshev, bitterly reflected later:

> When my regiment was on the way to the front, the units of the 139th Rifle Division were leaving the front line in panic. There was an endless flow of men of the 139th Rifles coming against us on the road. They were telling us all sorts of horror stories about their defeat. My men and commanders did not believe them. My unit had very high morale and fought stubbornly and bravely for over twenty-four hours. We had to retreat some 500 metres only due to the high casualties of commanders, lack of artillery support, and the panic

among the remains of the 139th Rifles. My 3rd Battalion, without its 9th Company, arrived in the afternoon. The reason for our defeat is that units were thrown into battle piecemeal. Units were split up and I had to command not a regiment, but a battalion, and the battalion commanders had to lead companies. Not all units of the regiment took part in the battle; it was chopped into smaller units. We lacked proper artillery support.

Komandarm 1st Class Grigory Kulik, the personal envoy of Marshal Voroshilov, removed Belyaev from command of the 139th Rifle Division. The chief of staff and commissar of the division were also replaced. Kombrig Ponedelin, former Chief of Staff of I Rifle Corps, took up Belyaev's place with the task of making the 139th a fighting unit again.

As of 18 December 1939 the condition of the 139th Rifle Division was pitiful. The losses were 50 per cent or more. The division lost the bulk of its heavy equipment in the Battle of Tolvajärvi. The 718th Rifle Regiment had around 1,000 men left with three heavy machine-guns and six light machine-guns. The 364th Rifle Regiment had 1,031 men with fourteen heavy machine-guns and twenty-one light machine-guns. The 609th Rifle Regiment, which was sent off into the rear to recover, had 1,491 men, one heavy machine-gun and thirty-four light machine-guns.

The NKVD investigation into the disaster at Tolvajärvi and Ägläjärvi was carried out in late December and completed by 2 January 1940. After a series of interviews and interrogations, the NKVD investigators found the commander of the Eighth Army Khabarov, Member of the Military Council of the Eighth Army Shabalov, commander of the 139th Rifle Division Belyaev, and commander of the 75th Rifle Division Stepanov personally guilty for the disaster at Tolvajärvi. The NKVD recommended the immediate dismissal and arrest of these commanders. However, this did not take place. Commanders were only removed from their offices and demoted. Khabarov was demoted to commander of I Rifle Corps and was replaced by Komandarm 2nd Class Shtern. The latter arrived at the front on 16 December and started tightening morale and discipline by bringing up NKVD investigators, representatives for courts martial, and a military prosecutor. Some men were executed on the very day of Shtern's arrival. Apparently, the executions were designed to intimidate the men, rather than punish those really guilty for the defeat of the 139th Rifle Division. However, these measures did not help. The 139th and 75th Rifle Divisions lost Ägläjärvi and were pushed back eastwards.

The front line stabilized at Aittajoki, the place of the first victory of the 139th Rifle Division on 4 December. This river was to become the 'Alamo' for the 75th and 139th Rifle Divisions. The order for the defence of the Aittajoki line, issued to the troops on 25 December, stated (among other things):

> The main defence line is Rantola–eastern bank of Vegarusjoki–
> Aittakoski–eastern bank of Salonjärvi. The enemy must not advance
> beyond this line under any circumstances. Every man, commander
> and political worker must know this by heart.

The 75th Rifle Division estimated its own casualties during the period 14–24 December to be:

	Killed in action	Wounded	Missing in action	Total
Senior and middle-level commanders	33	88	20	141
Junior commanders	109	129	55	293
Privates	812	1,312	1,544	3,668
TOTAL	954	1,529	1,619	4,102

In March 1940 the 139th Rifle Division received replacements and was planning a new offensive 'along the road that we all knew', as a staff worker of the 364th Rifle Regiment put it, but the offensive did not start before the arrival of peace.

CHAPTER 4

Northern Finland, Lapland and the Arctic Front

The Fourteenth Army attacked Finland in the extreme north, in the area of Petsamo. The army fielded the 104th Mountain Rifle Division, the 52nd Rifle Division (still on the way to the front at the outbreak of the war) and the 100th Detached Tank Battalion, transferred to the Fourteenth Army from the 35th Light Tank Brigade. The mission of the Fourteenth Army was:

> jointly with the Northern Fleet to destroy the enemy's forces and capture the Rybachi and Sredni peninsulas, and capture the area of Petsamo. Consolidate positions in the area and forbid the transportation of personnel and weapons from the Norwegian port of Kirkines, as well as prohibit landings on the Murmansk coastline.

The mission of the Fourteenth Army was secondary: the main strike was delivered by the Ninth Army towards Oulu. It was for the Fourteenth Army that Directive No. 001340 was issued on 28 November 1939. This directive is always wrongly interpreted in Finnish and Western sources. In addition to instructions for handling the civilian population, the Directive defines the troops' actions when reaching the Swedish and Norwegian borders:

> When reaching the Swedish and Norwegian borders, do not cross under any circumstances and do not allow provocations. Greet Norwegian and Swedish border guards when meeting them at the border but avoid conversations.

The directive is very logical, as the right flank of the army was, in fact, the border with Norway.

Finnish units in the Petsamo area were extremely weak – only the 10th Detached Company and the 5th Detached Battery were in the area. It was impossible to hold the line with such small forces in the open terrain of the northern tundra. The Fourteenth Army's advance guard penetrated 150 kilometres into Finland and was then ordered to stop. In late December the Finns launched harassing assaults of mobile ski units on Soviet supply lines, but in the open tundra it was hard for the Finns to approach their prey unnoticed. Komdiv V. A. Frolov ordered the construction of wooden bunkers armed with machine-guns and 45mm guns every 4–5 kilometres along the highway. The supply route was patrolled by armoured cars. This made Finnish strikes at the supply lines even more complicated.

The 104th Rifle Division and the newly arrived 52nd Rifle Division were waiting for the order to attack towards Kemijärvi and Rovaniemi. The Fourteenth Army's commander, in turn, had to wait for the Ninth Army to achieve a decisive victory in the Suomussalmi area and cut Finland in half. As this victory was not achieved, all military operations in the area stopped. Total casualties of the Fourteenth Army were the lowest in the entire Red Army in the Winter War: just 197 killed and 402 men wounded, sick or frostbitten.

The 122nd Rifle Division of the Ninth Army attacked towards Rovaniemi and Kemijärvi, some 300 kilometres south from the lead elements of the Fourteenth Army. The unit's original advance into Finland was a success, but then the fresh Finnish 40th Infantry Regiment, which was hastily sent to this sector of the front, stopped the Soviet advance. Both sides used flanking manoeuvres but the Finns finally prevailed. Here, just as in the Battle of Tolvajärvi, the 122nd Division was spread too wide in small units, giving the Finns the perfect chance to defeat units one by one.

The 163rd and 44th Rifle Divisions were even further south, in the area of Suomussalmi and Raatte road. The fate of the entire offensive of the Fourteenth and Ninth Armies was sealed by the fighting that took place in those places.

The Battle of Suomussalmi

This was without doubt the most famous battle of the entire Winter War. This is explained by both a stunning Finnish victory and the vast publicity that the battle received in the press outside Finland. The purpose of this chapter is to give a balanced account of the battle and set the record straight.

The 163rd Rifle Division, under Kombrig Zelentsov, started its offensive with the 662nd Rifle Regiment, the 81st Mountain Rifle Regiment (from the 54th Mountain Rifle Division), and the 759th Rifle Regiment. The division was split into two groups. The 81st Mountain Rifle Regiment, followed by the 662nd Rifle Regiment, crossed the Finnish border at Juntusranta and advanced towards Suomussalmi from the north. The 759th Rifle Regiment attacked towards Suomussalmi from the east, along Raatte road.

The 81st Mountain Rifle Regiment had been stationed in Kandalaksha before the war. This was probably the best division of the entire Leningrad

Military District and was perfectly trained for operations in the forests of Finland. The regiment served as a battering-ram against Finnish defences and quickly marched forward, brushing aside the small Finnish delaying parties.

The regiments of the 163rd Rifle Division captured Suomussalmi on the evening of 9 December. The 15th and 16th Detached Battalions of the Finnish Army could do little to stop them. Kalevi Juntunen of Group Kontula:

> We could only retreat in the beginning. There was very little snow on the ground and the Russian infantry had the same mobility as us. Their tactic was like this: infantry attacked us from the front and at the same time their cavalry outflanked us through the woods. We could only fall back in order not to be encircled. This lead unit, the 81st Mountain Rifles, was well trained. Our entire unit was around forty men – we could do little. Then we were gathered in Suomussalmi and transferred to the southern bank of Niskaselkä. The Russians captured Suomussalmi.

At the same time the entire 662nd Rifle Regiment was left in the rear of the 163rd Rifle Division to guard the Juntusranta–Suomussalmi road. The 81st Mountain Rifles tried to assault Finnish positions on the southern bank of Niskaselkä with two companies, but were thrown back by the Finns with heavy casualties. The 759th Rifle Regiment remained passive and did not take part in the assault. There was no cooperation between the two regiments, especially in matters of artillery support. The 81st Mountain Rifle Regiment was exhausted, had suffered heavy casualties, and could not advance any further. There was no possibility of a continuation of the offensive towards Hyrysalmi. Again, riflemen had to bear the main responsibility in battle – artillery and armour was stuck behind while all the tanks were stranded in Juntusranta without fuel.

The Finns started the transfer of reserves to Suomussalmi almost immediately after the outbreak of war. Companies of the 4th Reserve Battalion arrived on 3 December, followed by the entire 9th Infantry Division commanded by Colonel Siilasvuo. He well understood how shaky his position was. Cold weather had already set in and in a matter of days the ice of Lakes Niskaselkä and Haukperä would be thick enough to support the weight of Soviet light tanks. The arrival of armour would have made holding the southern bank of Niskaselkä and Haukperä a very difficult task. Siilasvuo was also aware of the 44th Rifle Division marching to reinforce the 163rd Rifle Division in Suomussalmi. His poorly equipped 9th Infantry Division did not have a chance against two Soviet rifle divisions with powerful artillery and armour support. Siilasvuo made a radical decision – probably the only correct one in his situation. He decided to separate the two Soviet divisions and deal with them one by one. He also decided to launch a counter-offensive in order to dazzle Zelentsov and gain the initiative in battle.

On 9 December 1939 Siilasvuo had at his disposal the 4th Reserve Battalion, 15th Detached Battalion, 16th Detached Battalion, 27th Infantry Regiment, Battle Group Kontula (two detached companies formed from local reservists) and the 5th and 6th Ranger Groups formed from elite Border Guard Rangers. Each Ranger Group was the size of a platoon.

Siilasvuo left a small force of infantry, with almost all the heavy machine-guns, on the southern bank of Haukperä. The force comprised two machine-gun companies of the 27th Infantry Regiment and some machine-gun crews from the 4th Reserve Battalion. All nine infantry companies of the 27th Infantry Regiment marched off to assault the Raatte road. After cutting the road, the Finns planned to build a defensive front facing east and then continue the offensive towards Suomussalmi.

The first Finnish offensive towards the Raatte road began on 11 December 1939. Battle Group Kontula cut the road, destroyed a Soviet convoy of six trucks carrying wounded to the border, and formed a defensive position facing east, against the approaching 44th Rifle Division. The Finnish troops manned a favourable defensive position on a river between Lake Kuivasjärvi and Lake Kuomajärvi. The infantry companies of the 27th Infantry Regiment and the 4th Reserve Battalion also reached the Raatte road and marched west, towards Suomussalmi, which was held by the 759th Rifle Regiment.

The 15th Detached Battalion launched harassing assaults on Cape Hulkoniemi from the west, while Light Company Hannilla tried to cut the Suomussalmi–Juntusranta road. The 81st Mountain Rifle Regiment repelled all these assaults.

Finnish units surrounded the 759th Rifle Regiment in Suomussalmi by 14 December and carried out several assaults on the village; all were repelled. The lead units of the 44th Rifle Division made contact with Battle Group Kontula on 15 December. The 25th Rifle Regiment of the new division tried to assault the Finnish positions with a company-sized force and failed. After that the 25th Rifle Regiment ceased all assaults and did nothing for a week. The most important result of the Finnish counter-attacks of 13–16 December was the moral effect on the commander of the 163rd Rifle Division, Kombrig Zelentsov. Unnerved by the continuous Finnish attacks on the supply lines of his division, Zelentsov considered the situation of his troops desperate. Time and again he requested permission to withdraw. He was forbidden to leave Suomussalmi due to the expected arrival of the 44th Rifle Division. However, the commander of the Ninth Army, Dukhanov, failed to arrange a coordinated operation by the two divisions. Dukhanov was removed from office on 22 December. Komkor Chuikov was appointed to replace him.

Despite the appointment of a new commander, the Soviet units were still reacting slowly. Preparation of the new offensive of the 44th Rifle Division towards Suomussalmi was postponed several times. Colonel Siilasvuo developed his own offensive plan in the meantime. He decided to strike simultaneously at the 662nd Rifle Regiment dispersed on the Juntusranta–Suomussalmi road and the 81st Mountain Rifle Regiment in Hulkoniemi.

Four Finnish battalions assaulted the positions of the exhausted 81st Mountain Rifle Regiment on 27 December and broke through the regiment's defences. The regiment had to fall back on the divisional HQ, and all men at the HQ had to take part in the battle. Continuing Finnish attacks completely unnerved the commander of the 163rd Rifle Division. Each day, Zelentsov bombarded Chuikov and Chief of the General Staff Shaposhnikov with requests to withdrawal from Suomussalmi to the border. Siilasvuo's strategy worked perfectly. Zelentsov was shocked by the Finnish assaults and depicted his division's situation as desperate. He received permission on 27 December and immediately started planning the evacuation of his regiments from Suomussalmi over the ice of Lake Kiantojärvi. The withdrawal began on the morning of 28 December. The 81st Mountain Rifles and the 759th Rifle Regiment formed a long column on the ice and marched off to the north. Tanks guarded the flanks of the column. The Air Force covered the withdrawal from the air. By the evening of 28 December the two regiments had safely arrived at their destination. However, Zelentsov seems to have completely forgotten about his third regiment, the 662nd Rifle Regiment, which was split into two battle groups guarding the Juntusranta–Suomussalmi road. The regiment was left on the road alone and suffered a crushing defeat. The regiment commander Sharov, and the regiment commissar Podhomutov, abandoned their troops at the very beginning of the battle and escaped to Juntusranta through the forest. The result was the near destruction of the 662nd Rifle Regiment. Sharov and Podhomutov were arrested, tried and executed in front of the remains of their own regiment.

Defeat of the 44th Rifle Division on Raatte Road

The withdrawal of the 163rd Rifle Division from Suomussalmi doomed the 44th Rifle Division on the Raatte road. It was left facing the 9th Finnish Division alone. The 44th Rifle Division stretched out for 20 kilometres along the road from the border to the Finnish defence line between Kuivasjärvi and Kuomajärvi. The division HQ was on the Soviet side of the old border in Vazhenvaara. The Medical Battalion of the division was stationed in the building of the Finnish border station. The 312th Detached Tank Battalion and the 56th Anti-Tank Battalion were stationed some 18 kilometres from the border. The 1st and 3rd Battalions of the 146th Rifle Regiment, the 122nd Artillery Regiment and the 3rd Battalion of the 305th Rifle Regiment followed them. The 9th Company of the 146th Rifle Regiment was guarding the left flank of the division in the area of Sanginaho, some 5 kilometres south from the Raatte road. The 2nd Battalion of the 146th Rifle Regiment, under Captain Pastukhov, was in positions on the bank of Lake Kuivasjärvi. The 25th Rifle Regiment held the front line at the river with two rifle battalions. The 4th Detached Scout Battalion was also on the way to the front. The 3rd NKVD Border Guard Regiment was also present at the front, but in fact Major Lvov, commander of the regiment, only had two companies at hand.

Chuikov and his staff made a quick analysis of the tactical failures and flaws of the 163rd and 122nd Rifle Divisions and sent recommendations to the staff of the 44th Rifle Division. Colonel Volkov, Chief of Staff of the division, completely ignored the recommendations and simply filed it in his in-tray.

Chuikov was quite sceptical about the battle value of the 44th Rifle Division in the terrain of Suomussalmi and requested the fresh 130th Rifle Division from Stavka. He noted that 'the 44th Division adjusts to the local conditions very badly' and also requested ski troops from Stavka. Shaposhnikov, Chief of the General Staff, replied that the 130th Rifle Division was never meant for the Ninth Army and that the Ninth Army would have to form its own ski units from rank-and-file men who could ski.

The 44th Rifle Division remained passive and did not assault the weak Finnish roadblock between the lakes. Orders for the offensive were shifted time and again. When the 163rd Rifle Division withdrew from Suomussalmi, the 44th Division was ordered to form an all-round defence formation and hold on.

Kombrig Vinogradov, commander of the 44th Rifle Division, and the division's Chief of the Political Department Parkhomenko, went to the front to oversee the preparations of the 25th Rifle Regiment. They arrived at the regimental HQ on 31 December.

The Finnish offensive plan was to go deep into the rear of the 44th Rifle Division and strike at the division's left flank. The 65th, 64th and 27th Infantry Regiments, as well as the 22nd Light Unit, 1st Ranger Battalion and 15th Detached Battalion, were earmarked for the operation. The Finns had a numerical superiority – they fielded twelve battalions against Vinogradov's seven. Vinogradov's advantage was in artillery and armour, but he could not deploy these properly in the forests and deep snow. The weakest spot of the 44th Rifle Division was the deployment of the troops. The division was spread out thinly in separate battalions and companies. The road was jammed with traffic, and the division did not have any significant supply of ammunition or food. Morale in the division was not at its best, as the terrain of northern Finland was completely strange and unfamiliar to men from the steppes and fields of Ukraine.

The Finnish offensive started on 1 January 1940 at 1400 hours. The 1st Ranger Battalion and the 1st Battalion, 27th Infantry Regiment, assaulted the positions of the 2nd Battalion, 146th Rifle Regiment, under Captain Pastukhov. Pastukhov's battalion inflicted heavy casualties on the Finnish rangers and repelled all their assaults. The Ranger Battalion had to be replaced with the 3rd Battalion, 27th Infantry Regiment.

The 1st Battalion of the 27th Infantry Regiment managed to bypass the Soviet flank and attacked the firing positions of the 3rd Battalion, 122nd Artillery Regiment, late on the night of 1 January. The artillerymen were exhausted by a long march. The commander of the battalion, Captain Revchuk, ordered his men to set the guns in firing positions and organize sentries. The men of the battalion replied that they were exhausted and Captain Revchuk permitted them to complete the job next morning. The 7th and 8th Batteries were thus in firing positions, but the guns were not ready to fire. The artillerymen had dinner and prepared for their night's rest. There were too few sentries and no rifle units nearby. The Finns poured a hail of fire at the battalion at 2300 hours. The men of the battalion were caught completely offguard. The 9th Battery was still standing on the road and the unit was wiped out to the last man, even before the men could prepare their guns for firing. The artillerymen, drafted from the reserve, panicked. Captain Revchuk tried to set up some sort of defence but had to fire his guns personally with a handful of veteran artillery-men. A few minutes later Revchuk ran towards the front line, to the 146th Rifle Regiment, to ask for help. His Chief of Staff, Captain Getmantsev, had fled in that direction even earlier. The commander of the 146th Rifle Regiment refused to send riflemen and only gave Revchuk two lightly armoured T-20 Komsomolets gun tractors. The Finns immediately knocked both out. The outcome of the battle was the loss of the 3rd Battalion's guns and heavy casualties in dead and wounded. The surviving artillerymen and Revchuk joined the 146th Rifle Regiment.

The 3rd Battalion, 27th Infantry Regiment, resumed its assault against Captain Pastukhov's battalion and inflicted heavy casualties on it (over 211 men were killed or wounded). Pastukhov's battalion had to withdraw to the road. The 1st Battalion, 146th Rifle Regiment, was thrown into battle and managed to restore the situation. Pastukhov's men manned their old defences at the lake. After that his battalion was virtually forgotten by the staff of the 146th

Regiment. No one maintained contact with the battalion, no one brought supplies.

The result of the battle on New Year's Day 1940 was that the Finns cut the 44th Rifle Division's supply route. Although the Finns could not hold the road, all traffic along the road stopped. Colonel Volkov, Chief of Staff of the 44th Rifle Division, reported the encirclement of the 146th Rifle Regiment and the 3rd Battalion, 122nd Artillery Regiment, on the morning of 2 January 1940. A small task force was sent to break through the encirclement: an armoured car company, a dismounted squadron, two companies of border guards and two platoons from the 3rd Battalion, 146th Rifle Regiment. The Finns repelled this assault. As soon as the Finns reached the road, they blocked it with trees, planted landmines and held the barricades in their sights.

The 22nd Light Unit reached Sanginaho and stormed the positions of the 9th Company, 146th Rifle Regiment. Isolated from all other units of the division, the company managed to repel all Finnish attacks on 1 January. Colonel Siilasvuo ordered the 4th Reserve Battalion of Lieutenant Karhunen to march off to Sanginaho, destroy the enemy and reach the Raatte road. The reserve battalion assaulted the 9th Company from the rear at 2100 hours on 3 January 1940, but the 9th Company held on. The Finnish battalion was ordered to repeat the assault on 4 January. The 15th Detached Battalion cut the road from Sanginaho to the Raatte road and marched north. Soon it ran into the 7th Company of the 146th Rifle Regiment, sent to assist the besieged 9th Company. The Finns easily stopped the Soviet advance and knocked out the tank that the 7th Company had as reinforcement. The 4th Reserve Battalion repeated the assault during the day on 4 January and destroyed the 9th Company after two hours of heavy fighting. Men of the 9th Company fought bravely and the Finns had to assault every hole in the ground. Commanders of the 44th Rifle Division on the Raatte road could only write down in their war diaries: 'We have no contact with the 9th Company, we hear that the firefight is abating.' The Finns counted 260 dead Red Army men on the battlefield after everything was over. Some forty men were taken prisoner. Finnish casualties were forty-two men, with fourteen killed and twenty-eight wounded.

The supply situation of the encircled units of the 44th Rifle Division worsened by 2 January 1940. Units were given permission to butcher horses for food. The flawed supply situation became obvious – the units at the front did not have any significant stores of food or ammunition.

Colonel Volkov requested an airdrop of supplies from the Ninth Army. He asked for over 50 tons of ammunition and supplies. Volkov calculated that, in order to continue the battle, the 44th Rifle Division needed:

9 tons of rifle ammo
8 tons of 76mm rounds
1.2 tons of 122mm rounds
2 tons of hand grenades
1 ton of rifle grenades
12 tons of straw
10 tons of oats
8 tons of bread
2 tons of meat
800 kilograms of fat
270 kilograms of sugar
240 kilograms of salt
500 kilograms of butter
8,000 tins of preserves

The Ninth Army did not have such vast supplies. To make things worse, the Soviet Air Force in the area was rather weak. Chuikov tried to send supplies by four TB-3 and R-5 planes, but they were all grounded.

It was obvious to Chuikov that the Finns controlled the road, but one could easily make it to and from the encircled division on foot through the woods. The Finns did not have enough troops to completely seal the encircled troops of the 44th Rifle Division. And so Chuikov began preparations to send a convoy of men on foot in order to deliver supplies to the 44th Rifle Division through the taiga north of the Raatte road.

Colonel Volkov informed the Ninth Army that a link with the encircled troops was re-established; that the Finns had been knocked out from the road; and that supplies were pouring in again. This message was a total lie: Vinogradov tried to break out several times on 3 and 4 January, but failed. The Scout Battalion, reinforced with armoured cars, also failed to break through to the encircled troops from the east. The lie was uncovered on 4 January. The condition of the encircled troops, in the meantime, continued to deteriorate.

Chuikov informed Stavka and the general staff about the dire situation of the 44th Rifle Division and the measures he had managed to take. The army only managed to drop several bags of dry tack to the encircled troops and recommended butchering horses for food. A new offensive was planned for 5 January in order to re-establish connection with the encircled regiments of the 44th Rifle Division. Vinogradov's group and Battle Group Lvov were supposed to strike at the Finnish encircling ring simultaneously. Everything went wrong and the plan was never accomplished. The most serious problem for the Ninth Army was that it had no more reserves to assist the 44th Rifle Division.

The 2nd Battalion, 146th Rifle Regiment, under Captain Pastukhov, abandoned its positions on the evening of 4 January, retreating to the HQ of the 305th Rifle Regiment. Captain Pastukhov explained the retreat by the fact that his battalion had not eaten for four days, had run out of ammunition, and was not in a condition to fight. This meant that the flank of the division was exposed. Vinogradov ordered the battalion to eat and then return to its original positions, but it was too late. The Finns seized the opportunity and cut Vinogradov's battle group off from the rest of the division. Now there could be no simultaneous strike by the two battle groups. Lvov's group attacked separately but failed. According to some reports, Major Lvov was badly wounded in the combat and was evacuated from the battlefield on a sled. A senior lieutenant, the commissar of the 3rd NKVD Border Regiment and a Representative of the NKVD Special Department escorted the sled. The commissar of the regiment had a psychological breakdown, lost his mind and became delirious. Major Lvov suffered bitterly from his wound and asked the escorting commanders to finish him off. After some time the commanders thought they had run into a Finnish ambush, but it was probably just a hallucination of the commissar. The commissar grabbed his pistol, killed Lvov, shot the senior lieutenant (only wounding him), and then shot himself in the head but survived.

The Finns launched an all-out offensive against the 44th Rifle Division on the Raatte road, but in most places men of the 44th Rifle Division held their ground. Nevertheless, the division's forces were all but spent. Units were running low on ammunition and food, which had a clear impact on the troops. On the evening of 5 January the Finns destroyed the HQ of the 25th Rifle Regiment and started their assault against the HQ of the 146th Rifle Regiment. The wounded commander of the 146th Rifles, Major Ievliev, sent an uncoded radio message: 'Give help us, we are dying here.' This message was repeated several times and after that the radio went silent. The HQ of the 146th Rifle Regiment also ceased to exist. Most of the commanders and political workers survived the onslaught, however, and withdrew from the battlefield.

Vinogradov informed the Ninth Army on 6 January that he could not break out with heavy equipment but could get most of the men of the division out through the woods. He requested instructions. Chuikov replied that in this case the division had to hold on and wait for help. At the same time Chuikov requested Stavka's permission for the 44th Division to break out without its heavy equipment.

On the evening of 6 January the division HQ had radio contact only with the 122nd Artillery Regiment. The HQs of the rifle regiments were destroyed. Radio contact with the tank battalion was also cut. Weak radio contact could still be maintained with the 305th Rifle Regiment.

The situation had deteriorated even further by the evening of 6 January. Finnish units cut the road at the very border, building a barricade between the HQ of the 44th Rifle Division and the Medical Battalion of the division. Personnel of the HQ had to man the trenches and set up all-round defences. Sappers and riflemen were sent to protect the Medical Battalion. A battalion of the 305th Rifle Regiment, which had not taken part in the battle, was urgently sent to Vazhenvaara from Juntusranta.

Vinogradov summoned his commanders on 6 January at 1600 hours and briefed them on his decision to break out on the same day at 2200 hours. The remaining units of the division had to break out along the road through Finnish barricades with heavy equipment. Two rifle companies of the 25th Rifle Regiment, under the command of Major Plyukhin, commander of the 25th Rifle Regiment, were at the head of the column. They were supported by 45mm guns loaded with canister. They were followed by two batteries of the 122nd Artillery Regiment, tanks, supply units and trucks loaded with wounded. Asya Kotlyar, Senior Medic of the 146th Rifle Regiment, later stated that only walking wounded were loaded on the trucks. Around 200 severely wounded men were left at the mercy of the enemy. When Asya Kotlyar asked Vinogradov what to do with the severely wounded men, he replied: 'Let me take care of the healthy men first.'

The commanders of the column on the road received instructions what to do in case the breakthrough failed: they had to destroy all heavy equipment and break out through the woods.

The second column led by Vinogradov had two rifle companies of the 305th Rifle Regiment, the Guard Platoon, a machine-gun company and the commanders of the 44th Rifle Division. This column was supposed to march through the woods from the very beginning. A rifle platoon took point, then the HQ of the 305th Rifle Regiment, then Vinogradov and his staff, the machine-gun company, the 8th Rifle Company and the rearguard, which comprised the Guard Platoon armed with submachine-guns and light machine-guns.

The breakout began on the night of 6 January. The Finns opened a hurricane of fire at the column on the road and the breakout along the road failed immediately. Chaos and panic followed; the men of the 44th Rifle Division abandoned the heavy equipment and ran into the woods north of the road. The commanders lost all control over their troops. Intensive Finnish fire prevented the Soviets destroying the heavy equipment on the road. The artillerymen were only able to remove the breeches from the guns and hide them in the snow. The men of the division fled eastwards along the Raatte road for a distance of 2–3 kilometres. They gathered at the old border in Vazhenvaara at the HQ of the 44th Rifle Division. The commander of the 122nd Artillery Regiment vanished during the retreat, when he went to the end of the column to pick up his wounded wife. Three writers assigned to the division as military correspondents were also missing. The trucks with the wounded were left on the road. Those wounded who could still move joined the night retreat through the woods.

The column of the 305th Rifle Regiment did not meet any opposition from the Finns and reached Soviet lines without casualties. There is a common myth in Finnish books that Vinogradov escaped the encirclement in an armoured car or plane, but this is not so. In any case, Vinogradov acted like a coward, leaving the battlefield under the protection of two rifle companies and a well-armed Guard Platoon.

The 1st Battalion of the 305th Rifle Regiment, under Captain Chervyakov, was the only battle-ready unit of the division at the border. This was exactly the battalion that was urgently transferred by trucks from Juntusranta. The battalion took over the defences at the border. Supply of the battalion was so poorly organized that 40 per cent of the men did not have gloves or mittens.

The staff of the 44th Rifle Division immediately ran into difficulties with feeding the troops that had escaped the encirclement. All field kitchens and other heavy equipment were left in Finnish hands. The Finns captured 4,822 rifles, 190 light machine-guns, 106 heavy machine-guns, twenty-nine anti-tank guns, fourteen anti-aircraft truck quads M-4, seventy-one field and anti-aircraft guns, forty-three tanks, ten armoured cars, 260 trucks, two cars and 1,170 horses. War correspondents from all over the world arrived at the battlefield to see the picture of death and destruction. The Battle of Suomussalmi was announced as the greatest Finnish victory of the Winter War and immediately became a legend. The world's press announced the complete destruction of two Soviet divisions and the acquisition of vast amounts of war booty.

But the losses of the 44th Rifle Division were not as high as is described in the West. Total casualties of the division during the first week of January were 4,674 men, with 1,001 killed, 1,430 wounded and 2,243 missing in action. Total casualties of the 44th Rifle Division are summarized in the table below.

Unit	Killed	Wounded	Missing in action	Total
25th Rifle Regiment	?	?	1,551	2,031
146th Rifle Regiment	271	699	453	1,393
305th Rifle Regiment	25	15	280	280
4th Detached Scout Battalion	34	38	69	177
61st Sapper Battalion	6	35	49	110
122nd Artillery Regiment	145	117	408	670

The Ninth Army carried out an investigation by court-martial into the division's demise. Surviving commanders and political workers of the division were interviewed and some interrogated. The standard questions were:

'Describe the actions of the divisional commander and his staff.'
'Describe the breakout and defeat.'
'What are the main reasons for the division's defeat?'

All the commanders agreed that the main reason for the defeat was the separating of the division into smaller units, plus the large number of supply vehicles on the road that had to be guarded. Doctors and medics also blamed Vinogradov for leaving the badly wounded behind. The court-martial found Kombrig Vinogradov, Commissar Parkhomenko and Chief of Staff Volkov guilty and sentenced them to death. All three commanders were executed in front of the remaining men of the 44th Rifle Division in Vazhenvaara in January 1940. The NKVD reports indicated that rank-and-file men of the 44th Rifle Division mostly approved of this punishment.

The Commissar of the Ninth Army, Furt, was appointed acting commander of the 44th Rifle Division. His main task was to make the division a fighting unit again and prepare a new offensive by mid-March 1940.

One cannot underestimate the strategic importance of the Finnish victory at Suomussalmi. The offensive of the entire Ninth Army towards Oulu was stopped and its units badly mauled. The 163rd and 44th Rifle Divisions needed time to recover (the latter only regained fitness after the war was over). The sad fate of the 163rd and 44th Rifle Divisions stunned the Soviet senior commanders so much that they decided to pull the 122nd Division back towards Märkäjärvi, fearing another Finnish attack. The Finns took the initiative from the Soviets. The Finns held the front with small delaying parties, as Soviet activity at the front stalled. Siilasvuo's victorious 9th Division was free to be relocated to other sectors of the front. The Finnish High Command made the decision to use Siilasvuo's troops 100 kilometres to the south, in the area of Kuhmo, in order to defeat the 54th Mountain Rifle Division with the same tactics. The passivity of the Soviet Ninth Army after the defeat at Suomussalmi also gave the Finns a chance to relocate the 40th Infantry Regiment and two reserve battalions from the Märkäjärvi front to the Karelian Isthmus when a critical situation developed there. The Swedish Volunteer Corps took over the front at Märkäjärvi on 28 February 1940.

In contrast, the victory had a huge impact on the morale of the Finnish Army and the nation's Home Front. News of the stunning Finnish victory made headlines around the world. The Raatte road (blocked with the abandoned vehicles of the 44th Rifle Division), the march of hundreds of prisoners, the frozen corpses of Red Army men – these images became the defining symbols of the Winter War. The reputation of the Red Army suffered a serious blow worldwide. The legend of the Battle of Suomussalmi lives on. The newly built memorial on the Raatte road has 10,000 stones on a single field. Each stone symbolizes a fallen Finnish or Soviet soldier. Although the combined losses of the 163rd and 44th Rifle Divisions were not so high, no one can doubt the extent of the Finnish victory. Colonel Siilasvuo chose the correct tactics and his troops executed their missions with excellence. Kombrig Vinogradov's tactic of splitting his division into smaller units was a great gift to the Finns.

Captain Pastukhov, who managed to keep his battalion together and brought it to Vazhenvaara, was interviewed by the court-martial of the Ninth Army; he stated: 'the main reason for our defeat was that the regiment was split in battalions and battalions were split in companies, which fought independently'. After Pastukhov's battalion made it to Vazhenvaara, it had left seven commanders out of thirty-one, six junior commanders out of ninety-six and ninety-eight men out of 650.

A thorough analysis of the disaster was made by the Soviet staffs. It became obvious that the Red Army urgently needed mobile ski groups to succeed in Finland. Due to the deep snow, the riflemen of the Red Army could only move on roads, while Finnish ski troops could move freely over almost any terrain. Ski battalions were formed in each Soviet division. A ski battalion normally comprised young soldiers in good physical shape who could ski. However, the tactical deployment of such units was yet to be developed. In order to improve the overall situation on the Finnish front, the Komsomol (the youth section of the Bolshevik Party) called for patriotic young men to join the volunteer ski squadrons and battalions. These battalions were issued special ski uniforms and equipped with automatic rifles and submachine-guns. The average age of these men was twenty years. Several dozen such ski battalions were formed in January 1940.

Komkor Chuikov, commander of the Ninth Army, is better known in the West as the commander of the Sixty-Second Army and, later, the Eighth Guards Army, where his forces played a crucial role in the Battle of Stalingrad. Chuikov is one of the greatest war heroes of the Red Army in the Great Patriotic War. In his memoirs, entitled *From Stalingrad to Berlin*, he did not write a single word about his role in the Winter War and the Battle of Suomussalmi . . .

Suomussalmi Repeated: Fighting on the Kuhmo Front

After the Finnish victory at Suomussalmi the threat of the Soviet offensive towards Oulu was liquidated. The Finns had enough time and resources to strike at the 54th Mountain Rifle Division, which was stopped 15 kilometres south-east of Kuhmo.

Siilasvuo's 9th Division completed its deployment against the 54th Mountain Rifles on 27 January 1940. The Finnish plan was exactly the same as the offensive plan against the 44th Rifle Division on the Raatte road: cutting the supply routes of the division in the rear with mobile ski groups, splitting the division into individual pockets and destroying these pockets one by one. The tactics became known as *motti* tactics – in Finnish, 'motti' means a stack of wood and the tactic can be described as chopping up and stacking wood in different places.

The Finnish offensive began on 29 January. The 27th Infantry Regiment immediately succeeded in cutting off the rear units of the division at Reuhkavaara, breaking through the defences of the 305th and 529th Rifle Regiments. The Finns attacked even deeper into the Soviet rear at Löytövaara on 30 and 31 January.

Chuikov and his staff took immediate measures after the first Finnish assaults. The Ninth Army did everything possible to avoid a repetition of the catastrophic scenario on the Raatte road. All reserves were to assist the 54th Mountain Rifles, including improvised battle groups and freshly formed ski battalions. The first improvised group was Battle Group Kutuzov, which comprised the 3rd and 17th Detached Ski Battalions and the 11th Sapper Battalion. Battle Group Kutuzov (Major Kutuzov was a deputy commander of the 54th Mountain Rifle Division) launched a counter-offensive against the Finns at Löytövaara on 30 January 1940, but failed to achieve any success. Before Major Kutuzov formed his staff and established contact with his units, the Finns counter-attacked and virtually wiped his group out. Major Kutuzov himself was killed in action.

The Finns successfully chopped the 54th Mountain Rifle Division up and started planning the offensive for its destruction. However, all their plans were skewed by the arrival of Colonel Dolin's ski brigade, which fielded three ski battalions. The brigade skied through the snow-covered wilderness and arrived on the battlefield on 13 February, when the head of the brigade reached Vetko Farm. The brigade was some 7 kilometres from the encircled Mountain Rifles. At that moment, two companies of the 65th Infantry Regiment, the 4th Company of the 27th Infantry Regiment and the 3rd Company of the 5th Ranger Battalion, hit the brigade from three directions. Dolin's ski troopers managed to repel the first assault on 13 February 1940 but the Finns destroyed the Soviet troops at Vetko on the evening of 14 February. This was a lethal blow to the brigade, as the staff of the brigade occupied Vetko Farm. Captain

Yrjö Hakanen, commander of the 1st Battalion, 65th Infantry Regiment, led the assault against Dolin's men at Vetko:

> The ski brigade had excellent equipment and weapons, but lacked battle experience of operations on Finnish terrain. This is especially true for the brigade's officers, Colonel Dolin and his deputies.
>
> As the arrival of Dolin's brigade completely messed up our offensive plans, the 9th Division was very interested in the course of the battle at Vetko Farm between the lakes. We had to destroy this brigade as quickly as possible. This was easier said than done. First of all, we had very few men; secondly, the brigade was scattered over an area of 40 kilometres. We needed time to spot them, while the terrain was completely covered with forests without any roads. To make things worse, one company was removed from my battalion. I requested reinforcements. As there were no reserves available, the division's staff asked me if a Swedish field gun would do. They proposed to set it to fire over the open sight. I agreed with joy. My men picked the gun up from its position in Lutjanjärvi.
>
> The field gun arrived and we set it up to the right of the road with great pomp and ceremony. Both my infantry companies and the machine-gun platoons were concentrated in a jump-off area on the ridge. My entire battle group was ready for the attack. I had no reserves and could not even ask for them. All men from the rear and supply units of the division were already in front-line duty guarding the isthmus between the lakes west of Vetko.
>
> My plan of 'artillery preparation' was to fire at Vetko Farm first and then shift fire at the sauna, as Russian ski troopers used the house as a weapon emplacement. After this the field gun was to continue firing to suppress other enemy weapons that frustrated the advance of my companies. Machine-guns were supposed to join the artillery preparation five minutes before the attack, in order to pin the enemy down at the moment when my men would start their assault. If I remember correctly, the gun was to open fire at the Farm at 1415 hours.
>
> The field gun opened up at both targets according to the plan. All eight machine-guns joined the battle a bit later. It was quite a noise, as all my heavy weapons were concentrated on a front 400 metres wide.
>
> One of the disadvantages of a narrow assault sector was that we could only use frontal fire. Covering assaulting infantry with a creeping barrage was also impossible, because as soon as my men

rushed forward, they blocked the view of the targets for the machine-guns. Our machine-guns went silent almost immediately. The ridge was not high enough to use indirect fire over the heads of our attacking infantry.

As soon as the fire support of the attack stopped, the enemy opened fire. This forced our attacking line to return fire and start a firefight prematurely. Of course, this also meant that the attacking line stopped and had to take cover. It was hard to get men to stand up again due to insufficient fire support.

This was exactly what happened. Our men advanced a bit and then got stuck in a firefight.

Our left flank advanced further than the others. Second Lieutenant Mäkinen's assault party managed to bypass Vetko Farm in the twilight and attack it from the rear. They were in a hand-to-hand fight with the Russian ski troopers several times, but finally Mäkinen's men made it to the very house. Hand grenades rained on them from the windows and trenches around the house, so they could not stay there for long. Before withdrawal the assault party managed to set the house on fire, thus completing the mission.

The fire illuminated all around and the enemy could not deliver accurate fire any more. We, in turn, saw the enemy very well against the fire. Our men charged again during the fire. We mopped up the entire area rather quickly. I would like to praise Junior Sergeant Rintamaa and the runner of the 1st Company, Private Katajamäki. Second Lieutenant Mäkinen, leader of the assault party, also deserves high praise. Lieutenant Saikku made a good decision to send an assault party to set the house on fire.

Dolin's ski brigade was very well equipped and armed. Their uniforms were warm, lined with sheepskin. Snowsuits and ski gear were very professional.

The brigade did not carry any heavy weapons. The most common weapon was a bolt-action rifle, but many men also had submachine-guns and automatic rifles. They had very few light machine-guns. We only captured a few of those at Vetko. They also carried several small-calibre mortars and mortar rounds in specially designed bag packs.

The brigade did not have any supply sleds or carriages. Apparently, the brigade was to get supplies through airdrops. They had no equipment to evacuate the wounded. However, medics carried all the instruments with them, including instruments for surgery.

The brigade did not have any accommodation with them, not even tents. We found several boat-shaped sleds of plywood. However, they looked like toys and there was probably very little use for them. The brigade was equipped with mobile radio sets for communication.

Apparently, the brigade maintained close contact with their Air Force. Soviet airplanes followed the brigade so closely that we often spotted ski troopers by the presence of airplanes. However, the situation at Vetko was so chaotic that the Russian pilots probably had no idea where the brigade's units were.

The Russian skiing style was different from the Finnish. A Russian ski trooper's body swayed from left to right when he skied, so we could tell a Russian from a Finn at a long distance. Finns always skied straight, following a line. Russian ski poles were longer, so they had to lift their hands higher. Probably this caused the swaying from left to right.

Russian skis were similar to Finnish, but sliding in snow was poor. The ski grease was completely unfit for use by Finnish standards. We only used it to grease the sleds.

We estimated casualties of Dolin's brigade at Vetko as high as 250 men killed. These were the numbers that I reported to the division. They thought that we were exaggerating the enemy's casualties. However, later it turned out that our estimate was too low. After the war, the Russians evacuated forty burnt bodies from the ruins of Vetko Farm, twenty-five bodies from the sauna, and ninety bodies from the garden. Our men picked up and buried 118 killed ski troopers. So the total death tally was 273 men. One must also count the men killed in the woods, and there must have been a lot of them.

Units of the 9th Finnish Division attacked the encircled 54th Mountain Rifles on numerous occasions, but only managed to destroy one garrison at Reuhkavaara. The rest of the garrisons of the 54th Mountain Rifles held out and repelled all Finnish attacks. The 54th was an elite unit of the Red Army, stationed in Kandalaksha, Soviet Karelia before the war. Many men of the division were local Karelians and were a match for the Finns in survival skills and tactics. Commanders of the division took energetic measures to set up strong defensive perimeters immediately after the division was encircled. Sectors of fire were cleared, trenches and bunkers were built.

The Finns concentrated all their resources on the destruction of three Soviet garrisons on the northern tip of Lake Saunajärvi. The Finns launched the first attack against the so-called 'HQ Hill', but their assault was repelled with casualties. Then the Finns assaulted the western garrison with two companies on 27 February, but again failed. Major Hakanen's battalion launched a new offensive against HQ Hill on 2 March, after a powerful artillery barrage of 4,500 rounds. Finnish companies assaulted at 2000 hours on 2 March 1940. They managed to reduce the Soviet positions after a whole night of fighting. Some of the Soviet defenders managed to withdraw from the area into the western and eastern garrisons under cover of darkness. The Finns counted about eighty Red Army dead on the battlefield as morning came. Some sixty men were taken prisoner. The Finns continued their attacks and launched an assault against the eastern garrison on 3 March. The garrison repelled Finnish assaults three times. The Finns managed to get the upper hand in the battle as late as 8 March 1940. The Finns estimated that around half the defenders had left their positions and moved to the western garrison over the frozen lake. The Finns also estimated total casualties of the 54th Mountain Rifle Division to be as high as 420 men. The Finns took a total of 215 prisoners from 25 February– 8 March. Major Hakanen's battalion casualties were also high and grew to 460 men killed, wounded or missing in action.

Chuikov was well aware of the difficult situation of the 54th Mountain Rifle Division and managed to relocate more reserves to the area. The recovered 163rd Rifle Division arrived from the Juntusranta area and launched its own offensive westwards, in order to relieve the encircled 54th Mountain Rifle Division. By the end of hostilities, the 163rd Division had only managed to advance 1 kilometre, but was getting close to achieving a breakthrough.

The Finns began an artillery barrage against the western garrison on 11 March. This was the last remaining garrison at Lake Saunajärvi and the garrison also had the HQ of the 54th Mountain Rifle Division in it. Finnish companies assaulted Soviet positions in the evening of 12 March, after a day-long barrage. The firefight lasted all night long, and the Finns managed to close in on the Soviet trenches. News of the armistice reached the front-line units at 1000 hours on the morning of 13 March 1940. Nevertheless, an intensive exchange of fire at the front continued during the last two hours of the war.

Siilasvuo's Division suffered heavy casualties in the battles against the 54th Mountain Rifle Division. According to Finnish sources, the losses were 4,595 men, with 1,340 killed, 3,123 wounded and 132 missing in action.

The casualties of the 54th Mountain Rifle Division were also very high. During the entire campaign the division lost 6,431 men, with 2,118 killed, 3,732 wounded, 573 missing in action and eight frostbitten. Some 720 bodies were found in the area of Dolin's ski brigade. According to official information, the dead ski troopers were all evacuated and buried in the Soviet Union, but recent research indicates that they were all buried on the spot and still lie on the battlefield in unmarked graves. Many graves are now on privately owned land.

The strategic importance of the deadlock at Kuhmo was high. The 9th Finnish Division, a battle-hardened and experienced unit, was locked in battle with an equally well-trained and motivated opponent. The 9th Division was tied down in battles until the end of the war. It could not be transferred to any other sectors of the front, when fresh troops were badly needed on the Karelian Isthmus. The situation at Kuhmo became critical for the Finns with the arrival of the replenished 163rd Rifle Division. The division stormed Finnish positions from the east, trying to re-establish a link with the encircled 54th Mountain Rifle Division.

To sum things up, the pre-war plans of the Finnish Army were correct. Indeed, the fate of the whole war was sealed not in the wilderness of Northern Finland, where the Finns had their spectacular victories, but on the Karelian Isthmus, where the Red Army launched its new grand offensive in February 1940.

CHAPTER 5

Breakthrough on the Mannerheim Line

The Soviet units on the Karelian Isthmus spent January 1940 in training, reconnaissance of Finnish lines and the destruction of Finnish positions. The number of Soviet rifle divisions on the Karelian Isthmus grew to twenty-three from the original ten. Heavy artillery was brought to the front in order to destroy Finnish fortifications. The artillery spent around 7,000 rounds each day in January, 'softening' the Finnish defence lines. The Right Group of the Seventh Army became the separate Thirteenth Army. The divisions were redistributed and the two armies fielded a total of seven rifle corps. The main axis of attack was clearly towards Vyborg, as the Seventh Army fielded fourteen divisions and the Thirteenth Army only nine.

Harassing attacks by battalion-sized forces began on 1 February 1940. The real large-scale offensive started on 11 February 1940. The breakthrough was planned for the Summa village sector, where the 100th Rifle Division attacked. The 42nd, 43rd, 113th, 138th and 70th Rifle Divisions on the Western Isthmus only managed to tie down the Finns, but did not penetrate the Finnish lines. The 113th and 70th Rifle Divisions only managed to capture one strongpoint, 'Bear', on Marjanpellonmäki Hill, but this was the only small success. Finnish lines held out across the entire isthmus, but a breakthrough at Lähde developed into a crisis the Finns could not deal with at the main defence line.

January 1940, Lähde: Soviet Preparations

The Finns rotated their units on 4 January 1940. The 1st Battalion of the 15th Infantry Regiment was replaced with the 1st Battalion of the 8th Infantry Regiment.

There were some changes on the Soviet side as well. The commander of the 123rd Rifle Division, Colonel Stenshinski, was removed from office. Colonel Alyabushev was appointed the new commander, and he brought order to his unit, instructing the men to build dugouts with stoves to warm themselves. After minimal living conditions were arranged, Alyabushev launched a training programme and prepared for a new offensive.

All three regiments of the division spent January in hard battle training. The new division commander stubbornly trained the division for the assault. Combat training covered such areas as skiing, machine-gun marksmanship, squad combat, platoon combat, and cooperation of armour and rifle units. Combat training sessions took place every day, even in mid-January 1940, when temperatures on the Karelian Isthmus dropped to as low as minus 45 degrees Celsius. Some Finnish officers stated that the scale of the thermometer was too small to measure the extreme low temperatures. All three regiments of the 123rd Rifle Division were stationed some 2 kilometres from the Finnish main defence line. Only company-strong forces were in contact with the Finns.

Captain Nazarov, from the staff of the 123rd Rifle Division, later commented on the new divisional commander and his actions:

> Our Division commander – I have no idea if he had any sleep at all, but he was always at the front and bitched about even the smallest detail. He achieved extremely high levels of readiness in his troops. All had received so much training and had such high morale that the breakthrough happened naturally.

Indeed, the men of the division spent so much time and effort on training that this brought a new spirit of confidence and a will to win. Men were impatient to go into battle.

Soviet scouts tried to get across the Finnish lines every night and snatch a prisoner. However, in most cases the Soviet scout parties were too large and easily spotted.

The division's supporting artillery units were also prepared. New guns were brought into position, and there was so much artillery that sometimes artillery commanders had arguments about the location of guns. There was almost no space in the rear of the division's sector to set all the guns.

Despite the failures, the scouts managed to spot both key forts in the area: Millionaire bunker on Tongue Hill and Poppius bunker in the centre of the Finnish defences. It is interesting to note that Soviet scouts originally thought that the two casemates of the Millionaire bunker were separate fortifications.

As the 123rd Rifle Division was carefully rehearsing the assault, the 24th Corps Artillery Regiment set two 152mm guns into firing positions to destroy the Millionaire bunker. Trenches for the guns were built well beforehand. Shelters for the gun crews were covered with three layers of logs. The guns were set into the firing positions by the evening of 25 January 1940, but the fire mission was cancelled due to thick fog.

Two 152mm guns under the command of Lieutenant Grachev opened fire over open sights at the Millionaire bunker at 1200 hours. A Finnish artillery observer, Second Lieutenant Esko Kallio, in the eastern observation tower of the bunker, was barely able to send fire data to his battery in order to suppress these guns before the Soviet crews scored a direct hit on the armoured tower. This killed the young Finnish officer and blew off the top of the tower. The next round hit the armoured tower on the central part of the bunker. Artillery observers of the 2nd Detached Artillery Battalion barely made it out of the tower before it was hit. Both Soviet guns continued firing at the bunker unhindered and as a result made a hole of 2 × 2 metres in the eastern casemate of the bunker. Several heavy rounds exploded inside the bunker. Proud Soviet artillerymen asked all commanders at the front to sign an official certificate verifying the bunker's destruction. The official paper was signed by the commander of the 5th Company, 272nd Rifle Regiment, and the commander of the 4th Battery, 402nd Howitzer Artillery Regiment, and the Chief of Staff of the 24th Corps Artillery Regiment.

Poppius bunker was subjected to similar fire on 28 January. The result was the death of four men of the bunker's garrison and the destruction of the bunker's western casemate.

The Breakthrough

The Finns rotated troops in the sector shortly before the Soviet offensive. The 1st Battalion, 8th Infantry Regiment, was replaced with the 2nd Battalion, 9th Infantry Regiment. The 9th Regiment was completely Swedish-speaking (Swedish is the second official language of Finland and 6 per cent of Finns speak Swedish as their mother tongue). This only added to the communication difficulties among Finnish troops.

The Soviet artillery opened up at 0840 hours on the morning of 11 February 1940. The barrage lasted two hours and twenty minutes. Four artillery regiments fired at the Finnish positions. The 24th Corps Artillery Regiment alone fired 14,769 rounds at the Finnish defences. Soviet artillery commanders were themselves impressed with the scale of the artillery preparation:

> For the first time our regiment took part in such a powerful and well-prepared artillery barrage. The artillery barrage at Lipola was just a rehearsal compared to this. At the beginning of our barrage the enemy tried to open fire but was silenced quickly. The regiment completed the fire support mission.

The 245th Rifle Regiment, supported by heavy T-28 and light T-26 tanks, assaulted Poppius bunker at 1100 hours and the red banner was lifted above the ruins of Poppius at 1224 hours. This caused cheerful shouting at the division's HQ and encouraged the men of the 245th Rifle Regiment even more.

Lieutenant Malm's company, which was defending Poppius bunker, could do little to oppose the onslaught. Lindman's battalion had been in quieter sectors of the front before being shifted to Lähde. The battalion had no experience of fighting in open terrain against masses of Soviet tanks. The men were shocked by the sight of several dozen Soviet tanks. Nevertheless, the men did what they could. By the end of the day Lieutenant Malm's company had sixteen men left out of 100. The commander of the 2nd Battalion, 9th Infantry Regiment, Major Lindman, lost control over his troops at the very beginning of the battle. Some Western sources claim that Lindman was wounded, but according to the war diary of the 8th Infantry Regiment, he was unharmed but lost control and did not take an active part in the battle.

Soviet tanks and riflemen proceeded to the test bunker, where they stopped and dug in for the night. On the morning of 12 February the Soviet offensive continued. The Finns had to give up the idea of holding the first trench in the afternoon and fell back to the rear line, which had only field fortifications under the protection of an impressive anti-tank ditch.

The commander of the 5th Infantry Division, Colonel Selim Isacsson, called his superior, General-Lieutenant Harald Ökvist, in Vyborg in the afternoon and said: 'This is it, they broke through.' Ökvist tried to encourage the colonel as best he could.

The Millionaire bunker and Tongue Hill were assaulted by a battalion of the 255th Rifle Regiment. Assault parties pushed the Finnish infantry out of the trenches, approached the bunker and reached its roof at 1240 hours. The Finns could not hold the trench work south of the bunker, despite all their efforts. Private Rafael Forth, 4th Company, 9th Infantry Regiment, recalled:

> In the morning and before noon on Sunday, 11 February 1940, we could eat some pastry. The Russians did not shoot so much at the bunker itself, but assaulted to the right from the bunker at the so-called Finger Hill. The 4th Company tried to mop up the trenches with hand grenades and submachine-gun fire, but it was in vain. The Russians took a good hold on the hill and were coming closer and closer to the bunker through the trenches. Simultaneously with the Russian infantry approaching the right entrance, a Russian tank drove straight at the bunker, most likely with a plan to block the left entrance. Now it was the time for the AT gun to act. It was placed at the left entrance. The gun leader stood inside the bunker in the MG casemate and gave orders to the gun. The gun fired many shells that

had tracers, but the tank was just coming closer and closer to us. It was only when the tank was 150–200 metres away that our AT gun managed to score a direct hit. The tank stalled and started burning. The gun leader shouted 'Täysosuma!' ['Direct hit!']. I did not know what it meant but I jumped up and shouted the same word to the crew of the gun that was already rejoicing in the midst of thick gunpowder smoke. The destroyed tank was burning all night long. Lieutenant Ericsson came along with his notebook and wrote down the names of the gun leader and the gun layer. 'You guys are getting a medal' – was his short comment. If the tank managed to block the left entrance and the Russian infantry the right, we would all have been trapped inside the bunker.

Soon after the tank started burning, a Russian MG opened intensive fire at the left entrance. We had an MG in the casemate, but as the gun port was too narrow, we could not respond to that fire. We three men stood inside the casemate in front of the gun port, looking at the burning tank. Artur Hoijar stood to the left, Platoon Leader Höckerstedt in the middle and then I to the right. All of a sudden an MG burst hit the gunport. An MG bullet hit the inner part of the gunport, split into pieces and struck between Hoijar and Höckerstedt. The platoon leader swayed backwards, saluted, said 'Greet home for me!' and fell down. He was hit with a bullet splinter into his heart and died in my arms. Hoijar was hit in his right arm with bullet splinters. He ran down into the bunker, where the medics took care of him.

The Russians advanced through the trenches from the Finger to the right entrance. They climbed the roof of the bunker from there and took defensive positions. At the same time they started throwing down stones and sand from the roof to the right entrance and blocked it. There was no time left to waste for us.

Company commander Ericsson gave an order to storm the roof of the bunker from the left entrance. We quickly grouped for the assault and managed to collect thirty hand grenades – fifteen stick grenades and fifteen egg grenades. My squad leader, Gunnar Ingo, stood a bit higher than me and I stood a bit lower on the staircase. I was unscrewing the lids on the stick grenades and passing them on to Gunnar. He threw them as fast as he could, so that the grenades exploded on the roof. After we threw all the stick grenades on the roof, the guys from the 4th Company stormed the roof. They 'wiped the roof clean' with submachine-guns and light MGs. I threw the egg grenades at the other side of the roof at the same time. The Russians were forced to leave the roof and withdraw into the trenches after our assault.

But I did not manage to throw all the egg grenades before one of our guys fell back from the roof. As I stood below at the entrance, I took him to the medics inside the bunker. He was badly wounded in his back by bullets from a Russian MG that had opened fire against the left entrance. As I was helping the casualty and looked to the right, I saw the bullets from the Russian MG hitting dust and stones a mere metre from us.

As I brought the casualty inside, I shouted for medics. The medic was Finnish-speaking and shouted back that he had someone to bandage first. He was bandaging the right arm of Artur Hoijar. I put the casualty on the bunk next to Artur and the medic. The casualty wept and asked me to pray for him. I tried to explain to him that I had to go and help the others who were fighting on the roof, but he repeated time and time again: 'Do not leave me!' I told him that the medic would bandage him as soon as he was done with the others. I also told him that his mother must have definitely taught him to pray, and that God would definitely help him in that tough situation. I hurried up towards the exit and the guys had completed the assault on the roof, so I took my rifle and continued my guard duty outside the bunker. The guys, who came down into the bunker from the roof, told me that one of our men was killed and remained lying on the roof. It was impossible to confirm this in the overall confusion.

Lieutenant Ericsson was satisfied with results of the assault. The situation was stabilized, at least for the moment. We were about thirty men left inside the bunker. Most of us were from the platoon of Second Lieutenant Skade; eight of the guys were from our MG company. The wounded that could still walk left the bunker in the evening. The badly wounded were taken away in sleds. Both Hoijar and the man wounded in his back (it was Andersson from Petsamo) were transported away in sleds. In the evening I was relieved of my guard duty. I had my pocket watch with me. It was strange, but I wanted to keep it with me. I put both the watch and the chain into the pocket in my pants and tied up my snow camouflage suit tightly. That was a wise thing to do as later I was taken prisoner by the Russians on Monday afternoon. It was all quiet during the evening and night. The knocked-out tank burnt and illuminated the terrain. The Russians were probably sleeping after a hard day. One after another our men found a reason to 'go out' and we were fewer and fewer men left inside the bunker.

The 6th Company Commander, Lieutenant Malm, came to the bunker later during the night in order to discuss the situation with Lieutenant Ericsson. I heard part of their conversation, as I was relieved of guard duty and was busy with a Primus heater, trying to boil something drinkable. Malm had four or five men with him. He had previously sent runners to the Millionaire bunker, but none of them made it through. They were all lying dead in the trenches.

The lieutenants spoke about the situation for about an hour. I could not quite understand what they were talking about. Later in the night, Lieutenant Ericsson took his bag pack, his overcoat and said: 'I am now out of here. I am not planning to be buried in this bunker alive.' So he left. After Ericsson had left, my squad leader, Gunnar Ingo, said: 'but those few of us that are left here will, of course, let them bury us alive!'

After some time Skade came back into the bunker. Before that he had met Ericsson in the trench. Ericsson ordered Skade to go back and stay in the bunker. Apparently, Ericsson went to the dugout of Second Lieutenant Finne in order to discuss the situation. At the same time, Finne was wounded by a shell and taken away. Finne died of his wounds in a field hospital on 21 February.

Junior Lieutenant Lekanov, leader of a Soviet assault party, commented:

Having spotted the forward concrete fortifications, we were transferred to the left flank, where we spotted the largest, bunker 11. It was located on Tongue Hill and swept with fire through cuttings in the forest the dragon teeth and trenches to the right of bunker 6 and to the left up to Lake Summajärvi. This bunker and the entire hill dominated our left flank.

On the day of the breakthrough of the Mannerheim line, Engineering Battalion Commander Senior Lieutenant Grabovoi ordered my assault party in reserve. Two assault parties under Junior Lieutenants Markov and Yemelianov were sent against bunker 11.

One hour later the liaison officer arrived with an order for us to meet the unit commander at his observation post: 'Assault party of comrade Markov,' he said, 'is to the right from the bunker in the dragon teeth, pinned down by strong enemy fire. Tanks cannot assist them, as the hill is too steep. The second assault party under comrade Yemelianov, which is also to the right, is under a hurricane of artillery and mortar fire. Yemelianov is wounded. Immediately advance to assist our comrades and destroy bunker 11.'

We walked out of the forest towards the hill and were immediately hit by mortar fire. We crawled towards the trenches with heavy boxes of explosives. I ordered my soldiers to take off their white overalls, as they only made it easier to spot us against the black background of soil ploughed by artillery fire.

It was severely cold, but we were all covered with sweat. Finally, we reached the nearest trench. Together with the infantry we tried to inspect the bunker, but a White Finn emerged at that moment and threw several hand grenades at us. A short burst of a machine-gun and the enemy was destroyed.

The White Finns locked themselves in their underground fortress. We crawled on the roof of the bunker with the boxes of explosives. We started to look around, where to put the charge. It was soil all around. The bunker pierced the hill like a tunnel. Soldiers threw grenades in the ventilation pipes of the bunker, but this apparently did not cause too much damage to the Finns.

Then Sapper Zavialov got into a trench from the rear and approached the doors of the bunker. Although the door had a gun-port, no one fired from it. Zavialov saw that the enemy did not return fire and decided to throw a grenade, But as soon as he stood up, a shot was fired and the brave sapper fell down. We all got angry. Soldier Mokrov approached Zavialov to assist him, but the enemy pinned him down by fire.

We had to rescue our comrades. Engineer Solin thought up how to do it. He proposed blocking the door of the bunker with stones. The Finns spotted it and opened mortar fire, but it was too late. The door was buried under the stones, the gunport was blocked.

The bunker was huge. I realized that the amount of explosives we had would not be enough to destroy the stronghold. But returning to the rear for additional explosives would mean letting the White Finns out of the bunker. We set the charge at the door and detonated it. The explosion tilted the doors: the White Finns are in our hands, they cannot get out. Infantry quickly surrounded the bunker and occupied the rear trenches.

I reported my actions to the rifle battalion commander and retreated together with my group to the starting point, where my commander prepared explosives for us.

Apparently, Second Lieutenant Skade reported to Lieutenant Ericsson in the trench that most of his men had deserted from the bunker. This outraged Ericsson and he ordered Skade to return to the bunker and hold it at all costs. Junior Lieutenant Lekanov stated in his memories that the bunker was blown up by 0500 hours on 12 February:

> We became part of Lieutenant Prudnikov's assault party. We had to carry several hundred kilograms of explosives to the bunker. Despite the strong fire of the White Finns, the engineers rapidly made their way to the bunker. After that we took the boxes with explosives from the trenches and laid them on top of the left [western] casemate. A huge pile of boxes with explosives grew on top of the bunker. The infantry withdrew to the trenches. Fuses were lit at my command. A tremendous explosion. A huge flame shot into the sky. We were all covered up with soil. Ears were ringing for a long time, our heads were spinning.
>
> We walked up to the site of the explosion [. . .] there was a crater up to 10 metres in diameter. The iron reinforcement vanished into dust. Everything was blackened 50 metres from the explosion site. The huge bunker, along with its garrison, ceased to exist. This was at 0500 hours, 12 February 1940.

Soviet archive documents repeat the story. Operation reports of the 255th Rifle Regiment mention two explosions on the western casemate of Millionaire bunker on 11 February. The regiment's staff still thought that the western and eastern casemates were two separate bunkers. However, the Soviet reports also mention that the bunker was still operational on 11 February. The final destruction of the bunker took place at 0315 hours according to the Soviet reports.

However, Finnish soldiers defending the bunker state the bunker was destroyed one day later, on 13 February:

> The night passed by and the morning of 12 February grew light. The number of men in the bunker had decreased to just six: Second Lieutenant Skade, Gunnar Olin, Arvid Aura, Johannes Bengs, Karl Holmberg and I, Rafael Forth. Everyone was from the MG company, except for Second Lieutenant Skade.
>
> Later we realized that there were two more men inside the bunker. They were Gunnar Storm from Malax and a Finnish guy who was most likely a sapper.

It is important to note that Forth did not mention the group of forward artillery observers under Lieutenant Uggla from the 2nd Detached Heavy Artillery Battalion in his memoirs. He also mentioned nothing about the blowing up of the bunker late at night on 11 February.

Lieutenant Uggla, who was not under the command of Ericsson, decided to leave the bunker on the morning of 12 February. According to his account, his group had to break out, as Soviet sappers were preparing the next explosion of the bunker on the roof. Uggla made it to the Finnish lines at 1207 hours and reported to the commander of the 8th Infantry Regiment that eighteen men out of Ericsson's company were still inside the bunker, and the men had locked themselves in and were afraid to exit due to the explosion that had taken place the previous night. Apparently, the artillery observers and infantrymen did not communicate with each other too much. Otherwise it would be hard to explain why Uggla did not know that there were only six men left in the bunker. Nevertheless, the staff of the 8th Infantry Regiment issued orders based on Uggla's report.

An infantry company, supported by four machine-guns, was sent to relieve the besieged bunker. The attempt failed. Soviet machine-gun fire was too strong and the Finns were pinned down several hundred metres north from the bunker. The attacking Finns could already see the ruined bunker and the red banner that the men of the 255th Rifle Regiment had set on the bunker's roof. The Finns saw no one leaving the bunker, and so the legend was born about the entire Finnish platoon killed inside the bunker.

Apparently, the crew of the anti-tank gun at the eastern casemate of Millionaire bunker had also left the battlefield in the evening of 11 February, as their gun was captured by the 255th Rifle Regiment on 12 February. Rafael Forth described the last hours of the defenders of the Millionaire bunker:

> It must have been around noon when two runners made it through the trenches and told us that we were ordered to leave the bunker immediately. Lieutenant Ericsson had plans to draw the whole company back to the second line of defences. I saw that the runners Hjortell from Kvevlax and Ström from Österhankmo were very much worried. They called for us to leave the bunker immediately. Second Lieutenant Skade said that he had an order from the company commander to go back into the bunker and that he was not going anywhere.
>
> The runners told us time and again: 'Let's go now.' But Skade did not listen to them. Finally, we all said that if the company commander gave an order to leave the bunker, we would all go.

Skade answered: 'So let's go, but first let's have something to drink.' Someone lit up the Primus heater, but it did not work, so we did not manage to have any coffee.

The runners were about half an hour inside the bunker and were now heading for the exit. I followed them. I don't know who left the bunker after me, but Aura, Bengs and Holmberg definitely left the bunker. Skade and Olin were both from the same town, Brändö in Vaasa and for some reason they lingered inside. Some 20–30 metres from the bunker I stopped and looked back, but I did not see anyone coming out of the bunker and no one was seen on the roof. Before I left the bunker, I took the camera of Second Lieutenant Uggla, some small things and two map cases. I don't know who they belonged to. After picking up those things I took the rifle and followed the runners.

The runners ran along the trench quickly, although there were pieces of torn phone cable and other small things lying on its bottom. When we were some 200–300 metres from Finne's dugout, the runners stopped. They were searching for their comrades. Their comrades were there when the runners were sent to the Millionaire bunker with an order for us. Now there was only a gasmask and a few small things lying on the ground. When we looked out of the trench, we saw three Russian tanks driving towards the second line of our defences. The trenches were collapsed in the places where the tanks had driven over them.

We rushed further on and reached a spot where the trench divided into two. We ran to the right, runners first and me after them. I hoped and believed they would be able to find their comrades. Soon we came to a passage dugout that was built into the trench. We went through this dugout and came to another dugout. But that was it. The Russian artillery fired hundreds of guns and countless shells were falling on the Finnish lines. It was an ear-splitting noise.

We returned to the place where the trench divided in two. We took a new direction and ran some 100 metres to the left. There the trench finished and a supply road started. I recognized the place because that was where I picked up food with the guys on Saturday. When we came up from the trench on the supply road, we were visible to the Russians. We came under fire from small arms. We threw ourselves to the left of the supply road, where the Russian artillery fire had wiped away snow and from there we could crawl about 100 metres forward, creeping through dirt and sleet.

But suddenly we reached the border of the artillery fire area and found 1-metre deep snow on a swamp, which was impossible to move on. All three of us crept into a shell crater to hold a military council. First of all, we took off all extra clothes and threw away everything that we took from Millionaire bunker. We threw away map cases and bread bags. We even left our rifles there. As well as uniforms we had snowsuits that were black with dirt. On our hands we had gloves. We came to a common decision to get back to the supply road, by creeping and, where possible, by short rushes.

One of the runners jumped up first. When he was some 20–30 metres away; I was ready to follow. However, the second runner made it before me, so I was left last. Snow cover and some bushes offered a bit of protection in the beginning, but later it was just plain field with no place to hide. I jumped up from the crater and ran some 10–15 metres when bullets started whining and whistling around me. I threw myself down and crept a bit. I jumped up again and fell down to creep further. I managed to make about 100 metres from the crater. There I saw one of the runners lying on the ground, hit by bullets. I threw myself at his side. He did not say a word. Apparently, he was already dead.

I continued and made 50–60 more metres. There were a lot of dead men lying there and I thought that here the 4th Company was wiped out to the last man. Later I learned that it was a gathering point for the fallen. From here they were supposed to be transported further by horse-drawn sleds. However, it was now impossible. The dead remained there.

I saw someone wave to me from about 100 metres away. At the same time the bullet shower somewhat abated and I could make a longer rush. I thought that those were our boys in the second line of defence who were calling for me. I could only see a head sticking out of a trench. I ran the last bit towards him. When I was about 10 metres away, about twenty soldiers jumped up from the ground. And what did I see? Russian soldiers in great numbers. I stood on the supply road as if dumbfounded. I did not know if it was a dream or reality. Dozens of soldiers walked up to me and it became lively and noisy. They all spoke at the same time and started to dig in my pockets. Someone picked up Second Lieutenant Uggla's camera and took it away. Some more men searched my pockets. Now it was good that I left both my pocket watch and the chain fastened in the small pocket in my pants, covered by the dirty snowsuit. No one took my gloves.

So I managed to keep my pocket watch and my wedding ring. A Russian officer ran up to me, took me back to the Russian lines under guard, and my captivity started. When I looked around as I walked, with the Russian officer walking in front of me and two guards carrying rifles with fixed bayonets, it was like a fog in my head. I saw the Russian military equipment – the mechanized forces and armour. The thought struck me that it would not be long before the Russian Army paraded on Senate Square in Helsinki.

And the number of soldiers – there were thousands of them! It must have been more than a battalion in one place. These were probably the same soldiers that we saw from the gun port of the Millionaire bunker, marching as one gigantic river towards the weakest point of our defences in the swamp by Lähde.

After his return from captivity Rafael Forth managed to find out what happened to the last defenders of the famous bunker:

What happened to the other guys inside the bunker? Arvid Aura, Johannes Bengs and Kurt Holmberg left the bunker soon after the three of us, but they were so slow in the trench that we three had already traversed the passage dugout and turned to the right. They also went to the supply road and moved along it. When the Russians opened fire at them, they went back into the trench and hid in a small foxhole dug in the wall of the trench. After some time a Russian patrol appeared on the supply road. They jumped into the trench and the guys were quite anxious whether the Russians would bother to look into the foxhole. But the Russian patrol passed by and walked some 100 metres along the trench, coming back the same way. The Russians did not bother to look into the small foxhole on the way back either. They walked past our guys twice – and were just a couple metres away. The guys stayed there till darkness fell.

When it grew dark, the Russian tanks drove back to refuel and replenish their ammunition. Russian soldiers also withdrew, made campfires and cooked food. This is what our guys saw when they sneaked to the second line of defences under cover of darkness.

Four men were left inside the Millionaire bunker: Second Lieutenant Skade, Private Olin, Private Gunnar Storm (from the 6th Company) and an un-identified Finnish soldier. The men prepared to break out, leaving all heavy equipment inside. Second Lieutenant Skade was the only officer among them, and knew the Finnish trench work well. The men relied on him. When a good moment for the breakout came, all four rushed out of the bunker. They only made it 20 metres before they saw a group of Red Army men in the trench. As a result, the Finns had to retreat into the bunker and lock themselves up there. Red Army men immediately surrounded the bunker and invited them to surrender. This was not an option for Skade. Red Army men started throwing hand grenades into the bunker via the gun ports, but all four men survived.

After some time the Soviets got tired of the negotiations and the bunker was blown up. The massive explosion ruined the bunker and killed three men inside; Gunnar Storm was wounded and passed out. After he woke up, he saw that his left wrist was smashed to pieces. Storm crawled to the hole in the bunker's wall, which the explosion had made. When he emerged at the hole, he was greeted by rifle fire but was not hit. A Soviet commander ordered his men to cease fire, ran up to Storm, and helped him out of the bunker. So Gunnar Storm was the last man to leave the bunker, crippled, but alive.

The legend of the Millionaire bunker lives on. A Finnish veteran of the 8th Infantry Regiment visited the ruined bunker in 1999. He had taken part in the fruitless Finnish counter-attack towards the bunker on 12 February. In 1999 the veteran still believed that eighteen of his comrades were killed inside the bunker.

In the centre of the sector, the 245th Rifle Regiment continued its advance towards Kämärä Station along Lähde road. Improvised Finnish defences at the command bunker started to collapse during the day and the Finns retreated in disorder to the support line. It is important to note that the entire phone network in Lähde was completely destroyed by the artillery barrage of 11 February and could not be restored. Runners with messages were either killed or arrived at their destinations too late. There was no front line; units of the 245th Rifle Regiment, sappers, signals operators, runners, tanks, the retreating remains of the 9th Infantry Regiment and the counter-attacking companies of the 8th Infantry Regiment were all mixed together on the battlefield. During 12 February, when the Finns had already received orders to fall back to the second defence line, it turned out that a group of radio operators, sent to the command bunker, had established radio contact with the 8th Infantry Regiment. The 8th Infantry Regiment ordered the group to fall back as quickly as possible, but it was already too late. The group was trapped inside the bunker as Red Army men surrounded it. According to Captain Oksanen, twenty-nine wounded men, mostly from the 9th Infantry Regiment, were also inside the bunker; the Red Army men forced the Finns to surrender, threatening to blow the bunker up; but of twenty-nine men taken prisoner, only nine made it back home after the war. Other sources do not support this story.

All Finnish units had retreated behind the second defence line by the evening of 12 February. The Finns transferred reserves to the place of the breakthrough – the 13th and 14th Infantry Regiments – with a mission to counter-attack and restore the line early in the morning of 13 February. Two battalions of the 14th Infantry Regiment were supposed to attack from the northern part of Lake Summajärvi and reach the River Majajoki, while the other battalions were supposed to join the attack on the Kämärä road. The battalions of the 14th Infantry Regiment managed to complete their mission and reached the River Majajoki sector, but ran into the advancing elements of the entire Soviet 7th Rifle Division and were forced to fall back. The 13th Infantry Regiment was used for plugging holes in the collapsing Finnish defences and did not even start the assault. The commander of the 14th Infantry Regiment, Colonel Väinö Polttila, was mortally wounded in the morning battle.

The Soviet artillery opened fire at 1100 hours. Shortly after this, Soviet tanks and riflemen stormed the Finnish defence line. The Finns hoped that the anti-tank ditch would be able to stop the armour, but Soviet sappers blew up the steep walls of the ditch. The way for Soviet tanks was open. All Finnish anti-tank guns had been lost at the main defence line, so the Finns could only rely on satchel charges and petrol bombs. However, Soviet tanks did not approach the Finnish trenches but preferred to blast them from a range of 100 metres, staying out of reach of hand grenades and petrol bombs. A whole Soviet tank battalion drove over the Finnish trenches and attacked the 2nd Heavy Artillery Battalion from the rear. The attack caught the Finns completely by surprise. As Soviet Captain Arkhipov put it:

> Within several minutes we were at our destination. The forest grew thinner and among the snow-covered fir trees I saw gun trenches in a clearing. Howitzers were positioned in those trenches, firing on some targets behind the forest – their barrels at a high angle of elevation. Next to the gun positions we saw well-built dugouts. A soldier in a white apron, and with a spoon in his hand, walked out of one of the dugouts and froze, his eyes wide open, when he saw our tanks.
>
> As agreed, I relayed the assault signal on the radio, repeated it with flares, and tanks drove into the firing positions from three sides. Apparently, the artillery crews were not trained to fire at tanks. Or, probably, they just panicked – they ran in all directions from the guns. As there were three batteries, located at significant distances from each other, the fleeing Finns, both officers and men, covered the whole field. We captured twelve guns intact, three warehouses of ammunition, equipment and food. The only thing we did not find

was transportation means – there were neither horses, nor trucks, nor tractors. We did not even find track marks on the ground. This fact, as well as the well-built firing position of the battalion and dugouts, meant that we were still in the main defensive area of the Mannerheim Line, but already in the rear, in the last positions.

Most Finnish artillerymen fled the battlefield; some men locked themselves in a dugout. A Soviet tank drove over the roof of the dugout, but the structure did not collapse. After a brief discussion and a Finnish refusal to surrender, Soviet sappers blew up the dugout with all the men inside. Thirty-two Finns met their destiny inside. Seven of these men were the forward observation team who had escaped death in the Millionaire bunker the day before.

The breakthrough of the second line at Lähde on 13 February meant a complete collapse of the Finnish main defence line. The Finns had no fortified lines built up to the intermediary defence line. Marshal Mannerheim issued orders to fall back to the intermediary line at 1600 hours on 15 February 1940.

Many men and commanders of the Red Army were awarded the Gold Star of the Hero of the Soviet Union. Among them were Lieutenant Yemelianov (killed on 11 February 1940), commander of the assault party that stormed Millionaire bunker, and the commander of the 2nd Battalion, 245th Rifle Regiment, Captain Soroka, who was killed in action on 13 February 1940, when storming the second Finnish defence line.

Major Arthur Viking Lindman, a professional officer in the Finnish Army, perceived the demise of his battalion and the breakthrough of the Mannerheim Line as his personal disgrace. In August 1941 he commanded the 2nd Battalion, 13th Infantry Regiment, and in one of the attacks walked openly in front of the attacking line, searching for death. Deliverance came in the form of a Soviet bullet. Major Lindman died of his wounds in the 19th Field Hospital on 13 August 1941.

Summa Village Holds Out

The Finns rotated their units in the first days of New Year 1940 at Summa village. The front was taken over by the 1st and 2nd Battalions of the 7th Infantry Regiment. The first days of the new Finnish battalions were rather quiet at the front. Soviet artillery continued pounding the Finnish positions; both sides sent out scouts at night.

New units were on the way to the front from other military districts of the USSR. The 100th Rifle Division arrived in the Summa village sector from the Byelorussian Military District. The division arrived at the old border in the Pesochnoe–Sertolovo area in December and marched off to the front. The division was fully supplied with warm winter uniforms. Ivan Chetyrbok, platoon leader of the 3rd Battalion, 85th Rifle Regiment, recalled the march:

> From Pesochnaya we marched on the Vyborg highway to the Summa–Hottinen area. We arrived at the Mannerheim Line when it was still in Finnish hands. There were some rifle divisions before us there; they were dressed in an old fashion, in autumn and summer uniforms. They had boots with leg-wrappings and *budyonnovka* winter hats. When we were in Pesochnaya, we all received winter uniforms. We were dressed like Santa Claus – for the first time we received Russian *shapka* hats, for the first time in the history of our army – before that we only used *budyonnovkas*. Besides that, we had woollen helmet liners, which protected the entire face, with only the eyes and mouth exposed to the elements. Without those two things we would have all been frostbitten. We were dressed in the following manner: a warm under-shirt, *gimnastyorka*, padded jacket and a greatcoat on top of it. It was hard to turn around in such gear, never mind fight. Despite all these clothes, it was still cold. When we were on our way to the front, a lot of trucks were moving in the opposite direction – the road was narrow and we would spend a lot of time in traffic jams. There were a lot of frostbitten men moving from the front to the hospitals. They had to keep moving – so cold they were. We had our *valenki* felt boots, but they only had boots with leg wrappings. Those who walked from the front told us about the bunkers. We did not quite understand what they meant.

The division immediately started preparations for the assault on the Finnish main defence line. The village was still considered the best place for the main strike, and this was the reason for the daily artillery barrages on the village. The 355th Rifle Regiment manned the line west of the highway, and the 331st Rifle Regiment east of the highway. The 85th Rifle Regiment of the division took up positions on the left flank of the division at the River Summanjoki. The 355th Rifle Regiment had 3,028 men when it arrived at the front (178 commanders, 437 junior commanders and 2,413 privates).

Scout parties were sent out on a regular basis, but again the Red Army had not yet developed proper tactics for scout parties and sent groups that were too large. They were easily spotted and repelled by the Finnish sentries.

During the night of 13 January a Soviet raid did lead to success. A scout party of the 355th Rifle Regiment, under Senior Lieutenant Vatagin (twenty-five riflemen, twelve sappers and eight signals operators), managed to sneak behind the Finnish lines unnoticed. The group approached bunker No. 3 (its exact location was already known to the Soviets) and blew it up. The Soviet scouts first blew up the door of the bunker, grabbed the very first man who rushed out, and then threw multiple hand grenades into the bunker.

Four Finnish soldiers were killed, and one soldier (Private Toivo Mäkelä, 1st Machine-gun Company) was taken prisoner, being heavily wounded. The staff of the 355th Rifle Regiment had to send him to a dressing station immediately. Toivo Mäkelä died of his wounds in the Soviet Union. In Finland he is still considered missing in action.

This was the first prisoner of war taken by the division in the Winter War. The scout party also captured a Finnish sled and skis, as well as the personal belongings of the wounded prisoner. Senior Lieutenant Vatagin was allowed to keep a Finnish knife belonging to Toivo Mäkelä. All men and commanders who had taken part in the assault on the bunker were recommended for decorations. Senior Lieutenant Vatagin and squad leader Kirillov were awarded the Gold Star of the Hero of the Soviet Union. Squad leader Gerasimenko was awarded the Order of Lenin. The Finns sent an officer to investigate the reason for the bunker's explosion and only realized what had happened on the evening of 14 January.

The continuing artillery barrage destroyed bunker No. 7 on 15 January. The bunker was used for ammunition storage and no loss of life was involved in the incident. Bunker No. 15 took a direct hit on 19 January and was badly damaged. A crucial casualty was the bunker's stove, a vitally important asset, as temperatures dropped to minus 40 degrees Celsius in mid-January. The Finnish sappers who arrived to repair the bunker were shocked by its 1920s design: 'The roof of bunker No. 15: 1 metre of concrete without reinforcement, then 1 metre of sand and then 1 more metre of concrete without reinforcement!' Apparently, contractors of the Finnish Ministry of Defence, Granit Limited Company, helped themselves to construction materials in the 1920s.

The Finnish main defence line was an enigma for the 100th Rifle Division. There were so many cellars, foundations of burnt-down houses and farms in the village and each of them looked like a bunker. To make matters worse, some Finnish bunkers did not open fire for a long time and could not be spotted. One had to make them open fire.

The 355th Rifle Regiment carried out a reconnaissance in force west of the highway in order to spot new Finnish bunkers. The regiment's scout company and sappers of the 90th Sapper Battalion launched their assault towards bunker No. 2. The 4th Company of the regiment provided fire support for the attackers.

Bunker No. 2 'Terttu' opened fire during the reconnaissance in force. It had remained silent since mid-December 1939. The Soviet scouts spotted one more bunker to the left of bunker No. 2 (bunker No. 1). Sappers made a passage in the barbed-wire fence during the assault and then sappers and scouts were immediately pinned down by deadly fire from bunker No. 2 and the trenches around it. Political Worker Fomichev, of the 4th Company, saw the difficult situation and launched an assault with his entire company, which distracted the Finns for a while. The scouts made it back to their lines. Eight scouts were wounded and eight more killed in the firefight on the Soviet side. The Finns lost the commander of the bunker, Second Lieutenant Penttinen, who was mortally wounded in the firefight.

Bunker No. 2 was subjected to heavy artillery fire on 19 and 21 January and took several direct hits. A heavy round penetrated the roof and made a hole about 1 metre square. The bunker took more direct hits on 23 January. The Finns rotated their units at the front again on 24 January: the 2nd Battalion was replaced with the 3rd Battalion, 7th Infantry Regiment.

In the meantime, the 355th Rifle Regiment was carefully preparing for the assault on the bunker. The riflemen launched a series of attacks on Finnish outposts south of the bunker and drove them back to the bunker itself. In late January the jumping-off positions of the regiment were some 400 metres south of the bunker.

Bunkers at the highway continued taking hits from Soviet heavy artillery. Bunker No. 15 took several direct hits on 21 January, and bunker No. 5 took a direct hit at 1430 hours on 22 January.

A 45mm anti-tank gun from the 331st Rifle Regiment's anti-tank battery fired at bunker No. 5 for two days on 22 and 23 January and inflicted severe damage. The Soviet gun fired twenty armour-piercing rounds at the bunker's gun ports and armoured turret on 22 January and then 180 rounds on 23 January. The gun crew reported: 'the turret of the bunker is penetrated, the size of the hole is 45–50 centimetres'. The Finnish sappers who had to repair the damaged bunker reported: 'the armoured turret and the roof of the search-light casemate are broken into pieces. We built a temporary wall of logs and filled the destroyed part of the bunker with soil.'

Second Lieutenant Paitula (platoon leader, 1st Machine-gun Company, 7th Infantry Regiment), assumed that the Soviets had built the trench for the gun well beforehand and only brought their gun into position during the day. Despite several requests to suppress or destroy the gun, the Finns failed to do so, and the small Soviet gun continued to harass bunkers No. 5 and No. 6 with its fire on 25 January. It fired a total of thirty rounds on that day and scored several direct hits on both bunkers. Apparently, Finnish artillerymen were keeping their ammunition for a larger and more attractive target.

A bridge, destroyed by the Finns during the retreat.
(*Author's collection*)

Southern parts of Vyborg burnt by Finns during the retreat.
(*Colonel Skvortsov's collection*)

Grave of Red Army men.
(*Author's collection*)

The ruins of Äyräpää
Church, 1942.
(*Author's collection*)

Cannon of the 267th Corps
Artillery Regiment in
Vyborg, March 1940.
(*Colonel Skvortsov's collection*)

Artillery commanders of
the Red Army posing in
Terijoki, April 1940.
(*Natalia Filippova collection*)

Volunteer ski troopers return from the front after the end of hostilities, Leningrad, spring 1940.
(*St Petersburg State Photo Archive*)

A Finnish grave of unknown soldiers in Taipale, 1943.
(*Author's collection*)

Lieutenant-Colonel Yevgeny Skvortsov in 1945. After the Winter War he fought through the Great Patriotic War, ending that conflict in Berlin.
(*Colonel Skvortsov's collection*)

A Finnish artillery crew with a 122mm howitzer at summer camp at Perkjärvi during the 1920s.
(*Author's collection*)

Heavy 150mm howitzers fire during training at summer camp at Perkjär during the 1920s. These howitzers were captured on 13 February 1940 at Lähde.
(*Author's collection*)

A heavy French 152mm howitzer model 1915–1917, as used by the 4th Detached Heavy Battalion.
(*Author's collection*)

Taipale bridgehead, seen from the south-west. (*Pavel Murashov for Bair Irincheev*)

Kelja Christmas battlefield, seen from the south. (*Pavel Murashov for Bair Irincheev*)

Kiviniemi, seen from the south. (*Pavel Murashov for Bair Irincheev*)

The ridges of Äyräpää, seen from the west. (*Pavel Murashov for Bair Irincheev*)

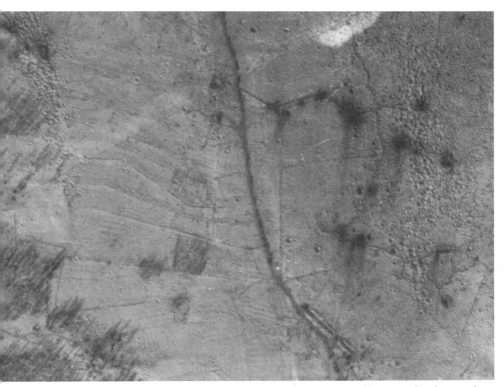

...mma village photographed by a Finnish scout plane. The black spots are blown-up bunkers and ...gouts. (*Finnish National Archive*)

...e result of Soviet bombardment of Finnish positions in the Lähde sector. Aerial photo by a ...nish scout plane. (*Finnish National Archive*)

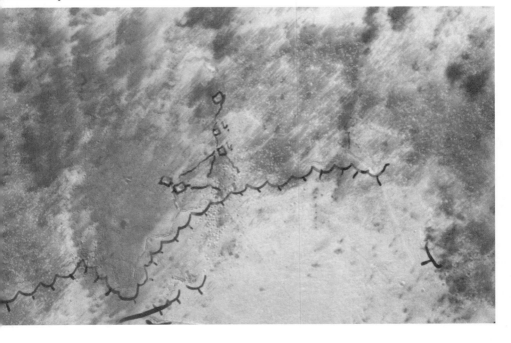

The Tassionlammet sector of the Mannerheim Line in February. Aerial photo by a Finnish scout plane. (*Finnish National Archive*)

A Finnish trench in the Suurniemi sector. (*Russian State Military Archives*)

Inside a Finnish trench in
the Suurniemi sector.
(*Russian State Military Archives*)

Finnish bunkers at
Muolaa river.
(*Russian State Military Archives*)

Bunker No. 6 in the Inkilä
sector.
(*Russian State Military Archives*)

(*Left*) Finnish Nordenfeldt anti-landing cannon at Tuppura Fort. (*Russian State Military Archives*)

(*Right*) Finnish tower for a forward artillery observer. Such positions were mistaken for sniper positions by Red Army men. (*Russian State Military Archives*)

Barbed wire at Bunker No. 2 in the Summa village sector. (*Russian State Military Archives*)

Bunker No. 15 in the
Salmenkaita sector.
(*Russian State Military Archives*)

unker No. 1 in the Inkilä
ector seen from the side
of the Red Army.
ussian State Military Archives)

A ruined Finnish dugout.
(*Russian State Military Archives*)

An unidentified bunker in the Suurniemi sector. (*Russian State Military Archives*)

A Finnish dummy cannon in the Inkilä sector. (*Russian State Military Archives*)

A Finnish anti-tank ditch in Summa.
(*Russian State Military Archives*)

Soviet guard at the door of Bunker No. 7 in the Inkilä sector.
(*Russian State Military Archives*)

Defused Finnish anti-tank mines.
(*Russian State Military Archives*)

The destroyed cupola of Bunker No. 10 in the Salmenkaita sector. (*Russian State Military Archives*)

An armoured cupola blown away from the bunker. (*Russian State Military Archives*)

Gun port at the entrance to Bunker No. 3 in the Suurniemi sector.
(*Russian State Military Archives*)

The remains of bunker No. 11 in the Salmenkaita sector.
(*Russian State Military Archives*)

The destroyed armoured cupola of a Finnish bunker – presumably Bunker No. 2 in Summa village.
(*Russian State Military Archives*)

Bunker No. 10 in the Salmenkaita sector.
(*Russian State Military Archives*)

A high-ranking Russian commander studying a ruined Finnish bunker, place unknown.
(*Russian State Military Archive*)

Kombrig Belyaev, commander of the 139th Rifle Division. Defeat in the Battle of Tolvajärvi froze his career in the Red Army. He retired in 1948 as a general-major – the same rank he held in 1940.
(*Photo provided by Nikolai Ivanov, Belyaev's grandson*)

February: Fifteen Days of Ceaseless Fighting

The 2nd Battalion, 355th Rifle Regiment, launched a carefully planned assault against bunker No. 2 on 1 February 1940. This was part of the series of preparatory assaults on the Finnish defences in order to exhaust the Finns, close in with the Finnish defence lines, and confuse the Finns about the axis of the main strike. An artillery barrage was opened on the bunker on the morning of 1 February 1940. It aimed not only to destroy the bunker but also to make passages in the minefield south of the bunker, and in the anti-tank rock barrier and barbed-wire fence. Then a Soviet assault party moved out against the bunker. It consisted of the 4th Company (Commander, Junior Lieutenant Grishin; Commissar, Political Worker Fomichev), 1st Sapper Platoon (Lieutenant Kucherov) and a platoon of T-28 tanks under Senior Lieutenant K. A. Yegorov, 95th Tank Battalion. The regiment's artillery supported the assault party, firing over open sights.

The staff of the Finnish 3rd Battalion received a message from bunker No. 2 at 1215 hours. The message stated that the bunker had been under heavy fire for two hours and was badly damaged. Apparently, a direct hit on the bunker's roof collapsed the old part of the bunker, killing the platoon leader, Lieutenant Hinttala, and the artillery observer team leader, Lieutenant Mannerhovi.

The death of two officers was a serious blow to Finnish defences in the area. Second Lieutenant Kuutti took over command, dismantled the machine-guns from the bunker and set them up in the open. Then he sent a request for help to his battalion. This message was immediately forwarded to the regimental HQ, but no measures were taken immediately to deal with the crisis. Artillery Sergeant Kenttä from the artillery observers group inside the bunker sent a radio message to his battery: 'Manner is gone, I am still holding on.' One more message from the bunker at 1300 hours reported that three Soviet tanks had crossed the obstacle line and were heading for the bunker.

The Soviet artillery hit the bunker and trenches around it one more time at 1330 hours, covering the assault party that was on its way. The 4th Company was slowly making its way forward, advancing in the dead zone of the bunker's machine-guns. Bunker No. 3, which was supposed to protect bunker No. 2 from such assaults, was badly damaged and it is questionable if it fired at all. Soviet sources claim that bunker No. 3 did open fire and thus prevented the assault party from planting explosives on the roof of the bunker.

The Finns spotted the Soviet sappers loaded with explosives, and concentrated all their fire on the sapper platoon of Lieutenant Kucherov. As a result, the platoon took heavy casualties and had to withdraw, failing even to make passages through the obstacle line for tanks. Tank crews had to destroy the anti-tank rocks with fire from their main guns. Out of thirty men in Kucherov's platoon, only seven were left after they withdrew from the obstacle line.

The Finns did not have any anti-tank guns in the area, so tanks easily destroyed the anti-tank rocks and drove forward to the bunker. One of the tanks hit a land mine and was immobilized. It was Senior Lieutenant Yegorov's tank that was hit. Yegorov left his tank and ran to the bunker, following the two remaining tanks. He was killed on the roof of the bunker. Two of his tanks were on the roof of the bunker at 1440 hours. The garrison of the bunker requested a defensive barrage on the area south of the bunker, but this failed to stop the Soviet assault. The garrison reported the surrender of the bunker to the enemy at 1555 hours. The retreating 7th Finnish Company reported that two Soviet companies captured the bunker. In reality, a decimated 4th Rifle Company held the bunker. The Political Worker of the company, Fomichev, reported to the commander of the 2nd Battalion, Captain Sipovich: 'the company has twenty-eight men left. If there are no reinforcements, we will complete the mission anyway, the remaining men fight as a whole company.'

Despite losing the bunker, the Finnish decision to concentrate fire on the 1st Sapper Platoon was correct. The 4th Company only carried 100 kilograms of explosives, which was not enough to do any serious damage to the bunker. The company blew up a 50-kilogram charge on the roof of the bunker and it did not leave a scratch.

Descriptions of the later battle for the bunker are different in the Soviet and Finnish archive documents. The difference is a matter of several hours but it is worth mentioning. According to the Soviet reports, the assault party withdrew from the bunker, as it was obvious that more explosives were necessary to destroy the bunker.

According to the Finnish sources, the 9th Company and a bicycle company from the division's light unit counter-attacked at 2020 hours. By 2150 hours the bunker was again in Finnish hands. The Soviet assault party had planted charges in the gun ports but did not get chance to detonate them. Finnish sappers from the 28th Detached Sapper Company took the explosives as war booty and immediately started repairs of the crippled bunker. They brought nine loads of boulders to strengthen the roof of the bunker. Repairs were planned for the next day, but they did not take place due to the new Soviet assault.

According to the Soviet sources, Kombrig Yermakov ordered Captain Korovin, commander of the 90th Sapper Battalion, to personally lead the assault party and destroy the bunker. This order was issued at 2100 hours on 1 February, after Yermakov heard about the failure to destroy the bunker. Captain Korovin rallied all the men and formed a new assault party. It consisted of one sapper platoon plus the remnants of the 4th Rifle Company and Lieutenant Kucherov's sappers. The men carried around 600 kilograms of explosives. Late at night, his group was already on the bunker and immediately started preparing the explosion. More explosives had to be brought. Men had to carry the boxes sneaking on the ground due to strong Finnish fire from bunkers No. 1 and No. 3. Commanders and privates worked together. The following commanders and men showed exemplary actions in this dangerous project: Chief of Staff of the 90th Sapper Battalion, Lieutenant Lapshin, Lieutenant Ivanenko, Junior Political Worker Kirpaty, Junior Commander Smirnov, Sappers Anisimov and Koloskov, commander of the 4th Rifle Company Junior Lieutenant Grishin and Platoon Leader Groshev. All was ready for the explosion at 0415 hours on 2 February. The explosives were stacked at the eastern corner of the bunker. Junior Commander Tsvetkov, from the 90th Sapper Battalion, was left at the charge to guard it from possible Finnish counter-attack as the 4th Company was withdrawn from the bunker. The sapper killed three Finns who tried to defuse the charge. Soviet sources do not state whether the sapper later retreated to his lines or was blown up together with the bunker, but his name does not appear in the online casualties database. The explosion shook the air at 0620 hours. It completely destroyed the eastern wall of the bunker. After the explosion the 4th Company again manned the bunker.

According to Finnish sources, they still held the bunker in the early morning of 2 February. Finnish archive sources mention nothing about the explosion at 0620 hours. They do mention, however, the assault of the 4th Rifle Company, 355th Rifle Regiment, against the bunker on the morning of 2 February. The garrison of the bunker fired signal flares into the air, requesting a defensive barrage. Despite this, the Soviet riflemen were some 50 metres from the bunker at 0745 hours, advancing with fire support from heavy machine-guns. The Finnish 9th Company left the bunker at 0920 hours, reporting that the bunker was destroyed and impossible to hold. The Finns did not undertake counter-attacks during the day, but a company of the 3rd Detached Battalion launched the next counter-attack. The mission was to hold the bunker as long as possible.

The Finns assaulted the bunker again after a short artillery barrage at 0620 hours on 3 February. They reached the ruined bunker at 0740 hours but could only hold it for thirty minutes. A hurricane of fire from Soviet riflemen and tanks forced them to retreat. Before leaving the bunker for good, the Finns burnt its casemates and underground gallery with petrol bombs.

According to Soviet archive sources, bunker No. 1 was assaulted and destroyed in the first hours of 3 February. Fire from the trenches around the bunker prevented the delivery of additional explosives to bunker No. 2. The assault party consisted of riflemen of the 5th Company, 355th Rifle Regiment, two T-26 tanks and two squads of sappers. They made their way to the bunker via a hand-to-hand fight through the trench work. Then they piled up 1,200 kilograms of explosives on the bunker's roof and blew it up at 0420 hours on 3 February.

Delivery of additional explosives to bunker No. 2 began immediately. Around 3,500 kilograms of explosives were on the roof of bunker No. 2 and inside its western casemate late in the night of 3 February. A huge explosion destroyed the bunker in the first hours of 4 February 1940. The Soviet sappers used a total of 5,300 kilograms of explosives to destroy the bunker.

This was the first large bunker captured by the Red Army in the whole Winter War, and the commander of the 100th Rifle Division, Yermakov, concentrated all his efforts on this flank of the assault.

Attacks by the Soviet troops on the Finnish positions north of the captured bunkers continued for several days, but they could not make any further penetration of the Finnish lines. The Finns held out stubbornly in the forest north of the captured bunkers. The 355th Rifle Regiment lost five commanders killed and twenty-three wounded, plus seventy junior commanders and men killed and 527 wounded.

The 355th Rifle Regiment sent a tank landing party into the Finnish rear with the mission of reaching the school and Turta Farm, capturing enemy trenches and preparing for the regiment's advance. Five T-28 tanks with armoured sleds, three flame-thrower tanks, 105 men with four heavy machine-guns and two mortars were earmarked for the mission. Senior Lieutenant Lobodin led the task force and the Commissar of the landing party was Political Worker Chausov. The landing party failed to complete its mission: the tanks were hit by concentrated Finnish artillery and mortar fire and started to drive back and forth, threatening to squash the armoured sleds with the men inside. The landing party had to dismount in the anti-tank ditch. The crew of tank No. 108 lost its bearings and opened fire on Soviet riflemen and a battalion CP, mistaking it for a Finnish bunker. The Finns described this operation as: 'Russkies attack with 50–60 tanks with armoured sleds for the infantry' and 'around 300 men are attacking under cover of armoured shields'. The Finns claimed five tanks destroyed on 6 February and then two more tanks in Peltola strongpoint.

The 355th Rifle Regiment reported eight T-28 tanks lost on that day and praised the flame-thrower tanks for their efficiency. Soviet riflemen who tried to join the landing party in the anti-tank ditch were pinned down by intensive Finnish fire and had to stop. All units were withdrawn to the initial positions at

2000 hours. All attempts to break through the Finnish defences between bunker No. 2 and the highway failed during the period 6–15 February. A regiment sent an assault party without tanks to one of the bunkers at 0400 hours on 7 February but the attack was stalled by a minefield. Soviet artillery continued pounding Finnish trenches and bunkers. The armoured turret of Peltola bunker took a direct hit on that day, killing artillery observer Ruohomaa.

The 355th Rifle Regiment was supposed to receive flame-thrower tanks and teletanks for the destruction of the bunkers, but the 100th Rifle Division cancelled the order. The riflemen and tanks attacked again, working closely together. All assaults on 9 and 10 February also failed. However, these assaults were just a foretaste of the grand offensive to come on 11 February.

On 11 February the Soviet artillery rained a hail of fire on the Finnish defences: 'Our artillery fire on that day was especially destructive and precise.' The 34th Artillery Regiment of the division fired 6,030 rounds at the Finnish positions, the 21st Heavy Corps Artillery Regiment fired around 1,000 rounds.

However, the Finns repelled the assault of the entire 355th Rifle Regiment with great difficulty. Soviet attacking lines reached the barbed wire and were pinned down by fire from all the weapons the Finns had. Six T-28 tanks were driving back and forth in front of the Finnish trenches all day long, firing at the defences. Two of these tanks drove into the Finnish rear. Second Lieutenant Lehmuskoski tried to knock them out with satchel charges but failed.

The regiment sent out an assault party on 14 February but it was stopped by strong machine-gun fire and forced to return. The regiment lost two commanders killed and six wounded, twenty-five junior commanders and men killed and 180 wounded. Total losses of the regiment in the Winter War, according to the dressing station of the regiment, were:

	Type of casualties	Arrived at the dressing station of the regiment		Note
		Men of our regiment	Men of other units	
1	Killed	394	–	Men killed in action
2	Wounded	1,877	201	never arrived at the
3	Frostbite 1st degree	110	18	dressing station,
4	Frostbite 2nd degree	12	3	except for 7 men who
5	Shell-shocked	218	44	died of heavy wounds.

All attempts by the 331st Rifle Regiment to break through the Finnish defences east of the highway also failed. The regiment carried out a reconnaissance in force on 1 February against bunker No. 6 at the highway, but the companies were almost immediately pinned down by machine-gun, mortar and artillery fire. Bunker No. 6 was still operational, although artillery and T-28 tanks fired at it over open sights.

The 331st Rifle Regiment continued its assaults with two or three companies during the six days from 2 to 8 February, but failed to achieve anything. Their assaults were supported by T-26 tanks and flame-thrower tanks on 6 February, but the Finns knocked out four of them: two tanks were burnt out on the battlefields, while two made it back from the assault damaged.

Flanking fire from bunker No. 10 also prevented the regiment from advancing. The bunker was immediately spotted by Soviet artillerymen. The regimental commander, Major Buslaev, ordered the 3rd Rifle Company to destroy the bunker. The Finns stopped the assault party by their fire at the anti-tank rock barrier, and the assault party had to withdraw after taking casualties.

An assault party with three T-28 tanks drove off to bunker No. 6 on the evening of 7 February, but one tank got stuck in a crater, the second got wedged on a boulder, and the third tank lost the sled with explosives on the way. As the riflemen and sappers were left without armour support, they returned to their initial positions. The tanks were later evacuated from the battlefield, but the destruction of the bunker failed again.

The 331st Rifle Regiment attacked strongpoint Ruohonen at bunker No. 17 on 8 February, but the Finns repelled all assaults. After this, Soviet assault parties again stormed the Finnish strongpoints at the highway. At least three guns of calibre 76mm–122mm were set to support the assault parties with direct fire.

The regimental commander, Major Buslaev, ordered the destruction of the long-suffering bunker No. 6 by an assault party of riflemen and sappers without the support of tanks. The assault party was driven off by concentrated Finnish machine-gun fire.

Soviet guns firing over open sights finally destroyed bunker No. 5 with direct fire. Second Lieutenant Salonen reported at 1310 hours that the roof of the bunker had collapsed, burying the machine-gun, but its crew had made it out of the bunker. Salonen also reported that Soviet snipers were firing at the gun ports of bunker No. 6 with armour-piercing bullets, but the damage was insignificant. Three Soviet fighters strafed the Finnish trench network all day long, frustrating the movement of Finnish infantry.

The grand offensive of the Red Army began on 11 February. Political workers of the regiment held several meetings with the men, encouraging them to break through the Finnish defences. The 331st Rifle Regiment, supported by tanks, assaulted Inkilä strongpoint east of the highway at 0915 hours. The assault was repelled. Soviet tanks ran into the anti-tank gun of Second Lieutenant Valde Hämäläinen, camouflaged at the ruined bunker No. 7. Seven tanks were lost immediately. Second Lieutenant Inkilä reported the destruction of nine tanks by the end of the day. A Finnish artillery observer in the trenches estimated Soviet losses as 150 men killed. Finnish losses, as recorded in the war diary, were also significant – fifteen men killed and sixteen wounded.

The staff of the 331st Rifle Regiment could only reflect:

> the offensive was stopped by fire of the enemy from Stone, Egg and Tongue Hills, as well as from bunker No. 6 and trenches around the bunker. The enemy was especially keen on stopping our tanks, knocking out ten of them. Two Finnish Fokker fighters tried to strafe our riflemen during the assault.

The Soviet commanders had mistaken a single Finnish anti-tank gun for a powerful artillery bunker.

In twelve days of fighting, from 1 to 12 February, the 331st Rifle Regiment reported the loss of six commanders, fourteen junior commanders and 128 men killed. According to incomplete reports, the regiment lost seven commanders, eight junior commanders and 294 men wounded.

Finnish defences were weakened by the daily artillery fire and relentless assaults by the 355th and 331st Rifle Regiments. All communication trenches collapsed. Trench work, bunkers and dugouts collapsed partially. Finnish officers also noted that holding their ground against the Red Army assault parties was difficult: 'Enemy artillery fire over the open sight and machine-gun fire makes the battle especially hard' reads one comment in a Finnish war diary.

The Soviet offensive continued on 12 February. The 123rd Rifle Division had broken through the defences of the 9th Regiment the day before and continued its advance north. The Finnish units in Summa village had their left flank exposed. The commander of the 2nd Battalion sent an order to Inkilä strongpoint at 1655 hours:

> There will be no reinforcements. Hold your ground till the last man. Pay special attention to the junction with Tuomola strongpoint. Send sentries to no-man's-land during the night to avoid sudden night attacks by the enemy. Give soldiers as much time for rest as possible, but not to threaten the integrity of defences.

The last sentence describes the condition of the men very well, as battles had been raging in the sector for twelve days. At the same time the commander of the 7th Regiment reported to the division, saying eloquently: 'even if Soviet tanks drove over the trenches, the men would not wake up'.

A Soviet attack against Lempi strongpoint began. The Finnish battalion commander sent the same order there: 'hold your ground with all means'.

The Soviet offensive in the sector did not resume on 13 February but Soviet artillery continued pounding the Finnish defences. Apparently Soviet units in the sector were waiting for the situation to develop in the neighbouring sectors, where the 123rd Rifle Division was already battling for the Finnish second defence line. The Finns rotated their units in Summa village on this day: the 1st Battalion, 7th Infantry Regiment was replaced by the 3rd Battalion, 15th Infantry Regiment. The battalion held out for two days, and in the afternoon of 15 February 1940 Mannerheim issued orders to fall back to the Intermediary line. The Finns disengaged and left Summa village in the darkness. All intact fortifications were destroyed during the retreat – the Finns threw petrol bombs into the remaining bunkers and dugouts.

Two months of fighting in Summa village were over. Despite the numerical superiority of the 100th Rifle Division in this defence sector, the Finns managed to contain all Soviet assaults. Even the loss of the key bunker No. 2 did not break their will to fight. Withdrawal from Summa village began only on the afternoon of 15 February, and in good order. Soviet attempts to destroy the bunkers in this sector in January and February mostly failed: only bunkers Nos 1, 2 and 3 were destroyed by assault parties, the rest were dealt with by artillery. However, the 355th Rifle Regiment failed to build on the initial success after 3 February.

Summa village was completely destroyed during the battle. Villagers received permission to return to their home as late as 1942. They had to live through the winter of 1942–1943 in cardboard barracks provided by the Finnish Army and Soviet wooden dugouts built in the area in 1941. The final rebuilding of the village was planned for the summer of 1944; timber was harvested in autumn 1943. However, these plans were never accomplished due to the new Soviet offensive in June 1944. The village was not rebuilt after the war; a small summer cottage village was built on its spot in the 1990s. Aune Inkinen recalled a trip to her former home village:

> One summer in the 1990s we visited Summa village with my son and daughter. It might sound strange, but this trip brought peace to my heart. Fields and gardens disappeared in a new forest. I could not see bomb and shell craters any more. There were no more trees broken by artillery fire. Only three concrete steps, covered with moss, were left from our house.

Kombrig Yermakov, commander of the 100th Rifle Division, continued his career in the Red Army, took part in the Great Patriotic War and served as a Soviet military adviser in China.

Captain Sipovich, a career commander in the Red Army, fought as a regimental commander in the Great Patriotic War. In the spring of 1942 his regiment was trapped in the huge encirclement at Kharkov, but the energetic Sipovich managed to break out from the pocket. He served at the Battle of Kursk as a deputy divisional commander, then took part in the Dnepr crossing, and completed the war in Poland with the rank of general-major. He retired in 1968. He died in Moscow on 4 January 1984.

Sapper Captain Korovin, who received the Gold Star for blowing up bunkers No. 1 and No. 2, was taken prisoner by the Germans in 1941. This was considered a personal disgrace by the Soviet State, so his decoration was cancelled.

Senior Lieutenant Vatagin had led the party to bunker No. 3. He was killed in action in Czechoslovakia at the approaches to Prague. He carried the rank of major and commanded a rifle regiment at the moment of his death. He is buried in a Soviet military cemetery in Prague.

Squad Leader Kirillov, who also took part in the raid against bunker No. 3, graduated from Moscow Infantry Academy in 1940 and then from Frunze Academy in 1942. He took part in the Great Patriotic War and the war against Japan. He retired as a lieutenant colonel and passed away in Tambov on 28 September 1988.

Political Worker Fomichev, who was also awarded with the Gold Star for the destruction of bunker No. 2, was killed on 12 October 1941 during the Battle of Moscow, and is buried in Podolsk.

Senior Lieutenant Yegorov, the T-28 tank platoon leader, was posthumously awarded with the Gold Star of the Hero of the Soviet Union for his participation in the assault on bunker No. 2.

Second Lieutenant Paavo Mikkola, platoon leader, 6th Company, 15th Infantry Regiment of the Finnish Army, was lightly wounded in the Soviet artillery barrage on 14 February 1940. He was bandaged and refused hospitalization. He was torn to pieces by a Soviet shell on the way back to the front. His remains and dog tag were found on the battlefield as late as 1999. He is buried with his battle comrades in his hometown of Hämeenlinna.

When the collapsed casemate of bunker No. 2 was dug open, the remains of Lieutenant Hinttala and Lieutenant Mannerhovi were found. They were both buried alive on 1 February 1940 during the Soviet artillery barrage. According to some reports by their relatives, the bodies were very well preserved – the giant chunks of concrete that buried the officers served as a refrigerator. It was

minus 40 degrees Celsius on 1 February, and the bodies were frozen solid.
Lieutenant Hinttala is buried at Hietaniemi military cemetery in Helsinki. This
cemetery is also the resting place of Karl Gustav Mannerheim, Commander-
in-Chief of the Finnish Army. It was his wish to be buried next to the men he
led in the Second World War.

Junior Sergeant Ernest Daniel Pohjola was buried alive on 1 January 1940,
in the ruins of collapsed bunker No. 4. His body is still inside the bunker. An
empty grave lies under a cross bearing his name in his home village of Hattula.

Merkki Sector: the Breakthrough Expanded

The sector of attack for the 90th Rifle Division became even narrower in
February 1940, as the 80th Rifle Division took over the positions at the railway.
As a result, the 90th Rifle Division only assaulted a narrow sector of 2.5 kilometres. The division received significant reinforcements of artillery – there
were forty-eight 152mm guns, twenty 122mm guns, thirty-four 76mm guns
and twenty-four 45mm guns in the sector.

The artillery bombardment of Finnish positions began at 0940 hours on
11 February 1940 and lasted two hours. During these two hours the artillery in
the division's sector fired 15,719 rounds.

The 286th Rifle Regiment, with two tank companies of the 160th Tank
Battalion, assaulted on the left flank of the division. The 173rd Rifle Regiment,
with two companies of the 157th Tank Battalion, assaulted on the right. The
588th Rifle Regiment did not fit in the narrow sector of the front and stood in
reserve. The main strike was delivered in the direction of Hill 44.8, the sector
held by the 3rd Battalion of Major Ruotsalo from the 1st Brigade. Soviet tanks
and guns, firing over open sights, easily shot through the Finnish trenches on
top of the swamp. The Finns managed to repel most of the assaults but lost one
strongpoint. The brigade's reserve, the 2nd Battalion of Captain Karinno, was
thrown into a night counter-attack but failed to recapture the trench. Only
on the morning of 12 February, when the 1st Battalion, 3rd Brigade, was
fed into the battle, did the Finns manage to restore the line. Aimo Mursula, of
the 2nd Battalion of the 1st Brigade, recalled the battle against the 90th Rifle
Division on 11–12 February 1940:

> In the last moments of darkness before dawn we saw why we
> were alerted to man the trenches. Three enemy tanks had driven
> up to our trenches under cover of darkness. Two of them were still
> manoeuvring, looking for a better firing position. The tanks were
> painted white. There were bundles of logs and branches attached to
> one of the tanks in front of its turret – was it foliage for camouflage?

The tanks stopped some 60–70 metres from our trenches but they were out of range of our hand grenades. The tanks started rotating their turrets, looking for targets, and opened fire at our machine-gun nests. In this way they managed to break most of our positions, which is no wonder, as there was nothing we could do against them. One had to watch the tanks very carefully and notice where the tanks aimed. Then we had to quickly give signs to our men so they would have time to flee from the section of trench under fire.

The tanks attacked our positions for a long time unhindered, as we did not have any anti-tank guns. The only Bofors anti-tank gun was in the 3rd Platoon, on our left, but it took a long time to get it from there because of the deep snow. One also had to proceed with caution, as the thin forest provided no cover or concealment.

The very first round fired from the Bofors at a distance of 70 metres hit the turret. The tank immediately ceased fire. One could clearly see the hole in the turret. The second tank was not clearly visible behind the first. Our gun fired several rounds but missed. Nevertheless, the second tank also ceased fire. The third tank turned around and left the battlefield immediately.

Enemy infantry assaulted at the same time. They moved forward slowly, pushing armoured shields on sleds in front of them. Regular rifle bullets could not penetrate them, but we picked up armour-piercing rounds from Russian machine-gun belts (the bullets had a black head) and after that we had no trouble at all. After my very first shot the closest armoured shield stopped. Apparently, there was no one left to push it forward. The same happened with the other men. When the enemy tanks withdrew and the infantrymen realized our rifle fire could penetrate their armoured shields, the assault was over.

On our right flank the situation was much worse. There, enemy tanks also approached our trenches under cover of darkness. Part of the trench in that area was built on top of a swamp and tanks calmly attacked the trench. Our infantry had to retreat and enemy infantry captured a section of trench 200 metres wide. They also managed to capture one dugout.

A swift counter-attack began on the morning of 12 February. It advanced well, and by noon the entire trench was again in our hands. Many were killed in that battle, but a new soldier immediately came to replace the fallen one. Wounded retreated through our positions in an unending flow, some by themselves, some supported by their comrades. The enemy also suffered heavy casualties, with a lot of dead left on the battlefield. The enemy had fortified the place of breakthrough very well – we collected eighteen machine-guns on skis with armoured shields.

The 90th Rifle Division was reinforced with the 43rd Detached Scout Battalion, which had chemical tanks and one armoured T-26. The mission of the 1st Company of BHM flame-thrower tanks was to set Finnish log barricades on fire, causing the detonation of charges and mines. The 2nd Company was to burn the Finnish infantry in trenches. The Finnish infantry only managed to damage one flame-thrower tank in combat with close-range weapons. The 286th Rifle Regiment assaulted the Finnish lines again and captured part of the trenches, but could not advance further. Finnish anti-tank guns knocked out six tanks; four tanks were lost after hitting mines. The armoured T-26 tank took six direct hits but was not damaged. The Soviet offensive continued on 13 February and the Finns repelled it with great difficulty. The 40th Light Tank even tried to deploy a sapper tank with a wooden bridge for negotiating obstacles, but this tank was knocked out by a land mine.

As the Soviet breakthrough in the Lähde sector deepened on 14 February 1940, the commander of the 1st Division, General-Major Laatikainen, made the decision to withdraw the 1st Brigade behind the River Peronjoki. As a result, the breakthrough in the Finnish main defence line widened. The Finns started to withdraw to the intermediary defence line on 15 February. During the four days of fighting from 11 to 15 February, the Finnish 1st Brigade lost about 60 per cent of its personnel, some 400 men remaining. Soviet casualties in the sector were also high. During the same period the 286th Rifle Regiment lost thirty-nine men killed, 419 wounded, eleven missing in action and fifteen frostbitten. The 173rd Rifle Regiment lost ninety-seven men killed, 376 men wounded, eighteen frostbitten and thirty-three sick. The 588th Regiment's losses were thirty-five men killed, 261 wounded, eighteen frostbitten and nineteen sick. The division lost a total of 1,351 men during the offensive.

Tassionlammet: One Boys Anti-tank Rifle per Brigade

The 14th Infantry Regiment of the Finnish Army easily repelled all the assaults of the 24th Rifle Division in the sector. This famous division of the Red Army, tracing its traditions back to the times of the Russian Civil War, was spread too thin and was partially demoralized by the death of its commander, Kombrig Veshev, on 6 December 1939.

The 24th Rifle Division spent all January preparing a new offensive. Artillery fired at Finnish bunkers in the Suurniemi sector over open sights. Bunkers

No. 4 and No. 5 were subject to fire from heavy artillery on several occasions. The first Soviet artillery pieces were set to fire in the open and were quickly suppressed by Finnish mortar fire. Then Soviet artillerymen built wooden bunkers on Suursuo swamp and fired from them. Finnish 81mm mortar rounds could not destroy such bunkers and Finnish artillery had to be summoned to suppress these guns.

The worst, however, was the methodical artillery fire at the Finnish trench network and obstacle lines. With each day, the trenches were becoming more and more shallow and dangerous to stay in, due to the unceasing Soviet artillery fire.

The 14th Infantry Regiment was replaced with units of the 2nd Brigade on 23 January. The 3rd Battalion of the brigade that manned the positions at Suursuo swamp bitterly observed the condition of the lines:

> the defences left to us by the 14th Regiment on 22 January are in bad and incomplete condition. Trenches are too shallow, in some places (strongpoint L1) one can only crawl in them. The trench between strongpoints K3 and L1 is built in open terrain, over the swamp. Communication trenches are either missing, or one can only crawl in them. Each strongpoint only has one or two dugouts. In the strongpoint of the 8th Company they are standing out above the ground and provide weak cover from shrapnel.

The Finns did their best in three weeks from 23 January to 11 February to improve their positions: they deepened trenches, planted more mines on the swamp, repaired the barbed-wire obstacles. Carrying out fortification works in swampy terrain had its difficulties – there were no stones to strengthen the defences, and even soil had to be brought to the trenches at night, in order not to draw Soviet fire.

The noise of axes and saws could also be heard from the southern side of the Suursuo swamp. Soviet sappers were building their own jumping-off positions for the assault, sometimes under cover of a smokescreen. The Finns did their best to harass the Soviet work with artillery and mortar fire. Soviet artillery continued its methodical barrage of the Finnish lines and managed to destroy two wooden bunkers. Soviet activity on the southern edge of the swamp intensified with each day and everything pointed to an imminent offensive.

Soviet mortar batteries delivered a powerful strike at the Finnish obstacle line on the evening of 10 February. A rifle company began a reconnaissance-in-force at 0930 hours on 11 February. After this, Soviet artillery hit the Finnish strongpoints K3 and L1 at the axis of the main attack. Second Lieutenant Savinen, platoon leader in the K3 strongpoint, had made a smart move and withdrew his platoon along the communication trenches before the artillery barrage. His platoon managed to avoid casualties. The neighbouring strong-point, L1, did not have communication trenches into the rear and the Finns suffered heavy casualties.

The Soviet assault itself began at 1240 hours. Under the cover of armoured shields, the 2nd and 3rd Battalions of the 274th Rifle Regiment, with support from T-26 tanks of the 155th Detached Tank Battalion, slowly moved forward. A 122mm cannon, firing over open sights, supported the assault. Soon they captured part of the Finnish trenches between strongpoints K3 and L1. The Finns noted that this success was largely due to the brave actions of four tank crews.

The Finnish 3rd Battalion immediately requested reinforcements and the 2nd Battalion managed to send them. At 1310 hours the Soviet assault started along the whole breadth of the Suursuo swamp, but the Finns clearly saw that the focal points were K3 and L1. Finnish reinforcements arrived at K3 at 1630 hours and the Finns managed to restore balance. The Red Army men did not advance further and dug in in front of the Finnish trenches under cover of tanks and armoured shields. One more rifle company made it across the swamp during the day. Finnish mortars were low on ammunition and fired few salvos. The 5th, 7th and 8th Rifle Companies of the 274th Rifle Regiment dug in on the southern tips of strongpoints K3 and L1.

Losses for the day in the Finnish 3rd Battalion were eighteen killed and thirty-six wounded. The 274th Rifle Regiment reported six men killed and 191 wounded on 11 February. As four tanks were standing right in front of the Finnish positions and two Soviet rifle companies were dug in behind armoured shields within range of hand grenades, the commander of the Finnish 3rd Battalion asked for permission to keep the reinforcements that had arrived from the 2nd Battalion. The exchange of fire continued during the night. The Finns managed to bring up ammo and food for the men at the front. The mortar crews received only sixty mortar rounds.

The Soviet assault continued on the morning of 12 February. The Soviet riflemen assaulted after an artillery strike: 'The pace of advance is slow, very skilful, they move under cover of armoured shields from crater to crater. We are facing well-trained units . . .' was the observation of Finnish officers. Luckily, the Finns had issued armour-piercing rifle rounds to the men in K3, in order to neutralize the Soviet men behind the armoured shields and in armoured sleds. Ten Soviet tanks broke into K3 at 1230 hours and more riflemen made it across the swamp under their protection. The real threat of a tank breakthrough into the Finnish rear appeared. All the brigades' units were alarmed and Finnish tank-hunter teams manned positions in the rear. Soviet tanks and riflemen captured the southern part of K3 at 1330 hours. The Finns lacked long-range anti-tank weapons and could only damage some tanks with satchel charges.

At the same time Soviet tanks left the swamp, outflanked L1 and forced the Finns to withdraw from the (now almost non-existent) trenches of strongpoint L1. There was a danger of encirclement of K3 and L1, and the Finns had to man flanking positions at the border of L1 and L2. The brigade commander informed the 3rd Battalion at 1405 hours that he was sending five infantry platoons and a machine-gun platoon from the 2nd Battalion in order to carry out a counter-attack. This reinforced company also had one 37mm anti-tank gun, but due to the difficult terrain it could not be delivered to the front line. The gun was left standing at the CP of the 3rd Battalion. After the counter-attack, the reinforced company was to return to the 2nd Battalion.

While the Finns were completing their preparations for the counter-attack towards L1, Finnish men in L2 saw with amazement a Soviet rifle company forming two attacking lines in the open and starting their assault. Finnish mortars and artillery could do little as their ammunition was all but spent. The Finns tried to stop this assault with two machine-guns urgently transferred from K3 and K1. At the same moment Finnish defences started to collapse in K3 itself, as Soviet riflemen made it into the trench and started mopping up towards the dugout area. A hand-to-hand fight raged in the trenches the entire afternoon of 12 February, men on both sides using hand grenades, pistols, submachine-guns and bayonets.

A Finnish counter-attack began at 1700 hours between K3 and L1, which eased the situation for a while, but the advance was immediately stopped by deadly machine-gun fire. Thirty minutes later Lieutenant Siuhkonen reported that he could not advance without hand grenades. There were no hand grenades in the battalion's ammunition storage, so the staff of the 3rd Battalion had to gather all hand grenades available at the CP and send them to the front. Second Lieutenant Savinen launched a simultaneous counter-attack in strongpoint K3 with his platoon, and made it to the southern tip of the strongpoint. There he was stopped by fire from Soviet tanks. The battle abated in darkness. Finnish supply units finally managed to bring hand grenades and satchel charges to the companies at the front. Finnish officers still considered the situation critical: some parts of the strongpoints were still in Soviet hands, losses were high, and the surviving men exhausted. The commander of the 3rd Battalion, Captain Virkkunen, informed the brigade that he could recapture the lost strongpoints in the night, but could not return the five platoons to the 2nd Battalion. This meant there were no more reserves left in the entire brigade. Virkkunen promised to return the anti-tank gun, as he could not deploy it anyway.

The reinforced Finnish company suffered such high losses in the counter-attack that its remains had to be merged with the 3rd Battalion. The brigade commander attached the 2nd Battalion to the 3rd Battalion, leaving one company and eight machine-gun crews in reserve. The Finns failed to recapture the southern part of K3 in the night. The situation in L1 was also unclear. No one on the Soviet or Finnish side could report casualties, as the battle did not stop for a minute. Dead Soviet and Finnish men filled the trenches and were stacked on top of each other in layers.

The exchange of fire lasted all night long, but in the early hours of 13 February the Finns received a British Boys anti-tank rifle – the entire brigade had only one such rifle. The Soviet assault in the morning of 13 February started at 0810 hours without artillery preparation. Light tanks supported the assault. The Finns were pushed back to the dugouts by 1036 hours. Bitter fighting in the trenches did not stop for a minute, as hand-to-hand fights erupted here and there. As Captain Kozhevnikov, commander of the 2nd Battalion, 274th Rifles, reported, an 'energetic exchange of fire and close combat' lasted all day in K3.

The staff of the 2nd Brigade informed the 3rd Battalion that the last 100 mortar rounds had been sent to the front: there were no more rounds left in the entire brigade. However, the Finnish heavy artillery managed to disperse attack formations of the 274th Rifle Regiment on the swamp, while the Finnish anti-tank rifle crew put their weapon to good use, knocking out four tanks in L1. Soviet tank men mistook the Boys rifle for a large-calibre machine-gun. Tank crews and riflemen blamed each other for passivity and lack of will to move forward. The Finns had continuous difficulties orchestrating artillery fire, as forward observers only had phone lines, which were almost permanently down, despite the superhuman efforts of signals operators to keep them working. When the situation was desperate, Finnish forward observers used signal flares to call artillery strikes.

The Finns thought that the situation had eased up a bit. In the evening they managed to bring the anti-tank gun to the front and knocked out three Soviet tanks, but four new tanks arrived to replace those destroyed. The Finns could only watch as Soviet armoured cars and tanks transported riflemen across the swamp into K3. The situation worsened again at 1600 hours. The main danger was that the 3rd Battalion did not have any reserves at the front in case of a Soviet breakthrough. The situation was reported to the brigade and the brigade commander urgently sent a company from the 1st Battalion to correct this. This company, under Second Lieutenant Zillacius, marched to the front, despite the presence of the Soviet Air Force. The phone line to K3 was restored at 1735 hours and Second Lieutenant Savinen reported that his forces were outnumbered and he was about to be surrounded by Soviet tanks. At the same time Savinen promised to hold out for thirty minutes more. Zillacius received an order to march off to K3 immediately, and twenty-five minutes later his company was in the strongpoint, despite the powerful Soviet barrage on the routes of approach. His company arrived at the very last moment to repel yet another assault of the 274th Rifle Regiment with rapid rifle fire. The Soviet men retreated into the trenches in the southern part of K3 and stopped their attacks for the day. Zillacius remained at the front line and his company was merged with the remains of the 3rd and 2nd Battalions. The southern part of K3 had been in Soviet hands for seventy-two hours and Soviet sappers used this time to build a strong wooden bunker there.

Eighty-one men were wounded in the 3rd Finnish Battalion on that day, and there was no information about the number of killed. The mortar crews were down to eighty-eight rounds. A promised reinforcement of ninety men had not arrived.

The men on both sides were exhausted after seventy-two hours of unceasing combat. On the morning of 14 February the temperature decreased to minus 31 degrees Celsius. The situation for the Finns remained hard, as there were no reserves available. Finnish battalion commanders counted their men. It turned out that 248 men held a 3-kilometre front. This was all that remained of the 3rd, 2nd and part of the 1st Battalions of the brigade. Battalion commanders of the 2nd and 3rd Battalions requested a withdrawal of their battered units from the front, but a negative answer came from the 1st Division at 0345 hours on 14 February.

The Soviet offensive resumed on the morning of 14 February. On that day the 24th Rifle Division attacked with the 274th and 168th Regiments on a wide front, from the railway to the eastern edge of Suursuo swamp, but all attacks were repelled.

In the afternoon the Finns made the decision to destroy the Soviet bunker in strongpoint K3. The Finns started their assault at 1730 hours, but the plan failed from the very beginning: the fuses of the mortar rounds failed due to the extreme cold, and most of the mortar rounds did not explode. The Finnish forces earmarked for the assault – three squads and one sapper squad – were insufficient. Men of the 274th Rifle Regiment opened such an intensive machine-gun fire at the Finns that the assault had to be called off. After that, the Soviets launched their own assault but the Finns held out.

The hand-to-hand fight lasted all night in strongpoint K3 around the dugout area. On the morning of 15 February the situation again became critical for the Finns. The brigade reacted to the desperate plea for help by sending twenty-five horse drivers from the 2nd Battalion – all the drivers from the 3rd Battalion had been fighting at the front for several days already. At 1149 hours men of the 274th Rifle Regiment managed to push the Finns from the first dugout. The Finns managed to blow it up and burn it with Molotov cocktails before the withdrawal. One minute later Second Lieutenant Savinen, who was firing back at the Soviets from the door of his CP, reported to the battalion that he could not hold out much longer. Company Commander Karttunen sent four machine-guns with crews and twenty-five replacements to the rear of strong-point K3. The replacements were close to panic and tried to leave the line unnoticed.

The Finns managed to stop the 274th Rifle Regiment only with a barrage of heavy artillery. The situation was stabilized again. Finnish battalions at the front received an order to fall back late in the evening of 15 February. The Finns managed to destroy all their dugouts before the withdrawal. Savinen's platoon, which had held out in strongpoint K3 for four days, had only eleven men left out of thirty-two.

The 274th Rifle Regiment lost from 30 to 40 per cent of its men. There is no precise information about casualties, as the 3rd Battalion failed to report casualties during the assault.

Casualties of the 274th Rifle Regiment, 11–15 February 1940 (without the 3rd Battalion) are as follows:

	Present on 11 February 1940	Present on 15 February 1940
Commanders	95	41
Junior commanders	249	112
Privates	1,636	903

The Central Isthmus

The Thirteenth Army also launched an offensive on 11 February, along its entire front, with the goal of tying down Finnish reserves. The main strike of the XV and the XXIII Rifle Corps was in the central Isthmus, between Lake Muolaanjärvi and the River Vuoksi.

The Finnish main defence line in the Central Isthmus ran along the Oinala–Parikkala–Muolaa Church village–isthmus between Lake Kirkkojärvi and Lake Punnusjärvi. The main line in this area only had field fortifications. The exception was the Muolaa Church village sector, with four weak bunkers dating from the 1920s. The rest of the concrete bunkers were some 15 kilometres behind the main defence line on the intermediary line.

The 136th Rifle Division, supported by the 40th and 39th Light Tank Brigades, launched its offensive towards Oinala and Parikkala, managing to capture one Finnish platoon strongpoint but failing to advance further. As the Soviet tank commanders noted, the artillery preparation for the offensive was not efficient enough. Trenches and wooden bunkers – the backbone of the Finnish defences – were not destroyed, and the Finns easily repelled all assaults.

The 17th Motor Rifle Division assaulted the positions of the Finnish 5th and 6th Infantry Regiments between Punnusjärvi and Kirkkojärvi and managed to advance some 100 metres into the Finnish defences, but the Finns still held on. The advance cost the division a lot of blood, especially among the commanders.

The 8th Rifle Division launched its assault towards Muolaa Church village with the support of the 39th Light Tank Brigade. During the preparation for the assault, passages in the anti-tank rock fence had been made. All hell broke loose on Church Hill on 11 February 1940, when eight Soviet artillery battalions opened fire. The hill was literally ploughed up with the explosions of heavy rounds. The beautiful church of Muolaa, which had been badly damaged in the December battles, was reduced to a heap of broken bricks.

The 2nd and 3rd Battalions of the 151st Rifle Regiment assaulted the hill. The 2nd Battalion, 310th Rifle Regiment, assaulted on the left. Men slowly moved forwards, pushing armoured shields in front. However, the assault was stopped by well-orchestrated Finnish small-arms fire. According to the memoirs of Finnish participants, a Finnish sergeant sneaked into no-man's-land, made a position in a shell crater, and opened fire at the flanks of the assaulting Soviet riflemen. An armoured shield only protected the upper part of the body of a rifleman, his legs remaining unprotected. The Soviet assault was stopped at the anti-tank rock fence.

The 3rd Battalion of the 151st Rifle Regiment was supported by twelve tanks of the 85th Tank Battalion and three flame-thrower tanks of the 204th Detached Tank Battalion. The tanks made passages through the anti-tank rock fence with armour-piercing rounds, destroyed barbed-wire fencing and opened intensive fire at the Finnish trenches with their main guns, machine-guns and flame-throwers. The Finns failed to knock out a single tank from the 85th Tank Battalion on that day. The battalion only lost a representative of the special department, Political Worker Bilik and tank commander Lieutenant Matkin. Both tank men were wounded when they came out of the tanks, rallying their own riflemen. Two Soviet tanks drove out on the ice of Lake Kirkkojärvi, trying to outflank the hill. The ice was too weak and both tanks sank.

The battle abated in the evening but Soviet riflemen remained at the anti-tank rocks. The commander of the 8th Division ordered a scout group to sneak into the Finnish trenches under cover of darkness and capture Church Hill. Scout parties moved out, but were spotted by Finns, took casualties and were forced to fall back on the morning of 12 February.

The regiments of the 8th Rifle Division tried to attack again on the morning of 12 February, but the riflemen could not stand up because of intensive mortar and small-arms fire from the Finnish side. Tanks of the 39th Light Tank Brigade charged forward alone. Eight cannon tanks and six flame-thrower tanks crossed the anti-tank rock fence, surrounded Church Hill from all sides and opened systematic fire at it. The Finns managed to knock out one cannon tank and three flame-thrower tanks with artillery. The cannon tank remained on the battlefield and one of the flame-thrower tanks burnt out.

The decisive assault on the hill began on 13 February. All Soviet artillery again opened up against the hill; some artillery pieces were set to fire over open sights 600 metres from the Finnish obstacle line. The commander of the 8th Rifle Division fed his reserves into the battle. They were the 1st Battalion, 310th Rifle Regiment, plus an anti-tank gun battalion and two tank companies. A company of cannon tanks of the 85th Detached Tank Battalion and two companies of flame-thrower tanks of the 204th Detached Tank Battalion attacked the hill. Tanks again quickly crossed the anti-tank obstacles, approached the hill and started the destruction of Finnish positions. Flame-thrower tanks poured burning liquid into the trenches, 'burning the enemy out of the trenches like insects'. Tanks stopped far enough from the trenches in order not to be destroyed by satchel charges or petrol bombs. Tanks drove up the hill several times, leaving the battlefield only to refuel and reload ammunition. Riflemen of the 151st Rifle Regiment started to gather behind the tanks at the jumping-off positions at 1600 hours. The commander of the regiment and the commander of the 3rd Battalion were also at hand, rallying their men for a decisive assault. A joint attack by tanks and riflemen began at 1725 hours. Despite desperate Finnish resistance, the hill was captured at 1800 hours. Soviet losses in the assault were around 500 killed and wounded. Two tanks were knocked out by Finnish artillery. Soviet riflemen were amazed to see that there were no formidable concrete bunkers on Church Hill.

The Soviet attacks continued from Church Hill to the north, towards Turulila Farm, but the Finns held their ground firmly until receiving the order to withdraw to the intermediary line.

Soviet tanks and riflemen deployed in four lines in the battles of Kyyrölä and Muolaa Church village. The first line consisted of cannon and flame-thrower tanks. They drove up to the Finnish defences, stopped 100–150 metres from the trenches and opened fire at possible positions of Finnish anti-tank guns. At the same time flame-thrower tanks drove close enough so that the Finnish trenches were within their effective range and poured burning liquid into them. The second line of tanks carried riflemen, who dismounted directly in front of the Finnish trenches. The tanks in the second line drove over the trench and attacked targets in the rear. The third line of tanks also carried riflemen and they only dismounted in the Finnish rear. The fourth line of tanks brought up heavy infantry weapons, ammunition and field guns. Step by step, these waves of armour and riflemen stormed Finnish positions.

The Finns often succeeded in breaking up this battle formation and tanks had to fight separately from riflemen. However, in February 1940 the tactics of the armoured units changed: taught by the bitter experiences of December 1939, the Soviet tanks crews did not drive into range of Finnish satchel charges and petrol bombs, but rather calmly executed the Finnish trenches at distances of 60–70 metres.

The 8th Rifle Division and its supporting armour continued their assaults on 14 and 15 February, but failed to achieve a decisive breakthrough. After the Finns received an order to fall back at 1600 hours on 15 February, they managed to disengage successfully. Withdrawal to the intermediary defence line at Lake Muolaa Isthmus–Sikniemi–Salmenkaita was only harassed by the Soviet Air Force. During the retreat the Finns burnt down all the buildings.

Rifle units suffered heavy casualties in the assault on the Finnish main defence line in the central Karelian Isthmus. The casualty rate rose to 60–70 per cent in some regiments. The 151st Rifle Regiment was reduced to a battalion after the battle for Church Hill. The 2nd Rifle Regiment of the 50th Rifle Division lost 1,175 men in three days of fighting and had to be withdrawn from the line. Just for comparison, the entire 90th Rifle Division lost 1,351 men in the same period storming a similar Finnish line. Finnish casualties were also mounting.

Eastern Isthmus: Taipale and Suvanto

The Thirteenth Army was delivering the main strike between Vuoksi and Muolaanjärvi with XXIII and XV Rifle Corps. These two large units had the 4th, 8th, 50th and 136th Rifle Divisions and the 17th Motor Rifle Division. The 62nd and 97th Divisions were on the way to the front. The 39th and elements of the 40th Light Tank Brigades supported the rifle units.

The offensive of the III Rifle Corps at Taipale was secondary. The III Rifle Corps fielded the 49th, 150th and 142nd Rifle Divisions. The reserve of the corps was the 101st Rifle Regiment of the 4th Rifle Division on the southern bank of River Taipale. The III Rifle Corps also had the 14th Detached Tank Battalion (with light T-37 and T-38 tanks), the 97th Ski Battalion and the 4th Detached Ski Squadron. In addition to the artillery of the divisions, the

III Rifle Corps had six artillery battalions. The main burden of battle rested with the rifle units – the tiny amphibious T-37 and T-38 tanks, armed with one machine-gun, were of little help in battle. Tank battalions of the 49th and 150th Rifle Divisions were also only equipped with T-37, T-38 and T-26 tanks model 1931, also armed only with machine-guns.

The Finnish 7th Infantry Division held a wide front from Haitermaa to Lake Ladoga. The division was under the command of Colonel Einar Vihma. The division's number, as well as the numbers of its regiments, changed in early January 1940:

Old unit number	New unit number
10th Infantry Division	7th Infantry Division
28th Infantry Regiment	19th Infantry Regiment
29th Infantry Regiment	20th Infantry Regiment
30th Infantry Regiment	21st Infantry Regiment
10th Artillery Regiment	7th Artillery Regiment
10th Light Unit	7th Light Unit

The division also had the 6th Detached Battalion under Major Oiva Saarelainen, which held four strongpoints in the Kirvesmäki sector.

The situation in the Lake Suvanto sector, from Kiviniemi to Kelja, was rather quiet: units of the 142nd Rifle Division and artillery on the southern bank confined their activity to scouting and systematic artillery fire at the Finnish positions. The situation at Taipale was much more difficult for the Finnish defenders.

The offensive of the III Rifle Corps was to start on 11 February, but preliminary attacks and reconnaissance-in-force began on 8 February. The 756th Rifle Regiment managed to capture strongpoint No. 1 in Kirvesmäki, on the very bank of Lake Suvanto. A rifle battalion of the 212th Rifle Regiment managed to break through between strongpoints No. 1 and No. 2 in Terenttilä. The Finns counter-attacked three times and recaptured all three strongpoints after the third try.

Both Soviet divisions launched offensives on 11 February 1940, after a three-hour artillery barrage. Just as on 15 December 1939, all six rifle regiments took part in the offensive.

Most of the Soviet assaults on the first day of the offensive were repelled. Only the 756th Rifle Regiment managed to make a small penetration of the Finnish lines, again capturing strongpoint No. 1 on the bank of Lake Suvanto, and also capturing bunker No. 1. The 1st Battalion, 21st Infantry Regiment, under Captain Valdemar Kilpeläinen, counter-attacked after an artillery barrage. The first Finnish counter-attack failed. The Finns made it into the trench on the second attempt and drove the Soviet battalions away from the trenches after a hand-to-hand fight. Soviet sources claim that the 756th Rifle Regiment withdrew only after the third Finnish assault. According to other archive evidence, the 756th Rifle Regiment failed to set sentries for the night and the Finns surprised the regiment in a night counter-attack. The regiment lost forty-seven men killed and 214 wounded during 11 February.

The entire main defence line was in Finnish hands. However, Finnish losses in the battle for the main defence line were also high and the 6th Detached Battalion had to be replaced by the 3rd Battalion, 21st Infantry Regiment, under Captain Berndt Polon.

During the four days from 11 to 14 February 1940 the Soviet regiments stormed the Finnish lines every day, and broke into the first-line Finnish trench on numerous occasions. However, there was no decisive breakthrough. The Finns managed to drive the Soviet riflemen away every night with a counter-attack. In the evening of 12 February the commander of the 150th Rifle Division, Kombrig Konkov, was removed from office and replaced by Kombrig Pastrevich, former commander of the 138th Rifle Division.

After four days of assaults the Soviet regiments were spent. The 101st Rifle Regiment, under Colonel Pimenov, had to be transferred from reserve to the front line. The regiment arrived at the front in Kirvesmäki to assist the 756th Regiment. The two regiments attacked towards bunker No. 1 on 15 February but failed to advance. Vladimir Grendal, commander of the Thirteenth Army, ordered the III Rifle Corps to take a pause in the offensive, bring its regiments in order and then resume the offensive on 18 February.

The 101st Regiment assaulted the area of bunker No. 1 on 16 February as well. Parts of the 9th Company managed to capture the trench at bunker No. 1 and a sapper platoon was immediately sent to the area, but before their demolition charge was ready, the Finns counter-attacked and drove the Soviets away.

The new Soviet offensive was planned for 18 February on a wide front. In addition to the offensive at Taipale, the 123rd and 19th Rifle Regiments were to cross Lake Suvanto at Volossula and strike at the right flank of the Finnish forces at Taipale. A mobile battle group, consisting of the Scout Battalion of the 49th Rifle Division, the 97th Ski Battalion, aero sleds and T-37 light tanks, was supposed to outflank the Finns via the ice of Lake Ladoga and capture the Järisevä Battery. The Finns stopped the mobile group with fire and after its commander was wounded, the unit was withdrawn from battle.

The Finns rotated their units at the front on 15 February. The decimated and exhausted battalions of the 21st and 19th Regiments were replaced by the

61st and 63rd Regiments of the 21st Division (a division formed in January 1940 from reserve units). Men of the 21st Division arrived at the front in white, shining, snow camouflage, closely shaved, clean and fresh. There were many young men among them. The Finnish front-line troops of the 7th Division – unshaven, dirty, and wearing torn snow camouflage – immediately dubbed the newcomers the 'porcelain boys' or the 'porcelain division'. Rotation of troops at the front line began on the evening of 15 February. The 1st and 2nd Battalions of the 61st Infantry Regiment made it to the front in the Kirvesmäki sector. Rotation of troops in the Terenttilä sector was not complete before the new Soviet offensive started.

The Soviet regiments resumed their offensive on 18 February. Soviet artillery delivered a strike at the Finnish positions from 1230–1300 hours. The artillery fire shifted into the depths of the Finnish defences and, as the rifle companies moved forward, Colonel Pimenov set all his regimental artillery to fire over open sights.

One and a half hours later, at 1504 hours, the surviving men of the 2nd Company, 101st Rifle Regiment, made it to the Finnish trenches. Ten minutes later the 7th and 9th Companies joined their comrades in the trench. A hand-to-hand fight followed. The men of the 101st Rifle Regiment took sixteen prisoners and consolidated their gains. The newly arrived 1st Battalion, 61st Infantry Regiment, under Captain Leminen, failed to hold its ground and retreated from all strongpoints in the Kirvesmäki area. The Finns counter-attacked at 1600 hours but failed. By 1600 hours the 101st Rifle Regiment captured bunker No. 2 and blew it up an hour later. According to some Soviet reports, a group of Finns locked themselves up in a dugout and refused to surrender, and the dugout was also blown up.

The 'porcelain boys' were driven some 500–700 metres from their positions, but managed to stop all further assaults. One of the reasons for this was the decision of Soviet commanders to consolidate their gains and stop in the first Finnish trench for a while. The 2nd Battalion of the 62nd Infantry Regiment, under Captain Larko, which had been in reserve at the Kirvesmäki sector, was ordered to man positions at the rear defence line. The battalion got lost on the way to the front and by mistake left the forest at Kirvesmäki, on the very front line. Lieutenant Rodionov, forward observer of the 328th Artillery Regiment, immediately spotted the battalion. He called in a strike of two artillery battalions and orchestrated their precise and deadly fire. One battalion of the 418th Howitzer Artillery Regiment joined the execution of the Finnish battalion. The Finns lost eighty-six men killed and fifty-seven wounded. Soviet artillerymen reported the complete destruction of the battalion, because: 'After the end of the barrage none of the Finns stood up. They were all dead.'

The Finns repelled the assault of the 123rd and 19th Rifle Regiments over the ice of Lake Suvanto. The Soviet battalions only managed to capture a shallow bridgehead at Volossula, and started cutting clearings in the Finnish barbed wire, but most of the men were pinned down on the ice. The Soviet units withdrew from the bridgehead on 19 February. The 123rd Regiment was transferred to the Taipale bridgehead after this. Other regiments on the Soviet bridgehead had suffered such heavy casualties that all attacks were cancelled.

The 49th Rifle Division penetrated the Finnish lines on 20 February 1940 and advanced 1 kilometre into the Finnish rear but was thrown back by a Finnish counter-attack.

The front line at Taipale stabilized after the dramatic events of 18–21 February. Exhausted Soviet troops tried to attack the Finnish positions again on 28 and 29 February, but all their attacks were repelled. In the first week of March the Thirteenth Army lost interest in Taipale, as the area of Vuosalmi looked more promising.

The Battle of Taipale became a symbol of the stoicism and heroism of the Finnish Army. The Commander-in-Chief, Marshal Mannerheim, personally thanked the commander of the 7th Infantry Division, Colonel Einar Vihma, and his Chief of Staff, Major Adolf Ernrooth, for their stoicism and bravery.

For the Red Army the Battle of Taipale was a slaughter similar to that experienced by the Allies on the Western Front in the First World War. As this was a secondary axis of attack, the only armoured units on the bridgehead were tank battalions of the 150th and 49th Rifle Divisions and the 14th Detached Tank Battalion. The 391st Detached Tank Battalion of the 49th Rifle Division had lost all its tanks by 24 February and was withdrawn from the front line. Repeated artillery barrages, stalled Soviet infantry assaults, high casualties for little or no gain – such was February 1940 at Taipale.

The Battle of Taipale was also the beginning of a long battle journey for the 150th Rifle Division in the Second World War. The division did not achieve anything outstanding in the Winter War of 1939/1940. On 1 May 1945 the banner of the 150th Rifle Division was lifted over the Reichstag in Berlin and became the Banner of Victory. Even today, it remains the most important symbol of victory in the Great Patriotic War for the Russian people.

The Mannerheim Line Abandoned

The Finns carried out a planned withdrawal to the intermediary defence line during three days from 15 to 18 February 1940. When the Finnish withdrawal was spotted, Meretskov ordered the formation of a mobile group that comprised armoured units with motorized riflemen. The group was tasked with a dashing raid into the Finnish rear and the capture of Vyborg by 18 February. However, this did not work out. Finnish resistance, the lack of open terrain and the Soviets' lack of experience in leading mobile battle groups all led to the failure of the Soviet plan.

The Finns held out at the intermediary defence line from 21 to 28 February 1940. After this they were forced to start a withdrawal to the last line on the isthmus – the rear defence line. Here we describe the battles for the two best-fortified sectors of the intermediary line: the Muolaa Isthmus and the River Salmenkaita.

Three Bunker Lines at Muolaa

The 4th Infantry Brigade defending the sector was exhausted by previous battles in Kyyrölä and Oinala. Casualties among officers were high and the Battle of Muolaa is rather poorly documented. Captain Tirronen of the 2nd Artillery Regiment recalled:

> The 1st Detached Battalion was in the first defence line together with the 2nd Light Unit and manned the bunkers at the front. Observation posts were distributed among our forward observation teams. The observers from the 1st Battery were in the old bunker at Lake Muolaanjärvi; the group of the 3rd Battery was in the old bunker north from the highway; while the group of the 2nd Battery was sent to Mutaranta.
>
> The 2nd Detached Battalion took up positions right of Muolaa, while the 1st Detached Battalion manned the lines at Mutaranta. The 4th Detached Battalion and the 2nd Light Unit were concentrated at Lake Alusjärvi.
>
> The enemy brought up artillery on 19 February, set their guns to fire over open sights and started chiselling our bunkers. Our artillery suppressed several guns. Enemy tanks tried to bypass our defences over the ice of Lake Muolaanjärvi in a new assault the next day. The first battery repelled the assault; one burning tank remained on the ice. The enemy guns destroyed one bunker and our artillery observers had to move into a trench.

The Finns had already retreated from Tassionlammet and the Väisänen sector of defence and held their ground at the northern tip of the lake. The Soviet command knew about the fortified line in front of the 136th and 62nd Rifle

Divisions and planned an outflanking manoeuvre across the lake against the exposed right flank of the Muolaa sector.

A combined battalion of the 24th Rifle Division and tanks of the 40th Light Tank Brigade were earmarked for this mission. The 3rd Company, 155th Tank Battalion, left for a scouting mission on the evening of 20 February 1940. The Finns knocked out two tanks on the ice. The remaining tanks retreated to the western bank. The BT tanks of the 236th Scout Battalion arrived at the western bank of the lake at 1915 hours. The combined battalion mounted the tanks and the task force drove off to the opposite bank across the frozen lake. The task force was hit with heavy artillery fire from the area of Hotakka. Chaos followed in the darkness, and the situation went out of control. The ice field was broken by artillery in some places. The tanks could not get ashore. The unit took heavy casualties and was forced to retreat to the western bank.

Five BT tanks were knocked out and burnt on the ice; one tank was knocked out, the other four sank. Company commander Senior Lieutenant Zubkov was among the men drowned with the tanks; platoon leader Junior Lieutenant Torgoboev was killed. The battalion's Commissar, Senior Political Worker Yevdokimov, was wounded. Six tankers were wounded, one was shell-shocked, and five were missing.

The 1st Company, 157th Tank Battalion, also took part in this assault. Two T-26 tanks broke into Hotakka and disappeared there; one tank was knocked out. The bypassing manoeuvre across the lake failed and a frontal assault along the eastern bank began.

The 136th Rifle Division attacked towards the isthmus between Lake Muolaanjärvi and Lake Muolaanlampi with all three regiments abreast: the 733rd Rifle Regiment on the left flank, the 387th Rifle Regiment in the middle and the 541st Rifle Regiment on the right flank. The 541st Rifle Regiment was reinforced with the 1st Company, 85th Tank Battalion. The 306th Rifle Regiment of the newly arrived 62nd Rifle Division attacked the ridges of Kangaspelto on the right flank of the 541st Rifle Regiment. The 306th was reinforced with the 317th Super Heavy Artillery Battalion and the 375th Howitzer Artillery Regiment, as well as a platoon of chemical tanks and two sapper platoons.

The Finnish 4th Brigade planned to use the first bunker line as a delaying position. The main battle was to start on the second and third bunker lines. The brigade's sector of defence was split into two subsectors: Muolaa and Mutaranta. The Mutaranta sector was held by the 1st Detached Battalion with 'the gun of Muolaa'. The Muolaa sector, at the highway and on the banks of Lake Muolaanjärvi, was held by the 2nd Detached Battalion with three anti-tank guns and a platoon section of the 4th Detached Battalion. The brigade held the 4th Detached Battalion and the 2nd Light Unit in reserve. The 1st Artillery Battalion, 2nd Artillery Regiment, supported the brigade.

The Military Council of the Thirteenth Army ordered the offensive to begin at 1330 hours, after an artillery barrage. The barrage lasted two hours and twenty minutes. After this, all four regiments began the assault. The 387th Regiment crossed the River Muolaanjoki and captured the bunker line in Muolaa village.

The 733rd Rifle Regiment spent the whole day storming Finnish bunkers No. 1 and No. 2 on the banks of Lake Muolaanjärvi. Finnish infantry withdrew, but a group of Finnish artillery observers locked themselves in the bunker and held it all day long. Soviet companies tried to advance several times, but were pinned down by Finnish artillery.

The commanders of the 136th Rifle Division knew about the Finnish bunker line. However, the latest information about the Finnish fortifications was from 1937, and the last bunker line remained unknown. Captain Shevenok, from the 137th Heavy Artillery Regiment, recalled the battle:

> I met the chief of artillery in the ditch, some 300–400 metres from the front. According to the map, there was a lake on the left and a small brook flowed into it. From the stories of my comrades, I knew that here, at the Muolaa–Ilves line, the Finnish main defence line began. Rifle units and tanks tried to break into the Finnish fortified area without preparation but failed.
>
> 'Right here,' the Chief of Artillery said, 'somewhere in this corner, between the lake and the river, there is a bunker. Well, it is your job to find its exact location. The Infantry tried to advance on the ice of the lake and the brook, but it all came to nothing. It looks like they have up to ten machine-guns in an area of 300 by 400 metres. We must knock that bunker out at any cost. The infantry said they saw its gun ports on the left as they attacked.'
>
> According to the Chief of Artillery's information, the gun ports were facing the flanks of our advancing troops and could only be seen from the flanks.
>
> After the first fifteen to twenty shots, the first round hit the bunker, ricocheted and exploded off the target, but nevertheless cut down one of the pine trees on top of it. Several minutes later the next round tore off the protective 'pillow' of stones from the roof of the bunker. Our infantry tried to advance on the right, but got pinned down. The bunker opened fire. And finally, we scored a direct hit on the armoured cupola of the bunker. I saw Finns fleeing the bunker.

Captain Tirronen of the Finnish 2nd Artillery Regiment recalled:

On 21 February, at 0700 hours, the enemy started a powerful artillery barrage, after which an assault on our positions followed at 0920 hours. Strong enemy forces stormed along the Kangaspelto–Hotakka road. Our own infantry were forced to retreat from their positions south of the road and consolidated their positions at Yrjonaho village. As a result of this retreat, forward observers of the 1st Battery, under Second Lieutenant Jorma Virtanen, with one machine-gun, were surrounded in the old bunker on the bank of Lake Muolaanjärvi. The enemy tried to capture the bunker, but Virtanen repelled the assault with shrapnel. [At] 1100 hours the 3rd Company of the 2nd Independent Battalion (Company Liikainen) received orders to counter-attack and rescue the surrounded artillerymen. The attempt was not successful, though. In the early afternoon the enemy's 203mm gun opened fire over open sights on Virtanen's bunker. After the bunker partially collapsed, Russian infantry again attempted to capture the bunker.

At that moment, Virtanen had already burnt all papers and maps. The garrison of the bunker managed to contain the enemy on the left flank, but on the bank of the lake the Russian infantry made it to the roof of the bunker and brought along machine-guns. The artillery observer did not give up: he gave the whole battery the coordinates of his own bunker! This desperate trick worked: the enemy suffered heavy casualties and withdrew from the bunker.

At 1320 hours the battery received the following radio message from Virtanen: 'If no relief comes, we will fight to the last man.'

Soon after this, the enemy managed to destroy the left casemate of the bunker with direct fire. The machine-gun was also destroyed. Soviet infantry then tried to enter the bunker through a hole in the destroyed wall, but Virtanen and his men repelled the attack with hand grenades. Then a short respite came. At 1700 hours the enemy again assaulted the bunker, but was repelled by artillery strikes of the battery, directed by the forward observers.

Our infantry also did not give up: at 1815 hours the company under Lieutenant Gummerus managed to throw the enemy back and rescue the artillery observers. Second Lieutenant Virtanen and his men left the bunker at 2015 hours, after ten hours under siege. On the roof of the bunker and all around it lay 200 enemy corpses. The fire of the battery was very precise!

Besides Virtanen, there were Sergeants Rossi and Partanen, as well as Senior Sergeants Ilvinen, Koiranen and Leppänen. They came through this ordeal more or less unharmed.

Colonel Tovantzev, commanding the Soviet 733rd Rifle Regiment, reported:

> In the evening the battalion attacked the Finnish lines, captured two wooden bunkers and one concrete bunker that was blocked by a group of men from the 9th Company, under Junior Lieutenant Beketov (now a Hero of the Soviet Union). This was a strong bunker, 35 × 12 metres in size, with three casemates, three gun ports and a metallic turret armed with a machine-gun. The enemy tried to attack several times but was thrown back.

During the night of 21 February, when Beketov's men surrounded the bunker, sappers brought up explosives under the command of the Chief of Staff of the 733rd Rifle Regiment, Major Smetanin, and blew the bunker up.

The 541st Rifle Regiment advanced, crossed the River Muolaanjoki and captured bunker No. 5. The staff of the regiment used the bunker as a CP. In the evening of 21 February the regiment's scout party and the 2nd Battalion continued their advance along the fields on the western bank of Lake Muolaanlampi. They entered Kirnumetsä Forest in the early hours of 22 February. Some Soviet riflemen reached Salmela Farm and occupied it. This move remained completely unnoticed by the Finns, and the 1st Detached Battalion left the edge of Kirnumetsä Forest unguarded, despite orders. Reports of the Soviet battalion in Kirnumetsä Forest came from Finnish sappers on their way back from the front. The sappers lived in Salmela Farm and had to kick out the Red Army men on the morning of 22 February. The Finns threw in a platoon to deal with the situation and then a company. Both attacks failed. Lieutenant Kostamo, from the 4th Detached Battalion, formed a battle group from all Finnish units in the forest and drove away the 2nd Battalion, 541st Rifle Regiment, back into the fields in the early afternoon.

The Soviet battalion had taken heavy casualties in the night battle. Most of the commanders were killed or wounded. The battalion made radio contact with the regiment HQ at 0900 and 1100 hours, requesting the support of tanks. A tank company from the 39th Light Tank Brigade, with seven cannon and five flame-thrower tanks, arrived at the CP at 0900 hours. The 3rd Battalion of the regiment moved out to the battlefield, escorted by tanks. Small T-38 tanks of the 18th Detached Tank Battalion carried ammunition and heavy weapons for the infantry. Both rifle battalions were in a very unfavourable position in the fields. They were under fire from Finnish machine-guns in the forest and, on the left flank, from bunkers No. 19 and No. 14. Nevertheless, the battalions stopped and started a firefight.

The small T-38 tanks of Lieutenant Vodopyan started the evacuation of the wounded from the battlefield. Tanks of the 39th Light Tank Brigade used all their ammunition and drove away to refuel and reload. Men of the 2nd Battalion, depressed by high casualties and loss of ground in the forest, panicked and retreated together with the tanks. This caused confusion and panic in the 3rd Battalion and some soldiers also withdrew. The remaining men withdrew to the regiment CP in the night, leaving some wounded on the battlefield. The regimental commander ordered the 1st Battalion to return to the battlefield and evacuate the wounded. This was done during the night of 22 February. During the night of 21 February the 2nd Battalion had lost up to 60 per cent of its original strength.

The 306th Rifle Regiment did not achieve any successes on 21 February. The Finns pinned down the riflemen after they had crossed the anti-tank ditch and barbed-wire fence. The Finnish positions were very well camouflaged. Artillerymen, tank crews, riflemen – no one could spot where the fire came from. All attempts to spot the Finnish positions failed. Weather conditions worsened in the evening and a blizzard started. The Soviets' only result of the day was closing in with the Finnish defence line and spotting two bunkers on the ridges. The commander of the 306th Rifle Regiment, Colonel Kryukov, decided to capture the ridges at night. Assault parties of the 306th Rifle Regiment started their attacks late in the evening and by the morning had cleared the ridges of Finnish infantry in close combat. The Finns lost all the bunkers on the ridges, two anti-tank guns and three machine-guns. Total losses of the 306th Rifle Regiment during 21 February were eighty-two men. Captain Tirronen again:

> At 1745 hours the assault by two companies supported by ten tanks forced company Mytty (2nd Company, 2nd Detached Battalion) to retreat from the sector to the north of the highway. An artillery observer of the 3rd Battery, Lieutenant Tamminen, was wounded in this incident.
>
> In the Mutaranta sector the artillery barrage started at 0900 hours. The attack followed at 1200 hours with the support of armour. Battle in the sector lasted all day long. We lost one bunker, which was destroyed, as well as one of our AT guns and two machine-guns. At 1715 hours the commanding officer in the sector received permission to retreat to the Kaivanto sector, to the main defence line. The lost positions were, from the beginning, merely meant to be covering

positions. The main defence line in the sector was in the process of construction – the 4th Detached Battalion was carrying out fortification works there.

It seemed that all four Soviet rifle regiments achieved spectacular success, breaking through the Finnish bunker line and only having to chase the retreating Finns. The Soviet commanders knew nothing about the third, and most powerful, bunker line. Bloody battles for the last bunker line lasted six days, from 22 February to the late evening of 27 February.

The main axis of advance was in the sector of the 387th Rifle Regiment in the middle of the Soviet attacking line. The other regiments continued to press on the left and right flanks.

The 306th Rifle Regiment continued its advance north towards Kaivanto Isthmus and bunker No. 15. The bunker protected a narrow isthmus between Lake Muolaanlampi and Lake Äyräpäänjärvi. The width of the isthmus was around 200 metres. The bunker was protected by an anti-tank ditch between the lakes and barbed-wire fencing.

The mission of the regiment was to capture the bunker, dominate Käenniemi Hill, and then steer to the right, attacking the Finnish defences in Ilves village from the rear. Assault parties of the regiment tried to approach the bunker on 22 February, but the Finns stopped them with concentrated machine-gun fire.

Then Colonel Kryukov ordered the 1st and 3rd Battalions of the regiment to outflank the bunker from the east, across Lake Äyräpäänjärvi, with an assault towards Koprala village. Battalions waded through deep snow on foot. Each squad formed a column. Men refused to form an attacking line despite all orders.

When the battalions were some 200 metres from the northern bank, the Finns opened intensive machine-gun and mortar fire. Men were pinned down and commanders failed to get them to assault again. Many were exhausted by the battle on the previous night. Some men lay down in haystacks next to the lake and fell asleep, despite the continuing Finnish fire. The battalions spent all day in the ice field, in dense formation on the lake, and later withdrew to Mutaranta. Total casualties of the battalions were thirteen killed and eighty-six wounded. Finnish newspapers reported the complete destruction of the battalions with 800 killed on the ice of Lake Äyräpäänjärvi.

After this, Colonel Kryukov ordered a new assault on the bunker with assault parties of the 3rd Battalion. The assault was to begin on 23 February. The 2nd Battalion of the regiment was to repeat the assault towards Koprala across Lake Äyräpäänjärvi. Kryukov strictly forbade his units to advance in dense formation and in large groups.

The 2nd Battalion was again stopped by Finnish fire on the lake; pinned down, its men refused to stand up. They pulled back in the evening. The assault party of the 3rd Battalion also failed to approach the bunker during the day. Then a company of tanks attacked the bunker. Seven cannon tanks of the 368th Detached Tank Battalion, two cannon tanks from the tank company of the 306th Rifle Regiment, and two flame-thrower tanks drove up to the anti-tank ditch and opened intense fire at the armoured turret. The Finnish infantry and machine-gun crews abandoned the bunker. However, a group of artillery observers of the 1st Battery, 2nd Artillery Regiment, stayed in the bunker. Tanks were standing side by side on the narrow isthmus and the Finns hit the group with mortar fire. This was the only thing they could do, as they had no anti-tank guns in the area. The result of the Finnish barrage was a destroyed track on one tank and a damaged driving wheel on a second. Senior Lieutenant Kirzhner, who was in command of all the tanks, ordered them to disperse and keep the bunker under constant fire. Then he ordered his tanks to bypass the anti-tank ditch from the left, across the frozen Lake Muolaanlampi. The leader of the flame-thrower tank platoon, Lieutenant Yegorov, opened fire at the bunker, making ten long bursts from the flame-thrower. In the meantime, the cannon tank of Lieutenant Polevich, the tank of the company commander, Senior Lieutenant Kirzhner, and the flame-thrower tank of Lieutenant Rodnev bypassed the ditch and approached the bunker. They opened fire at the gun ports and doors of the bunker and later attacked the wooden bunkers north of bunker No. 15. In the meantime, a party of sappers under the command of the division's Chief of Engineers, Major Sagoyan, made it to the bunker's roof and blew the bunker up. Riflemen to the south of the ditch immediately mounted the remaining tanks and they all drove off to the bunker.

The first explosion destroyed the armoured cupola of the bunker. Tanks and riflemen surrounded the bunker and provided a safe zone for the sappers. Sappers of the 93rd Sapper Battalion brought a lot of explosives to the bunker and blew it up at midnight. The sapper platoon leader, Lieutenant Pavel Fedorchuk, and the sergeant major of the sapper company, Boris Kuznetsov, distinguished themselves during the operation. They stood waist-deep in the water of the anti-tank ditch, passing boxes of explosives to the sappers in the bunker. Later, they carried all men of their platoon across the water-filled ditch. Both brave sappers were awarded the Gold Star of the Hero of the Soviet Union.

Some Finnish sources claim that the Red Army on the isthmus spent the whole of 23 February 1940 drinking and celebrating the 22nd anniversary of the Red Army. Drunken songs and shouts were allegedly heard even at the Finnish positions. This was definitely not the case at Muolaa, where the Soviet rifle companies stubbornly pressed on, grinding through the even more stubborn Finnish resistance.

The 733rd Rifle Regiment, assaulting along the eastern bank of Lake Muolaanjärvi, was stopped by fire from bunkers 10 and 16 and could not move forward. The 1st and 2nd Battalions of the 541st Rifle Regiment, supported by flame-thrower and cannon tanks, assaulted again towards Kirnumetsä but were hit by flanking fire from bunkers in Ilves village. As a result the battalions had to retreat to the bushes and groves on the western bank of Lake Muolaanlampi and form a defensive perimeter there. The regiment could only make it forward on 27 February 1940.

The 3rd Battalion of the 387th Rifle Regiment managed to surround two bunkers at Alhola Farm (bunkers No. 14 and No. 19) by the evening of 23 February, but the Finnish defenders refused to surrender. The riflemen only had 100 kilograms of explosives with them. When the charge was detonated, the riflemen saw to their dismay that it did not even leave a scratch on the surface of the bunker. The Finns inside still refused to surrender. A sapper platoon arrived at the bunkers around 2300 hours in complete darkness, bringing along about 500 kilograms of explosives. The sapper platoon leader agreed with the rifle company commanders that they would draw companies back only after the order: 'ignition'. However, the company commanders ignored the agreement and fell back too early. The Finns spotted this and again manned the trenches around the bunkers. The sappers were not ready to blow the bunkers and also had to fall back. Infuriated, Tovantzev ordered the recapture of the bunkers at any cost, and the 3rd Battalion assaulted the bunkers again. This time the Finns were forewarned and met the battalion with a hail of fire. After taking heavy casualties, the 3rd Battalion was drawn back. To make things worse, the forward battalions of Tovantzev's regiment were hit by friendly fire from the 136th Rifle Division's artillery twice: on 23 and 24 February.

Tovantzev fed the 2nd Battalion into the battle with the same mission. At a critical moment of the battle, when the commander of the 5th Company was killed, the Political Worker of the company, V. F. Ovchinnikov, personally led the assault and made it to one of the bunkers. The battle raged all night and into the next day. By 1400 hours on 24 February one of the bunkers was finally captured by the 2nd Battalion. Captain Tirronen recalled:

> In the morning of 24 February the enemy threw more armour into the battle. Among other things, flame-thrower tanks destroyed the entire garrison of a bunker by pouring burning liquid through its gun ports. Our men held these bunkers in very low regard.

Artillery observer of the 1st Battery, Lieutenant Heikki Tulikuora, described them like this:

> Black concrete bunkers stood in sparse forest without any communication cables or trenches. They were an intolerable place to be in combat, one had to be ready to leave immediately. Despite their high cost, they were hopeless rat holes and I am wondering why the enemy did not fry them all. If these bunkers were equipped with anti-tank weapons, one could defend himself against tanks. In reality, all we could do was sit inside the bunker and wait for a tank to drive up and do what he pleased.

The machine-gun platoon of the 4th Detached Battalion and a half-platoon of the 2nd Detached Battalion met their destiny in bunker No. 14. The assault party of the 2nd Battalion, 387th Rifle Regiment, with tanks of the 85th Tank Battalion, a flame-thrower tank and sappers, destroyed the bunker with all men inside. Junior Commander Bulatov was a participant in the operation:

> We took a couple of hundred kilos of explosives and walked off. We bypassed the bunker and approached it from the rear. All of a sudden, we saw our tank approaching the gun ports. As soon as it approached, the Finns threw several bottles with some liquid from the gunport. One of the bottles hit the rear of the tank and it caught fire. We tried to give the driver signs for him to drive away. In the meantime, our men Chupin, Zakharov, Sukharev and Sazonov, made it to the burning tank under fire and started throwing snow at it, trying to put out flames. After some time they succeeded.
>
> One more tank drove up in the meantime. This was our platoon leader, Junior Lieutenant Gordyushov, who brought us more explosives.
>
> I reported to the platoon leader that it would be difficult to blow up the bunker from the side. It was wiser to blow it up from the top – first destroy the armoured tower, then throw a box of explosives with a short ignition cable in order to deafen the defenders. This was what we decided to do. We set 75 kilograms of explosives at the tower and lit the fuse. An explosion sounded. It was strong, but the tower only cracked.
>
> Then we decided to blow the bunker up in a different way. We prepared the satchel charges. One man sat behind the turret of a flame-thrower tank, so that he could give signs to the tank crew,

when to burn the gun ports and when to cease fire. So our man hid behind the tank's turret and ordered: 'Fire!'

The tank fired. The Finns were afraid to be burnt alive and hid in the depths of the bunker. Then I decided to get out of the tank and listen to what was going on inside the bunker. I heard a conversation. All right then! I climbed the bunker and shouted: 'Surrender, you bastards!'

But the gang inside was silent. Then I threw a hand grenade into the crack in the turret. It blew up and the bunker caught fire. Those were the petrol bombs that the Finns used to burn our tanks. I heard screaming and strange noises inside.

The tank crew was given the signal to fire at the gun ports and then immediately cease fire. They did exactly so. In a second, we were at the gun ports and stuffing them with two boxes of explosives each. Then we lit the fuses. When the explosion took place, the gun ports were torn wide open. The flame-thrower tank started to pour burning liquid into these holes without stopping. Men stood at the door with machine-guns and hand grenades ready. The Finns had nowhere to run.

After some time we ceased fire from the tank and threw four boxes of explosives into the bunker. We advised the tank men to drive away. A powerful explosion shook the bunker. The turret was blown off, as well as the door. There was a dead silence in the bunker. Then we could report to the commanders that the bunker was neutralized.

There were fifteen dead Finns in the bunker.

Lieutenant Kauko Tiili, of the 2nd Artillery Regiment, described the last moments of the bunker and its garrison from the Finnish perspective:

A man from a garrison once arrived at our CP and told us about his concerns regarding the bunker's defence. The bunker was not completed and the steel shutters on the gunports were missing. If the enemy employed flame-thrower tanks in Kyyrölä, what would stop him from employing them here? The garrison prepared for the flame-thrower attack by blocking the gunports with stones and wet pillows. They could be kept wet with water from the well inside the bunker.

All of a sudden, the sky turned red in the direction of the bunker and a huge pillar of smoke shot into the sky. Helpless hatred filled our hearts. We could do nothing to help the men inside the bunker.

Then a blackened, wet, and petrol-smelling man ran into our bunker: 'I am the man who has just made it from there.'

From the voice of the man we could hear that he had just been through a great shock. He told us how a flame-thrower tank drove up to the bunker and poured burning oil inside. The stones and pillows did not help at all, the burning oil poured freely into the bunker like soup. The last thing he remembered was that he stood at the two gunports at the door and burning liquid was pouring in from both of them. He banged himself on his head with hands and managed to put out the flames in his hair. When the fire suddenly stopped, he thought that the tank was turning away. He saw from the gunport that the tank was driving towards the other side of the bunker, so he rushed to the door! It took him some time to open the door and when he rushed out, he saw that the tank was still there. The tank opened fire at him from a machine-gun. However, he had already managed to slip away from the bunker under the protection of the forest: 'All others are there, all eleven,' he said, shaking his head from shock. Someone noticed that the man was bleeding. It turned out that the tank indeed hit him in his hip, but he did not notice it, as he could still move. An officer went later to have a look at the fateful bunker: 'We should set a sentry at the door, so that no one can see what is inside,' he said quietly . . .

After this horrible incident the Finns would leave the bunkers immediately they spotted the approach of Soviet tanks. The tank platoon of Senior Lieutenant Kurganov, with two cannon tanks and one flame-thrower tank, attacked bunker No. 13 alone without infantry support. The Finns left the bunker as soon as they saw the approaching tanks. The tanks opened rapid fire at the gun ports and the door of the bunker. Then the tank men left their tanks and threw hand grenades into the bunker through the door and gun ports. When Finnish infantry tried to counter-attack, they manned their tanks again and repelled the Finnish attack with machine-gun fire. The heads of the Soviet armour-piercing rounds are still stuck in the wall of the bunker.

The battle at the third line of the Finnish bunkers raged day and night. Every day, the 387th Rifle Regiment was assaulting the Finnish positions. The Soviet flame-thrower tanks forced the Finnish infantry out of their trenches every day, driving them into the woods. During each night the Finns counter-attacked and restored their lines. Soviet tanks operated freely on the battlefield, as the Finns only had one anti-tank gun under Jaeger Sergeant Vasama from the 2nd Jaeger Battalion left to protect the entire sector.

The 306th Rifle Regiment at Kaivanto isthmus advanced using assault parties, and started the attack on the dominant Käenniemi Hill on 24 February. The Finns held out bitterly for three days, and the 306th Rifle Regiment captured the hill on the evening of 26 February. Soviet tanks could not support the assault parties due to the steep slopes and huge boulders. In two days of fighting for the hill the 306th Rifle Regiment lost nine men killed and eighty-two wounded, which demonstrated the efficiency of small assault parties.

After capturing Käenniemi, the regiment turned west towards Salmela Farm, thus threatening the Finnish bunker line in Ilves village from the rear. The Finns blew up the bridge at Salmela during the retreat, but two parts of the bridge were still intact. Battalions of the 306th Regiment crossed the bridge and made contact with the 541st Rifle Regiment.

Both sides had suffered heavy casualties and were exhausted by several days of fighting. The companies of the 2nd and 3rd Battalions, 387th Rifle Regiment, were down to 30 per cent of their original strength. The thaw that came on 22 February and the frosts on 23 February made combat even more demanding for the soaking, freezing soldiers of both sides.

The battalions of the 387th Rifle Regiment had lost their battle value by the morning of 27 February, most of their commanders being out of action. Only the 4th Company, under Lieutenant Golubev, assaulted the Finnish positions on the morning of 27 February. The remains of the 7th and 9th Companies were also supposed to join the assault, but fled the battlefield in panic. There were no commanders left to lead the men and keep them under control. It took the surviving lieutenants and sergeants of the companies a long time to gather their men and bring them to order. As a result, the 4th Company was almost surrounded by Finns and suffered heavy losses. Twenty men were killed and wounded out of fifty-seven that started the assault. The 5th and 6th Companies both had fewer than thirty men left and could not assist the 4th Company.

The 203mm guns of the 317th Super-heavy Artillery Battalion were set to fire over open sights in the afternoon of 27 February. They opened fire at the bunkers and destroyed or seriously damaged them. The fire mission against the bunkers was completed without losses, due to the skilful decisions of the Soviet artillery commanders. They agreed with rifle units and armour about support. Lieutenant Tarasov, awarded the Gold Star of the Hero of the Soviet Union, asked the tank crews to set two tanks on each side of his cannon. The tanks acted as a shield and protected the crew from flanking fire. Riflemen were in positions next to the cannon, in order to protect it from possible attack by Finnish infantry. Eino Hermunen of the anti-tank platoon of the Finnish 2nd Jaeger Battalion reported:

We anti-tank crews had a hard time – we had to repel tank attacks on the highway at Lake Muolaanjärvi and also at Äyräpäänjärvi. We did score hits on the tanks, but the no-man's-land was so narrow that the enemy evacuated the knocked-out tanks during the night, and sometimes in daylight. So we did knock tanks out but did not destroy them.

Air and artillery strikes were so strong that we had to hide the gun at the bunker wall. If we lost the gun, everyone would have been in trouble. I did not see any other anti-tank crews in our sector. We had to rush from one place to another all the time. Bunkers were no longer a safe place to be, as heavy artillery was firing at them all the time. The enemy air force dropped bombs on the bunkers and ploughed the whole battlefield with large-calibre bombs. The armoured turret on bunker No. 10 took a direct hit and cracked. The sentry in the turret lost consciousness. I learnt later that the armoured turret was finally shot off the bunker after numerous hits and the bunker itself was tilted like a ship in a sea storm.

We almost lost our minds from lack of sleep and exhaustion. We knew that we could not last long; a physical collapse was approaching us with lightning speed. But we fought on, gritting our teeth. A week passed like this, or it could be two weeks. We lost all count of time, we did not know which day of the week it was, which date, if it was still February or already March. We only knew one thing: day came after night and we were still living creatures on this earth. The earth was shaking and groaning, the war went on, and the closer its end was, the more merciless it was becoming.

In the evening of 27 February 1940 the Finns finally received the order to withdraw from the Muolaa sector. The withdrawal began immediately.

Late in the night on 27 February the Soviet assault parties approached the bunkers unopposed and blew them up. The 387th Rifle Regiment had suffered such heavy casualties that there were no riflemen left for assault parties. Riflemen of Junior Lieutenant Sinevykh's 6th Company were too few and had to be reinforced by volunteer artillerymen from the regimental batteries. The group only totalled sixty men. After blowing the bunkers up, the group realized that the Finns had withdrawn and started a careful advance.

The staff of the XXIII Rifle Corps saw that the Finns were about to start a withdrawal from their positions at Muolaa and prepared the 39th Light Tank Brigade for a dashing raid into the Finnish rear. The raid failed due to mines on the roads, forest barricades, deep snow and a skilful Finnish delaying action. The 232nd Scout Battalion with rifle units ran into a Finnish ambush at Heikurila. Soviet riflemen were pinned down and started a firefight with the Finns. The company commander of the 232nd Scout Battalion, Senior Lieutenant Vasily Moiseev, climbed out of his tank and personally led the sapper parties to clear mines. He was killed by a Finnish bullet when lifting Finnish mines. He was posthumously decorated with the Order of Lenin. He had a wife and four small children left at home in Rybinsk. Here is the story as told by his grandson, a Moscow-based engineer, Igor Moiseev:

> Grandmother could not bear grandfather's death and died in 1945. They loved each other very much. All four small children were sent to different orphanages. The oldest sister, Maya, later took all her younger brothers and sisters into her orphanage. My father, Leonid, followed the footsteps of his father and became a military pilot. I followed my father's example, and my son Ruslan also chose a military career. I hope that my grandson Dmitry will also go into a military academy. That's the story.

By noon on 29 February 1940 the Finnish delaying party was driven away and Soviet armour, aided by riflemen, captured Heikurila. The Soviet units were slowly approaching the last Finnish line of defence. The war ended two weeks later. At the end of the campaign the 387th Rifle Regiment had only 10–30 per cent of its original strength.

The River Salmenkaita

According to the plan of withdrawal to the intermediary defence line, the 6th Infantry Regiment withdrew from the main defence line on the evening of 16 February. By the morning of 17 February all Finnish units had withdrawn to the northern bank of the River Salmenkaita and Finnish sappers blew the bridges at 0900 hours.

The 6th Infantry Regiment took up defensive positions with all three battalions: the 1st Battalion occupied positions on the Kuusa–Äyräpää road, the 3rd Battalion manned the defences in Variksenkylä village, and the 2nd Battalion held the Heinjoki–Rautu railway bridge. The breadth of the defence sector was around 4 kilometres. In this area the Finns had around thirty-five concrete bunkers.

Wide fields are located on the southern and northern banks of the River Salmenkaita. The old Finnish bunkers were built right on the northern bank; the new bunkers for flanking fire were some 200–300 metres from the river. The Soviet commanders described the battlefield like this: 'Here the enemy had a field that was pre-sighted and we had to attack across this field.' During the assault on the Finnish defences, the men of the 17th Motor Rifles first had to cross the open fields on the southern bank of the river, cross the frozen river, and then assault the bunker line. The advantage of the Soviet position on the southern bank of the river was a range of tall hills covered with forest south of the fields. Artillery observers had a perfect view across the river from the hills and heavy artillery could be placed on the hills to fire over open sights.

The 6th Infantry Regiment spent 17, 18 and 19 February scouting the terrain, preparing bunkers for combat and clearing sectors of fire. According to a common rule, infantry companies manned the trenches while machine-gun companies set up their heavy Maxim machine-guns inside the bunkers. A Soviet scout party tried to approach bunker No. 20 under the protection of armoured shields, but was destroyed in close combat against Finnish troops. One more Soviet scout party tried to make it across the river on the night of 19 February, but ran into a minefield. Soviet artillery opened harassing fire against the Finnish defence sector on the morning of 20 February. The artillery fire intensified at 1000 hours and the Finns manned the trenches, preparing for a Soviet assault. The bulk of the 17th Motor Rifle and 50th Rifle Divisions arrived at the southern bank of the river on that day. Soviet units manned positions on the hills in the forest 1 kilometre south of the river. The three regiments of the 17th Motor Rifle Division attacked abreast, with the 55th Motor Rifle Regiment on the left, the 271st Motor Rifle Regiment in the centre, and the 278th Motor Rifle Regiment on the right flank. The 359th and 2nd Rifle Regiments of the 50th Rifle Division attacked on the right flank, from bunkers No. 3 and No. 4 to the southern bank of the River Vuoksi.

Soviet units carried out a company-sized reconnaissance-in-force at 1300 hours in the sector of the 2nd Battalion. The Soviet company managed to get a foothold on the northern bank of the river but was pushed back across the river in the evening. Regimental artillery of the 271st Motor Rifle Regiment fired at the Finnish obstacle lines over open sights all day. In the evening of the same day the Soviets delivered propaganda speeches against the 2nd Finnish Battalion.

Masses of Soviet aircraft emerged in the afternoon, bombing the entire sector of the 6th Infantry Regiment, while fighters strafed the Finnish positions, firing their machine-guns. However, the Soviet artillery observation planes were a bigger headache for the Finns. These slow biplanes directed artillery fire at any target they spotted. They quietly circled above the Finnish defences at a speed of 40–50 kilometres per hour. Their presence kept the Finnish artillery silent, as Finnish artillery officers feared their guns would be spotted and hit. In the evening the axis of the main strike became obvious for the Finns, due to the intensity of Soviet artillery fire – rounds rained down on the 3rd Battalion in Variksenkylä village. The Finns spotted more heavy artillery on the Soviet side. Two old bunkers were damaged by fire.

The Soviet artillerymen placed several guns on the southern bank and opened fire over open sights at the bunkers. The Finnish artillery could do little to suppress them. The presence of spotter planes, powerful artillery strikes, problems with phone lines – all these factors kept the Finnish artillery silent.

Soviet artillery opened intensive fire at all Finnish defences in the sector at 0830 hours on 21 February. However, the location of most bunkers was yet unknown to the artillery crews and their fire covered a vast area. The Soviet motor rifle units launched their assaults at 1230 hours. The 1st and 2nd Motor Rifle Battalions made it across the river, took cover behind the armoured shields and started a firefight with the Finnish 9th Company. One hour later Soviet companies captured Koivikkoniemi (Birch Cape) at the highway and forced one Finnish platoon to retreat. More units crossed the narrow frozen river at 1615 hours and the firefight continued.

Companies of the 359th Rifle Regiment surrounded the old bunkers No. 3 and No. 4 on Birch Cape. The Finnish garrisons refused to surrender, despite offers to do so and fire at the doors of the bunkers from machine-guns. In the evening both bunkers were blown up with all the men inside. Ten men were buried alive. Only two men from the bunkers remained alive: Corporal Peltola, who was sent for help before the Soviet assault, and Private Parkkonen, who was on sentry duty outside the bunker. When the Soviet assault began, Parkkonen tried to go inside the bunker but the door was locked and his comrades would not let him in. Then Parkkonen hid in the snow and was there until twilight, when the bunkers were blown up. He then struggled to bunker No. 36 and was sent to a dressing station as his feet were frostbitten.

The 1st Battalion, 278th Motor Rifle Regiment, formed an attacking line in the field in front of bunkers No. 15 and No. 36. The Finns waited for the attacking line to enter the sector of fire and opened devastating flanking fire at the Soviets at the barbed-wire fence. The machine-guns of bunker No. 15 fired all day without respite. Companies were pinned down at the barbed-wire fence. Some men made it to Luhtasaari Grove, east of the highway bridge. All other Soviet units were stopped by Finnish fire.

A blizzard started in the afternoon. Kombrig Batsanov, commander of the 17th Motor Rifle Division, decided to use the bad weather as a screen for the next assault. All three regiments attacked again in the evening of 21 February. The 3rd Company and some men from the 1st Company of the 278th Motor Rifle Regiment under Political Worker Senechkin again attacked across the field towards bunkers No. 15 and No. 36. They managed to surround bunker No. 15 in the evening. However, this was the end of Soviet success: the other companies could not break through to the bunker due to heavy fire. The 1st Company took heavy casualties at the bunker during the night and was pushed back to the river. Total losses of the 1st Battalion (278th Rifle Regiment) on 21 February were around 200 men killed or wounded.

The 1st Battalion of the sister 271st Motor Rifle Regiment also launched an attack in the evening, but lost the battalion's commissar when cutting passages in the Finnish barbed-wire fence. Senior Political Worker Zotov was killed. The commander of the 1st Battalion, Senior Lieutenant Kazanski, was wounded several hours later. The 55th Motor Rifle Regiment made it across the river and captured the old bunker No. 9 but was thrown back to the southern bank by a Finnish counter-attack.

The commander of the 6th Infantry Regiment ordered the 1st and 2nd Battalions to send a platoon each to the place of the Soviet breakthrough, as well as requesting a tactical reserve from the division in order to carry out a counter-attack. The divisional commander ordered the 26th Infantry Regiment to send a reinforced company under Lieutenant Hakalahti. The company had three infantry platoons, a machine-gun platoon and an anti-tank squad. The 5th Infantry Regiment sent an entire battalion to the Salmenkaita sector. The 1st Battalion, 5th Infantry Regiment, launched its counter-attack at 0500 hours on the morning of 22 February and managed to push the Soviet units toward the river by 0930 hours. However, the Finns failed to drive the Soviet units into the river – the destroyed bunkers No. 3 and No. 4 remained in Soviet hands. The Finnish battalion commander, Hanström, decided that his forces were too weak to hold this line and did not continue the assault. The Finns captured eight prisoners and twelve machine-guns in the assault.

The Soviet offensive continued on 22 February. Artillery increased the volume of fire, concentrating on the spotted Finnish bunkers. Direct fire against bunker No. 15 was especially strong. The bunker took three direct hits in the wall and the fourth direct hit knocked the armoured turret off the bunker. Soviet artillerymen also fired at bunkers No. 13 and No. 37, mostly over open sights.

Major Krylov, commander of the 278th Motor Rifle Regiment, sent the 2nd Battalion to assault the bunker line. The battalion mounted tanks and made it to the river, but had to dismount and attack on foot later. Tanks could not cross the river on that day. Riflemen managed to occupy Finnish communication trenches 150 metres from bunker No. 15 and recapture Birch Cape. As a result, Second Lieutenant Eloranta decided to withdraw his 8th Company to bunker No. 36, leaving the machine-gun crews inside bunker No. 15 alone. Men of the 359th Rifle Regiment continued their assaults from Luhtasaari Grove and managed to surround bunker No. 16 at 1415 hours. However, they could not hold and destroy the bunker.

The commander of the 6th Infantry Regiment ordered Hakalahti's company to march off immediately to the CP of the 3rd Battalion. He also requested the commander of the 5th Detached Battalion to send one more company urgently to the regiment's CP. The 278th Motor Rifle Regiment continued its assaults towards bunker No. 15 and the Finns had to dispatch all available reserves to the sector of the 3rd Battalion. In the evening one more battalion arrived at the regimental CP, forming the reserve of the regiment (Captain Leppälax).

The 55th Motor Rifle Regiment assaulted with one company on the left flank of the division, but the company was stopped by strong machine-gun fire and withdrew after taking losses.

A thaw came during the day of 22 February; it was sleeting and all the men were wet to their bones. The wind changed on the morning of 23 February, bringing colder air, and temperatures dropped to minus 10 degrees Celsius. All uniforms – overcoats, felt boots, mittens – froze solid. Anatoly Derevenets, signals operator of the 3rd Battalion, 278th Motor Rifle Regiment, described how it felt:

> Our overcoats were soaking wet from slush. Temperatures descended sharply in the first hours of the next day, and the overcoats were frozen solid in the posture that the men slept in. Most of the men were sitting at night, and their overcoats became stiff as a board. We went to the rear in this pitiful condition.

Despite the difficult weather, the 17th Motor Rifle Division continued its assault on 23 February. The Finns repelled the attacks of the 55th and 271st Motor Rifle Regiments on the left flank, and those of the 359th Rifle Regiment on the right flank. The 278th Motor Rifle Regiment was engaged in a heavy battle at bunker No. 15 in the centre of the Finnish defences. Three tanks attacked the bunker first, but the Finns knocked out two of them. In the evening a Soviet assault party reached the bunker and blew it up with a satchel charge. The Finns were forced to retreat.

The Finns counter-attacked in the evening of 23 February and recaptured Luhtasaari Grove and bunker No. 15. They took two light machine-guns and one heavy machine-gun as war booty.

Soviet artillery continued firing over open sights on the morning of 24 February, knocking down the armoured turret from bunker No. 13. The 278th Motor Rifle Regiment attacked again at 1230 hours, supported by six tanks. Two tanks got stuck in the anti-tank rock fence. The Finns were pushed away from the ruined bunker No. 15 and Rantala Farm at 1850 hours. The Finns had to replace the 8th Company, reinforce the 9th Company with one platoon, and launch yet another counter-attack at night. At 2100 hours the

Finns drove the Soviets out of the ruins of Rantala Farm, and from the grove to the south-east at 0400 hours.

Both sides were greatly exhausted by four days and nights of combat. The 278th Motor Rifle Regiment took heavy casualties. Finnish losses were lower, but nevertheless, the 6th Infantry Regiment observed:

> The men are extremely exhausted. During the night they must repair damaged trenches and during the day they have to be ready for battle. They can only fit in the bunkers and dugouts if they all stand.

The systematic work of the Soviet artillerymen started to yield results and most of the bunkers in the area had taken hits and suffered damage.

The 278th Motor Rifle Regiment was withdrawn from the front line on 25 February. The casualty rate in the regiment grew to well over 50 per cent. The war diary of the regiment describes the condition of troops like this:

> The 1st and 2nd Battalions of the regiment were withdrawn from the front line on 25 February. Only reinforced outposts were left at the front. Kombrig Batsanov, commander of our division, arrived to inspect our regiment on that day. The regiment was lined up and all men were counted.
>
> The 1st Battalion had left:
>
>> 1st Machine-gun Company 19 men
>> 2nd Motor Rifle Company 21 men
>> 3rd Motor Rifle Company 56 men
>> 4th Motor Rifle Company 32 men
>> Anti-tank Platoon 15 men
>> Mortar Platoon 15 men
>
> The commander of the battalion is Captain Vysotski; Commissar of the battalion, Comrade Senechkin, is seriously ill. He was sent to a hospital in the rear.
>
> The 2nd Battalion had just sixty men left, under command of Lieutenant Zakharov.
>
> The 3rd Battalion was the biggest, with:
>
>> Signals Platoon 27 men
>> Scout Platoon 15 men
>> 7th Motor Rifle Company 78 men
>> 8th Motor Rifle Company 62 men

9th Motor Rifle Company 75 men
Anti-tank Platoon 16 men
Mortar Platoon 25 men

The commander of the battalion is Lieutenant Pryanikov; the Commissar of the battalion is Comrade Kostrov, who was a Commissar of the Signals Company before.

Division Commander Kombrig Batsanov ordered that the men be given some shelter, that campfires be lit, that the men be kept in order, warm and dry.

Anatoly Derevenets described the moment like this:

When we came to the rear, we were planning to light bonfires to defrost our overcoats, but we were ordered to gather at the HQ tent. We were quite a pitiful sight when our divisional commander arrived at the regimental HQ on his armoured car [but] he was not shocked at all. Well-shaved, with shining red face, slightly chubby in a white sheepskin coat with a Finnish submachine-gun on his shoulder, the divisional commander rallied us to finish the enemy off and informed us that we were facing the Mannerheim Line. There was a pile of bodies next to the regimental HQ tent.

We first thought that they were all dead. But those were survivors of the previous assaults on the bunker, men of the 271st Motor Rifle Regiment. They had come back from the front line at night and were sleeping in the snow.

The commander of the 278th Motor Rifle Regiment, Major Krylov, reflected on the action of his battalions at Salmenkaita:

In some cases we repeated the same mistakes that we had made at the River Punnus-joki. Attacking formations were too dense, men walked openly. Commanders were too brave and walked openly in front of the attacking line, making themselves clearly visible to the enemy. This gave the enemy the chance to destroy our commanders and political workers at will. Units only used frontal assaults and gathered in large groups. Armoured shields were not used, although our advance was slow.

Anatoly Derevenets echoed his words:

We only had one battalion commander left in the regiment – commander of the 1st Battalion, Captain Vysotski. Finnish snipers hunt down our commanders with great stubbornness and success. Vysotski realized this. He walked around in the greatcoat of a private, without any commander's gear, armed with a rifle. I guess this was the reason he was still alive out of all our commanders. He is a good leader and losses in his battalion are not as high as in the others. However, it looks like he drinks all the time – his face is always swollen from vodka.

A combined group of the 271st and 278th Motor Rifle Regiments attacked the Finnish defences again on 25 February after an artillery barrage. The remains of the 2nd and 3rd Battalions of the 278th Motor Rifle Regiment attacked in the first line again. The 2nd and 3rd Battalions of the 271st Motor Rifle Regiment followed them. The Finns were forced to abandon the ruined bunker No. 15 and Rantala Farm again. The remains of the garrison from bunker No. 15 went into bunker No. 36. The Finnish counter-attack in the evening failed.

The Soviet Air Force delivered several strikes at the Finnish rear. One bomb hit the dressing station of the 6th Infantry Regiment, killing three doctors. Soviet fighters were strafing the roads in the rear all day long.

Using the captured bunker No. 15 as a jumping-off position for further assaults, the Soviet men stormed bunkers Nos 13, 14, 34 and 36. The remains of the 7th Company, 278th Motor Rifle Regiment, approached bunker No. 36 under a creeping barrage, climbed to its roof and hoisted the red banner on it. Political Worker Kostrov led the assault. The Finns left their bunker and a hand-to-hand fight started on the roof. Pryanikov's battalion did not assist Kostrov's assault party and the Finns managed to kill all the brave Soviet men at the bunker. Political Worker Kostrov and Private Boitsov, who were killed in this action, were posthumously awarded with the Gold Star of the Hero of the Soviet Union. Officers of the Finnish 2nd Artillery Regiment noted after this battle: 'The Russkies walk to our bunkers, singing and setting red flags on top of them. How is this possible?'

The assault westwards, towards bunkers Nos 13, 14 and 34, was more successful. A Soviet assault party with one tank attacked bunker No. 14 after a short artillery barrage. The Finns managed to halt the riflemen. They were forced to stop in the trench between bunkers No. 14 and No. 34. Despite this, the Soviet tank crew did not give up and attacked the bunker alone. The tank started driving back and forth at a distance of 100 metres from the bunker, staying out of range of Finnish close-range anti-tank weapons. Then the tank opened rapid fire at the gun ports and the door of the bunker from all its weapons. Seven Finnish machine-gunners were trapped inside. Corporal

Häkkänen, who tried to slip out of the bunker, was killed on the spot. Four defenders of the bunker were wounded, two remained unharmed. The Finns slipped out of the bunker in twilight, while Finnish infantry managed to destroy the brave Soviet tank that was left without infantry cover. Soviet artillery fire destroyed the roof of bunker No. 19 on the same day.

Soviet motor riflemen managed to capture bunker No. 13 during the day, but the Finns again threw them back to the ruined bunker No. 15 in the night. The Finns managed to recapture the ruins of Rantala Farm at 0400 hours on 27 February. The 6th Infantry Regiment received orders to withdraw to the rear defence line during the night of 28 February.

The 17th Motor Rifle Division prepared for a decisive assault, bringing more units to the northern bank of the River Salmenkaita on 27 February. Artillery continued pounding the bunkers with direct fire. The location of all bunkers was now well known.

The final assault on the Finnish bunker line began in the early morning of 28 February, and the 3rd Finnish Battalion reported a small breakthrough at Mattila Farm at 0800 hours. All Finnish attached units had already dismantled their phone lines and were on the move to the last Finnish line of defence on the Karelian Isthmus. There were no more resources left to repel the Soviet strikes. After this, the 3rd Finnish Battalion sent repeated messages of breakthroughs, and the commander of the 6th Rifle Regiment, Gruenn, had serious doubts whether the battalion would be able to hold the positions. The 1st and 2nd Battalions were ordered to secure the flanks in case of a Soviet breakthrough.

Despite the developing crisis on 28 February, the Finnish 6th Infantry Regiment successfully disengaged and withdrew to the River Vuoksi. After withdrawal from the Salmenkaita line, Finnish officers evaluated the action of the 17th Motor Rifle Division and the 50th Rifle Division and their artillery:

> At Salmenkaita the enemy tried to spot our bunkers and their sectors of fire immediately. Enemy infantry managed to close in with our positions under a creeping barrage of artillery, with armour, machine-guns and artillery firing simultaneously at our bunkers and their gun ports. Enemy infantry marched into battle in close formation, spreading into assaulting line only at the distance of final assault. Very often they just walked into battle, under the protection of overwhelming fire superiority. Enemy infantry did not use rifle fire at all in order to support their advance.
>
> Supporting fire of the enemy's automatic weapons was good, especially the machine-guns, which were often well placed.

Enemy artillery was extremely active at Salmenkaita, their marksmanship was good, which was the result of both exceptionally good terrain for observing targets at breadth and depth, as well as the calmness of the crews as they were aiming and firing at our bunkers over open sights. The effect of direct artillery fire on the crews of the bunkers was exceptionally high, the moral impact was very strong.

CHAPTER 6

March 1940: Last Stand-off on the Karelian Isthmus

The Finns completed their withdrawal to the rear defence line by 28 February 1940. According to the offensive plan of the North-Western Front, the X and XXXIV Rifle Corps were to reach Uuras archipelago, cross the Gulf of Vyborg and then assist the L and XIX Rifle Corps to capture Vyborg. Stubborn Finnish resistance on the rear defence line caused Meretskov, commander of the Seventh Army, to seek another solution. He formed the XVIII Rifle Corps from the divisions of the Seventh Army and the Group of Reserve of Supreme Command. It comprised the 86th, 173rd and 91st Motor Rifle Divisions. The corps received orders to cross the ice-covered Gulf of Vyborg and envelope Vyborg from the west. The XXXIV and L Rifle Corps were to break through the Finnish rear defence line and surround the city from the east.

Finnish pre-war plans of defence for the Gulf of Vyborg only had summer scenarios. The Finnish defence of the Gulf was confined to action against the Red Banner Baltic Fleet and the destruction of landing parties on the coastline. The extremely cold winter of 1939/1940 made it possible for the XVIII Rifle Corps to manoeuvre freely on the ice and bring heavy equipment, like tanks and artillery, across the ice-covered Gulf. This was a total surprise for the Finns. Suddenly, the whole coastline of the Gulf of Vyborg became a front line! There were no reserves left for this. The firepower of the coastal forts of Tuppura and Ravansaari was not enough to repel a full-scale attack of three Soviet divisions. The batteries of Satamaniemi and Ristiniemi also had only a minor impact on the course of battle. As a result, the detached battalions, formed from seamen or replacements lacking sufficient experience and training, opposed the three fresh Soviet motor rifle divisions and the 70th Rifle Division.

Soviet troops captured the islands of Tuppura and Teikari on 2 and 3 March. The garrison of Tuppura Fort used all the ammunition for their 6-inch guns and then fought as infantry. Soviet troops captured Kuninkaansaari Island to the north of Tuppura, cutting off the shortest route of retreat for the defenders of Tuppura. All Finnish counter-attacks failed. The 86th Motor Rifle Division and volunteer ski troopers, supported by armour, surrounded the island. On the evening of 2 March the garrison of the fort started the retreat, which turned into a partial rout. Some 650 men out of 800 reached the northern coast of the Gulf. The Soviet Motor Rifles and ski troopers lost 320 men assaulting the island, out of which sixty were killed. The garrison of Teikari Island repelled all Soviet attacks on 2 March, but had to withdraw late in the evening.

The all-out offensive of the XVIII Rifle Corps, under Kombrig Kurochkin, began on the morning of 4 March. The 86th Motor Rifle Division, supported by the 28th Tank Regiment, led the Soviet advance. The 70th Rifle Division charged across the ice to the right of the motor rifles. The bridgehead was immediately established at the Capes of Vilaniemi and Häränpääniemi. The 70th Rifle Division, under Kombrig Kipronos, captured Teikari and Melansaari Islands and continued its assault towards Nisalahti village on the mainland. The 173rd Motor Rifle Division, under Kombrig Martzinkevich, was sent across the Gulf to support the 70th Rifle Division.

All Finnish counter-attacks against the Soviet bridgehead failed. The Finns were throwing battalions and companies against reinforced Soviet regiments with armour and artillery. The result of these counter-attacks was heavy casualties for no gains. The 7th Detached Battalion of Major Varko lost seventy-five men killed on 7 March, when it was ambushed by Soviet troops and had to fall back.

Regiments at the point of the Soviet advance cut the Vyborg–Hamina highway on 9 March. Poorly trained Finnish detached battalions could not withstand the blows of the Soviet regiments. It was obvious that the total collapse of the Finnish defences was a matter of days away.

The situation to the east of Vilaniemi was less critical for the Finns. The battle-hardened 4th Infantry Division, which had been at the front since December 1939, defended the sector. Due to their extensive battle experience they easily repelled the assaults of the 113th, 43rd and 42nd Rifle Divisions. By the end of the war, however, the regiments of the 4th Infantry Division were driven away from the islands of the archipelago to the northern coast. The last Finnish reserves were thrown into the battle for the Gulf, including cadets from infantry training centres.

Soviet units hit the Finnish defences east of Vyborg with the XXXIV and L Rifle Corps. The L Rifle Corps was to assault from Tali Station towards Juustila, while the XXXIV Rifle Corps was to break through Finnish defences in Tammisuo, reach the Saima Channel, and strike at the flank and rear of Finnish troops in Vyborg through Monrepot park. This would have meant an encirclement of Finnish forces in Vyborg. The plan of operation was approved on 11 March. By the morning of 13 March units of the 123rd Rifle Division, with the support of the 20th Heavy Tank Brigade, reached the area of Portinhoikka. The 84th Motor Rifle and 100th Rifle Divisions fought their way to Lake Kärstilänjärvi. In the morning of 13 March all Soviet assaults east of Vyborg were halted.

The commander of the II Army Corps, General-Lieutenant Harald Ökvist, was concerned by events at the front. He could clearly see the idea of the enveloping Soviet strikes in order to encircle the Finnish forces in the city. Time and again he asked for permission to retreat from the city. The commander of the Isthmus Army, Heinrichs, refused each time. Ökvist knew nothing about the peace negotiations in Moscow that were already under way. Ökvist received permission to fall back to the rear defence line in Vyborg as late as 12 March. The rear defence line ran along the Seaport–Battery Hill–Railway depot line. Ökvist immediately issued orders to fall back. One regiment was to hold Battery Hill, the rest of the 3rd Division was to leave the city and take up positions on the other side of Saima Channel at Tienhaara. The 7th Infantry Regiment and the 3rd Light Unit took up positions in the city. The 8th Infantry Regiment, under Major Laaksonen, withdrew from the southern suburbs of the city early in the morning of 13 March and set the remaining wooden houses on fire. The Soviet 7th Rifle Division continued its offensive against Vyborg on the morning of 13 March, with all three regiments, and made contact with the last Finnish defensive line on Battery Hill. The Winter War ended at that place at noon Moscow time.

Downtown Viipuri remained in Finnish hands. Lieutenant-General Harald Ökvist watched the last parade of his troops in the inner yard of Vyborg Castle. The Finnish flag, which flew high over the castle during all 105 days of the Winter War, was taken off the Tower of Saint Olof with all proper military ceremony. Finnish units left the ghost city on the morning of 14 March and started their heavy march to the new border.

Battle of the River Vuoksi
After the withdrawal from the intermediate defence line in Salmenkaita, Finnish units withdrew to the last rear defence line on the Karelian Isthmus. The last line ran along the southern bank of the River Vuoksi, on the ridges of Äyräpää. The Finns managed to disengage the Red Army and successfully consolidate their positions on the ridges. Some delaying parties were left behind. Very few fortifications were built along the rear defence line; in most places the Finns had to fight without any fortifications at all.

Forward units of the XV Rifle Corps reached the rear defence line by 29 February. On the corps' left flank the 97th Rifle Division was still battling against Finnish delaying parties at the northern edge of Ristseppälä village.

During three days, from 1 to 3 March, the rifle corps and the exhausted 17th Motor Rifle Division and 4th Rifle Division, stormed Finnish positions at Kylä-Paakkola and Äyräpää in vain. The Finns held firmly to the natural defensive positions on the ridges, and losses in the Soviet regiments grew each day. Anatoly Derevenets again:

> On the evening of a cloudy day, when the firefight died out, we, a handful of men, gathered behind the stone wall of a burnt-out Finnish farm. Our thoughts were as dark as the coming night. Several men I knew from the rifle company were killed. Among them were Barski – a timid and educated homeboy. Vanyants, a tall and slightly over-weight student, whose father was a colonel, was also killed. Despite his high rank, his father never tried to get him a privileged position. Vanyants tried to evacuate a wounded company commander and a Finnish bullet killed him when he stood up. Ryzhov, the tallest man in the company, was wounded.
>
> We were all sitting silently, deep in our own thoughts. All of a sudden, Political Worker Andreiko broke the silence. He was trans-ferred to us from the 2nd Battalion, which was disbanded due to high casualties. 'You know, I want to say this,' he said. 'Which other army in the world could take all this – lying in snow for hours in bitter cold, storming enemy lines, drinking frozen vodka, always sleeping outdoors and in most cases without campfire? The Finns have a different war: they shoot us then go to sleep and rest in a warm house. What about capturing the unassailable bunker line just with infantry? We saw ourselves – the bunkers were not destroyed, they were almost intact. Of course our commanders are dumb, all they know is frontal assaults. But we overcame everything.'
>
> 'Are you preaching again, political worker? Did you not see how many casualties this cost us?'
>
> 'I am not talking on behalf of the commanders; I am talking about ordinary men like us.'
>
> 'The war is not yet over, pals.'
>
> Everyone was silent again.
>
> 'Do I also have to die here?' Andreiko said, as if he were talking to himself. 'I had a son born recently. Here is my wife.' He took a photo out of his pocket.
>
> I almost shivered when the political worker said these words: 'Do I also have to die?' This was a thought that we all had, but did not dare to say aloud.

We passed around the photo of a young woman with a baby, his wife with his son, and I had a spontaneous thought: if Andreiko gets killed, he has a son, at least some trace left of him on this earth. What would be left of us, former schoolboys? Just a photo in a family album? This thought was depressing. Spring was in the air. Behind the railway embankment there was a ridge that we had to take at any cost. Somewhere on the ridge there was an invisible enemy that saw us and could kill any one of us.

On 4 March the 39th and 220th Rifle Regiments launched assaults at the ridges of Äyräpää and managed to capture Church Hill, driving the 1st Battalion, 23rd Infantry Regiment, away from the hill. The 2nd Battalion of the 23rd Infantry Regiment managed to hold its ground between Church Hill and the ferry crossing, although the battalion commander, Captain Kaarlo Sihvo, was killed in action.

Church Hill was a dominant feature with perfect observation and a sector of fire towards Finnish positions on the northern bank of Vuoksi, as well as Vasikkasaari Island. Finnish officers regarded possession of the hill as crucial, and demanded it be recaptured. It was easier said than done, as Finnish units in the area had no reserves left. The 23rd Regiment of Lieutenant-Colonel Laurila had all three battalions engaged in battle. The 8th Light Unit, under Captain Leo Hävlä, was attached to the 23rd Regiment. This unit was transferred from the quiet sector of Kiviniemi. The counter-attack was supposed to begin during the night from 4–5 March, but started at dawn on 6 March, when it was already light. The squadron of the Light Unit marched into battle on foot, without taking any cover. Soviet machine-gun crews let the Finns close in on the hill and opened fire at a distance of 50 metres. The squadron lost forty-two men killed in a matter of seconds and the assault stopped. The squadron had consisted almost completely of men from Nurmo village, central Finland. Thirty-eight crosses bearing the same date now mark the tragic battle at Church Hill of Äyräpää (5 March 1940) in Nurmo cemetery.

After the Finnish counter-attack failed, the Soviet regiments attacked and captured Vasikkasaari Island. The 220th Regiment, which attacked the ferry crossing, was again stopped by Finnish fire. The regiment suffered exceptionally high losses in the first four days of March. Total losses were 1,233 men, with 317 killed, 752 wounded and 175 missing in action. The 8th Rifle Division joined the battle for Vasikkasaari. The remains of the 101st Regiment were also transferred to the Äyräpää area from Taipale. After the slaughter of the February offensive, the regiment had to be reorganized. The 1st and 3rd Battalions had suffered such heavy losses they were merged into one battalion with 300 men and two machine-gun platoons, while the 2nd Battalion was down to one rifle company and one machine-gun company.

The Soviet units continued their assaults and managed to capture a bridgehead on the northern bank of Vuoksi at Vasikkasaari. The Finns counterattacked twice on 9 March, but failed. The casualty rate in the Finnish infantry units was as high as 40–70 per cent. Battalion strength varied from 100–250 men. The Finns desperately held out with their last strength. Battles at Vuoksi raged on 11, 12 and 13 March. Soviet attacks and Finnish counter-attacks took place several times a day. The Finnish defences were on the verge of collapse but held on until the end of the war.

The Last Day and Hour of War

The Winter War was over at noon precisely Moscow time on 13 March 1940. The opponents at the front spent the last hours and minutes of war settling scores. Both Soviets and Finns fired as many rounds and bullets at each other as they could.

At noon Moscow time all the firing suddenly stopped. The war was over. All along the front the former enemies met in no-man's-land and discussed the practical matters of the peace treaty. Officers exchanged maps of minefields, discussed the schedule of troop movements, and took photographs together.

Such a sharp change from war to peace was a shock for everyone. Veterans on both sides described the moment as surreal. The memory of the sudden silence and the singing of birds instead of the roaring of guns stayed with these men for the rest of their lives. Anatoly Derevenets recalled:

> I was sent for duty on the phone for the commander of the 1st Battalion, Captain Vysotski. The battalion commander was a tall and handsome man, but apparently he had helped himself to alcohol too much, as his face was swollen and red. He had a lively conversation with the commander of the anti-tank battalion, Weinstein, and once in a while took a sip from a glass of vodka. The two commanders had some grilled meat for a snack. The dugout was illuminated with a glowing phone cable attached to the ceiling. I exchanged messages with phone operators from other units, just to keep myself awake. All of a sudden I heard somewhere far away a discussion about peace. The line was quite bad and I heard the conversation poorly.
>
> 'Can you hear what they are talking about?' I asked the phone operator at the regiment.
>
> 'I do,' he replied. 'But I cannot hear it clearly. The line is very bad. They are talking about peace or something.'

'Can you find out?'

'I will try. I guess the conversation is at divisional HQ.'

I started listening carefully to the conversation at divisional HQ. The line was awful, but I could hear what they said. It was true, today, on 13 March, hostilities were to stop at noon.

I interrupted the conversation of the battalion commander and the anti-tank commander: 'Comrade battalion commander, the peace is coming. The war will be over today at 1200.' The battalion commander was stunned:

'Who told you this?'

'I heard a conversation at divisional HQ.'

'Give me the receiver.' The HQ confirmed my words. 'Quite a surprise!', he exclaimed and immediately added: 'Now the fun is over ... .'

I did not understand what he meant. Either a lack of drill and discipline, or freedom to drink as much vodka as one could. Weinstein became ecstatic and started to plan his life in peace time. I called all phone operators. First, no one believed that the destructive Winter War was about to end. I heard great happy noise along all phone lines. All tried to share and discuss the happy news: 'The war will be over!'

The morning of this sunny day started with an irregular and lazy exchange of fire. At eleven o'clock the entire earth seemed to start vibrating. All weapons opened fire from both sides. Artillery, mortars, small arms were all in action. Lines went down immediately. The battalion commander ordered: 'Restore the line!'

I left the phone and walked towards the exit. The platoon leader also went out to see the situation. It seemed that the entire earth was on fire. Several shells exploded next to our dugout. We sprang back, and a shell exploded in front of the dugout, destroying the entrance. Air pressure put out our lamp – the burning cable. Quite a situation!

A frozen chunk of earth hit my side and broke two ribs. They said that two daily allocations of ammunition were spent in that last hour.

The thunder of guns did not abate until a complete, undisturbed, silence came at noon. This was peace. A bright, sunny, spring day. It was warm. A strong stench of explosions was still in the air. We all got out of the dugout. The screaming of wounded could be heard in the distance.

Not far from the bank there was an opening in the ice. Apparently, it was used for collecting fresh water. There was a young man lying there in a Finnish skiing suit with his head blown off. A sled approached our line from the Finnish side. An officer and three soldiers were in it. The officer asked for permission to pick up the dead man. Our regiment's commissar gave this permission. When the body was loaded on the sleds, the Finnish officer burst into tears.

I tried to talk to a Finnish soldier. He looked like a cultured man and turned out to be a pre-war schoolteacher. I used my poor knowledge of German and found out that the dead man was a friend of the officer. They had been together in the First World War, when Finland was still part of the Russian Empire.

The body was loaded on the sled. The older Finnish officer was crying all the time, not ashamed of his tears. The sled quickly departed towards a Finnish village. Amazing silence was around us, a silence that we had almost forgotten in the war. White snow was shining in bright sunlight. The fear and stress were gone. The Winter War was over.

Toivo Ahola of the 3rd Company, 15th Infantry Regiment, recalled:

The dawn of 13 March 1940 was beautiful. A sunny day was starting when we got out of our basement. We were in defence at the second line, behind the familiar Rat Hole strongpoint. Our positions were in thin pine forest, there was no defence line at all. We heard that the battle's intensity was growing, but it had not yet reached its peak. Our company commander was giving final orders at the second line when a runner came and brought a written order from battalion HQ.

Hostilities stop on 13 March 1940 at 1100 hours [Author's Note: this is local time; for the Russians, operating on Moscow time, the ceasefire was set for 1200 hours, noon]. Not a single shot must be fired after this. The company pulls back 1 kilometre from the present line and awaits orders there.

I looked at my watch – it was eight in the morning. We had to hold on for three more hours. I recalled the words of Second Lieutenant Andersson: 'Peace negotiations are under way in Moscow.' I was all the time looking at my watch, the hands were moving agonizingly slowly. The war was not over yet.

At the left flank of our battalion, at Tammisuo Station, the enemy had been attacking all morning. Second Lieutenant Matti Martela's platoon was almost cut off from the rest of the battalion. We received an order to help Martela and his men. We quickly formed a small task force under Second Lieutenant Andersson. We had to strike the enemy's flank and distract his attention from Martela's platoon. However, this was easier said than done because we had to attack across an open field. Success was very uncertain. It was almost ten o'clock – the war was supposed to be over in an hour! Luckily, the enemy that was pressing Martela withdrew and his platoon managed to link up again with the battalion. We had permission to go back to the second line of defence. We arrived there at quarter to eleven.

The time was almost eleven. All of a sudden it became silent. The symphony of death that had rung in our ears for three and a half months was over. A complete silence was there for some time, interrupted only by the engines of Russian aircraft, but they did not drop bombs any more. Soon they turned away and disappeared. Immediately after this, the Ivans shouted with joy loudly. We, Finns, were silent like a frozen lake.

We withdrew 1 kilometre into the rear, as we were ordered. We were forty-five men left in the company, just one-third of its original strength. Nevertheless, we managed to stop the enemy at Vyborg, no matter how hard they tried to capture the city in the last days of war. We went into a house with broken windows, but the stove was intact. We lit the stove and warmed ourselves a bit. It was still cold, although it was already mid-March. Three Russian soldiers came into our house in the afternoon to get acquainted with us. We could not have a normal conversation, as no one spoke the language.

From my point of view, I adjusted to peaceful life without difficulties. Some Finns took a certain pattern after the war – first they got drunk and then went to work. I did not drink and immediately went to work. Spring fieldwork was just beginning, and my help was greatly appreciated by my parents. My older brother had just married and moved out, while my younger brother was still recovering from his wound in a hospital.

Toivo Suonio, machine-gun platoon leader:

A runner skied downhill towards us and shouted: 'Peace! Peace is coming! Ceasefire at 1100 hours!' We were dumbfounded. This could not be true! Lieutenant Parkkola, the machine-gun company commander, was the first to react: 'Seize him! He has lost his mind; seize him before he spreads panic in other places.'

But no one managed to catch and seize our runner Pekka Mattinen, who rushed forward along the line to relay the important news. Could this really be true?

A sled appeared on the road, carrying mortar rounds. The driver was gypsy Ville Nyman from Savitaipale. He served as a driver in the mortar battery of Lieutenant Pajukari. The mortars were set and ready for firing at the ridge. We walked up to the mortar position. Lieutenants Suuronen and Pajukari were there. They all knew that the ceasefire was set for 1100 hours. We had less than an hour left!

During the night the mortar battery was out of ammunition. Now we had plenty of it. There were dozens of targets on the ice of Vuoksi and beyond. Would the enemy try to attack at the last moment?

Russian artillery was firing at Sintola ridges. Suuronen climbed a ridge to orchestrate our fire. He shouted: 'On my command! Battery, fire!' The mortars opened rapid fire. 'Guys, shoot faster!' Suuronen shouted from the ridge, 'Fatherland is still dear!' Our machine-guns fired non-stop. It sounded like they fired one belt after another. They fired at pinned-down Russian infantry on the ice without any opposition – they were too close and the Russian artillery was afraid of hitting them, too.

The fire intensified. Many women in Russia became widows in the last hour of the Winter War. We also had casualties from artillery fire. I saw a watch in Suuronen's hand. He seemed to be looking at the seconds ticking away and suddenly shouted: 'Cease fire!' We could not believe that the hell of war would be over at eleven o'clock sharp. But the impossible happened: when the watch showed eleven, a complete silence came. We heard birds singing in bushes at the river. It is impossible to describe the moment. It seemed that time stopped.

The next moment the Russians who had just been pinned down on the ice stood up and walked to our lines. Two airplanes flew low along the river – a Russian and a Finnish one! This made us confident that peace had come. We had not seen Finnish aircraft in the air for a couple of months.

I went to the CP of the 7th Company for detailed orders. My machine-guns were attached to this company under Mauno Kuhanen: 'Get the machine-guns off the island to the mainland!' he ordered. 'But don't tell the others, I am giving this order at my own risk. It will be faster and easier for all. I heard the schedule of withdrawal to the new border is tight.'

When I reached my machine-guns, the Russians were already there. They were all young and handsome men; as I heard, they were all cadets from military academies in Leningrad.

One of our machine-guns was Russian, a war prize. We had just repainted it white. Would the Russians make us return it? They did not. They even assisted us in loading the machine-guns on our sleds.

A young Russian lieutenant came up to me. He spoke a bit of Finnish: 'There are very few of you here,' he said with amazement.

I tried to explain that there were more soldiers on the northern bank of Vuoksi. In reality there was no one there. What can I say; we were a handful of hungry and exhausted men left.

A Finnish man from Ylämaa had a Russian rifle, war booty, on his shoulder. The Russian lieutenant walked up to the man, grabbed the rifle and said: 'A Russian rifle!' The guy turned around, stared the lieutenant in the eyes, held the rifle even tighter, and voiced his entire Russian vocabulary: 'A Finnish soldier!' The Russian lieutenant smiled, slapped our man on the back, and said: 'A good soldier!' Then he laughed. It was peace.

Lieutenant Viktor Iskrov, commander of the forward observers platoon, 68th Detached Mortar Battery, recalled:

All of a sudden there was a phone call. Senior Lieutenant Vnukov, our battery commander, called me. He said: 'Viktor, are you still fighting the war there? Are you planning to shoot?' 'Yes!' was my answer. I was in very high spirits: the Mannerheim Line had been broken, I could see Vyborg burning – I can very well remember that. On our left we could see both fire and smoke coming out of the city. 'So, the war is over,' he told me. I answered: 'No way! Let's go for Vaasa! We have just broken such a strong line, now we just have to go and capture Vaasa and other places!' Battalion Commander Sokolov did not know anything about the end of hostilities either. Senior Lieutenant Vnukov told me over the phone: 'You want to fight the war there, Viktor, but I am here at the firing positions, and I will not permit a single round to be fired. The war is over, they signed an armistice yesterday.' I asked Captain Sokolov. He called the regiment, and he was told there: 'Yes, this is it. There will be no fire mission, soldiers to stay in the trenches, do not go out of the trenches and wait for further orders.' He told me: 'That's the way it is, Lieutenant,' I answered: 'OK, got you.'

All firing immediately died out. No rifles or MGs, no mortars or artillery, and we could hear the birds singing – can you imagine? And all of a sudden we saw a man in white overalls getting down from a tree – a young Finn, with a red face. He shouted in a scared manner: 'War is over! War is over!' The Finns walked out of Karisalmi village with vodka bottles and shouted: 'Russkies, come and drink vodka with us! Come and drink with us!' I asked Sokolov what his commanders had told him. Sokolov answered that we had orders to sit in the trenches in order to avoid provocations. So we just sat in the trenches. The Finns saw that no one was coming to drink with them and went back into the houses. After that all movement died out.

Armas Paajanen of the 3rd Coast Artillery Regiment was in Kekkiniemi Fort:

An order about peace came in the morning of 13 March. At first, no one believed it, but we started to dismantle the guns. Second Lieutenant Tikka handed over the map of minefields to the Russians in the middle of the frozen lake. Tikka went to the middle of the lake and Russians came up to him. We were worried about him and held the Russians in our sights. We thought it was some sort of a trap. Everything went well, and the Russians invited us for a vodka shot in the evening, but we were not in the mood for a party.

Our empty fort and ploughed up soil were left behind. A beautiful pine tree grove in an area of two hectares was completely gone. We left the guns in Sapru School and were in Sortalahti in the evening. There we learnt about the peace terms and all became very depressed. The next morning our pals went to ask the officers whether it would be possible to see our home villages for the last time. The answer was negative. I addressed Second Lieutenant Tikka personally and asked if we could still do this: 'Those men, who were with me in the Battle of Taipale, can go. I am still your commander. Come back in forty-eight hours, do not let me down.' Everyone left and came back forty-eight hours later.

It was noon on 14 March when I came home. I walked around and looked at my home. Everything was empty, everything had been taken away. It was two o'clock sharp, when I locked the door and hid the key in a secret place I knew from childhood. I walked up my home hill, passed Leppoinmäki and arrived at Sirkanmäki. I stopped there and looked around again.

I saw the frozen Lake Kahvenitsanjärvi and the villages around it. My house and all my childhood memories were there on the opposite bank of the lake. The sky was dark, it was raining sleet. It seemed that the low clouds were also weeping for the fate of the Karelian people. I stood there for a long time, reflecting on many things. Although my cheeks were bitten by the frosts of Taipale and all human feelings were dumb because of the war, a tear rolled down my cheek. I walked away into the unknown future.

Aftermath and Closing Remarks

The Winter War ended on 13 March 1940, after 105 days. It is impossible to describe all the battles, skirmishes and raids of that war in a single book. The war at sea and in the air, diplomacy, and many other things are not in this book. It is amazing how much one can write on just 105 days in the history of humanity!

I hope that the book met the expectations of readers. I tried my best to describe the course of the war neutrally, with a discussion of myths and misunderstandings. I also hope that this book will assist the audience in the West to understand Finland and Russia better. Many features of the Russian and Finnish national character were revealed in that war.

Each battle and skirmish of that war deserves to be covered more fully. This book is simply an overview of the military campaign on land, and I would be very happy if it could be used as a starting point for new research on the Winter War.

During the period 1941–1944, the USSR and Finland were at war again, but that is a completely different story. After the end of hostilities in 1944 Mannerheim, Commander in Chief of the Finnish Army, addressed his troops with words of thankfulness and admiration in his Order of the Day No. 132 on 22 September 1944. The old marshal opened his message with the following words:

> Soldiers of the Finnish Army!
> The war in which our nation ended up three years ago, the war that demanded such high sacrifices from our nation, ended on 19 September 1944, with an armistice. After all our bitter experiences we see that that mainstay of peaceful future life is in building trustful relations with all our neighbouring nations.

Starting from 1944, a neutral and non-aligned Finland is the closest and best European neighbour of the Soviet Union and Russia. Let us hope that the peace between the two nations will never be broken again.

Appendices

I: Glossary of Finnish Terms

Finnish	Translation
harju	ridge
heinä	hay
järvi	lake
joki	river
kangas	sandy hill
kivi	stone
korpi	dense forest
koski	rapids
kylä	village
lahti	gulf
lehti	leaf
mäki	mountain, hill
marja	berry
metsä	forest
mylly	mill
niemi	cape
niitty	grass field
oja	brook, ditch
pelto	field
pieni, pien–	small
ranta	bank, beach
ruoho	grass
saari	island
salmi	narrow straight
suuri, suur–	large
vaara	hill, mountain (in the northern parts of Finland)

II: Typical Soviet Rifle Division Compared to a Typical Finnish Infantry Division

Soviet Rifle Division
(Around 17000 men)

Finnish Infantry Division
(Around 14200 men)

Rifle Regiment (around 4000 men)
Three rifle battalions
Regimental battery (four 76mm guns)
Scout company
Regimental anti-tank gun battery
  (six 45mm guns)
Four mortar platoons
  (eight 82mm mortars)

Infantry Regiment (around 3000 men)
Three infantry battalions
Gun company (four 37mm anti-tank
  or field guns)
Mortar company (six 81mm mortars)

Rifle Regiment

Infantry Regiment

Rifle Regiment

Infantry Regiment

Howitzer Artillery Regiment
  (around 1300 men)
36 howitzers

Artillery Regiment (around 2400 men)
36 guns

Artillery Regiment (around 1890 men)
36 guns and howitzers

–

Detached Tank Battalion
Could be armed with T-37 or T-38
  amphibious tanks, T-26 light tanks
  or chemical tanks. As a rule, fielded
  from 10 to 40 tanks

–

Detached Anti-Tank Battalion
18 45mm anti-tank guns

–

Detached Scout Battalion (328 men)
Cavalry Squadron
Motorcycle Company
Armoured Car Company
Tank Company

Light Unit (around 500 men)
Cavalry Squadron (around 180 men)
Bicycle Company (around 190 men)
Machine-gun Platoon

Detached Signals Battalion

Detached Signals Company

Detached Sapper Battalion

Two Detached Sapper Companies

III: Unofficial Table of Army Ranks

Finnish Army	Red Army	Red Army political branch	Designation in Red Army terminology
War Marshal	Marshal of the Soviet Union	–	Senior commanders and political workers
–	Army Commander 1st Class	Army Commissar 1st Class	
General of Infantry	Army Commander 2nd Class	Army Commissar 2nd Class	
Lieutenant-General	Corps Commander, Komkor	Corps Commissar	
–	Division Commander, Komdiv	Division Commissar	
General-Major	Brigade Commander, Kombrig	Brigade Commissar	
Colonel	Colonel	Regimental Commissar	
Lieutenant-Colonel	–	–	
Major	Major	Battalion Commissar	
Captain	Captain	Senior Political Leader	Middle-level commanders and political workers
–	Senior Lieutenant	Political Leader, politruk	
Lieutenant	Lieutenant	Junior Political Leader	
Second Lieutenant	Junior Lieutenant	Deputy Political Leader	
Non-Commissioned officers		–	Junior commanders

IV: Losses of the 20th Heavy Tank Brigade in December 1939 (Minus Attached Units)

Date	Landmines	Artillery hits	Burnt	Left on the battlefield
30.11.1939	1 T-28	–	–	–
1–2.12.1939	6 T-28	3 T-28	1 T-28	–
13.12.1939	–	–	3 T-28	–
14.12.1939	–	3 T-28	–	–
16.12.1939	–	3 T-28	–	–
17.12.1939	4 T-28 1 BT	8 T-28 2 T-26	5 T-28	8 T-28
18.12.1939	1 T-26	4 T-28 1 T-26	1 T-26	9 T-26
19.12.1939	–	13 T-28 2 T-26	4 T-28	7 T-28 1 SMK
20.12.1939	3 T-28	3 T-28	1 T-28	–

V: Losses of the 40th Light Tank Brigade in December 1939

Date	Landmines	Artillery
1.12.1939	3	–
2.12.1939	2	–
3.12.1939	2	1
8.12.1939	–	12
11.12.1939	–	8
13.12.1939	–	4
14.12.1939	–	2
15.12.1939	–	1
16.12.1939	–	1
17.12.1939	4	7
18.12.1939	–	1
19.12.1939	–	9
20.12.1939	–	1
28.12.1939	–	6

VI: Finnish and Soviet Slang from the Winter War

Designation	Translation	Meaning
aavetykki	Ghost cannon	A Soviet railway-based heavy cannon that fired at Vyborg from Perkjärvi Station.
Hopea makkara	Silver sausage	A Soviet artillery observation balloon.
Hyppy-Heikki	Jumper	A Russian siege cannon model 1877, used by the Finnish Army. The cannon did not have any recoil system and jumped back when fired.
Kivitalo	A stone building	A Soviet T-28 medium tank. Dubbed so due to its size.
Kristie-vaunu	Cristie tank	Finnish designation for any modification of a BT tank.
Laiska Jaakko	Lazy guy	A slow Soviet artillery observation biplane.
Lepakko	Bat	A Soviet artillery observation biplane.
naapuri	Neighbour	General designation of Soviet troops by the Finns.
piiskatykki	Whipping gun	A Soviet 45mm anti-tank gun or a regimental 76mm gun, firing over open sights.
Postijuna	postal train	A Soviet T-28 medium tank. The name was given to the tank because the entire field post and pay of the 91st Tank Battalion was found in one of the abandoned vehicles.
Vickers-vaunu	Vickers tank	Finnish designation for any modification of a T-26 tank.

Designation	Translation	Meaning
Cuckoo	A Finnish sniper	He takes a position in a tree, according to a common legend in the Red Army. However, Finnish snipers never took positions in trees. Finnish artillery observers used tree positions.
Karelian sculptor	A Soviet heavy cannon firing over open sights	So-called because it makes a bunker into a memorial for its garrison.
LTB	*Lichny tank boitsa*, a trooper's personal tank	A humorous name for an armoured shield on skis.
Lumberjack	A Soviet heavy cannon firing over open sights	So-called because it destroys the woods.
Valley of Death	A pre-sighted place	The fields south of Salmenkaita and some sectors of the front in Lähde were so named.

Archive Sources

Finnish National Archive
War Diary, 15th Infantry Regiment SPK 1071–1075
War Diary, 2nd Battalion, 5th Infantry Regiment SPK 1095–1097
War Diary, 1st Battalion, 15th Infantry Regiment SPK 1093, 1094
War Diary, 1st Machine-gun Company, 15th Infantry Regiment SPK 1087, 1088
War Diary, 2nd Machine-gun Company, 15th Infantry Regiment SPK 1089
War Diary, 1st Company, 15th Infantry Regiment SPK 1076, 1077
War Diary, 3rd Company, 15th Infantry Regiment SPK 1078, 1079
War Diary, 4th Company, 15th Infantry Regiment SPK 1080
War Diary, 5th Company, 15th Infantry Regiment SPK 1081
War Diary, 6th Company, 15th Infantry Regiment SPK 1082, 1083
War Diary, Gun Company, 15th Infantry Regiment SPK 1101
War Diary, 2nd Battalion, 5th Artillery Regiment SPK 1938
War Diary, 6th Infantry Regiment SPK 911
War Diary, 1st Battalion, 6th Infantry Regiment SPK 936
War Diary 2nd Battalion, 6th Infantry Regiment SPK 938
War Diary 3rd Battalion, 6th Infantry Regiment SPK 945
War Diary, 3rd Machine-gun Company, 6th Infantry Regiment SPK 930
War Diary, 7th Company, 6th Infantry Regiment SPK 926
War Diary, 8th Company, 6th Infantry Regiment SPK 928
War Diary, 9th Company, 6th Infantry Regiment SPK 929
War Diary, 2nd Battalion, 16th Infantry Regiment SPK 1116
War Diary, 2nd Battalion, 7th Infantry Regiment SPK 959
War Diary, 3rd Battalion, 7th Infantry Regiment SPK 962
War Diary, 7th Company, 7th Infantry Regiment SPK 952
War Diary 3rd Machine-gun Company, 7th Infantry Regiment SPK 954
War Diary, 1st Company, 24th Infantry Regiment SPK 3476
War Diary, 1st Battalion, 24th Infantry Regiment SPK 1190
War Diary, 3rd Battalion, 24th Infantry Regiment SPK 1197
War Diary, 24th Infantry Regiment SPK 1187
War Diary, 1st Battalion, 2nd Artillery Regiment SPK 1890
War Diary, 3rd Department of Staff of the 4th Infantry Brigade SPK 2770
War Diary, 4th Jaeger Battalion SPK 1806, 1807
Collection of archive documents of the fortification department of the General Staff of the
    Finnish Army T17764
Memoirs of Corporal Toivo Ahola
Memoirs of Lieutenant Paavo Kairinen

Russian State Military Archives
Armoured Units

Operation and battle reports of the units of the 20th Heavy Tank Brigade. Fund 34980, Document List 11, File 138

War Diary of the 20th Heavy Tank Brigade. Fund 34980, Document List 11, File 141

Information on materiel of the 20th Heavy Tank Brigade. Fund 34980, Document List 11, File 156

Information on presence, condition and losses of battle vehicles of the 35th Light Tank Brigade. Fund 34980, Document List 11, File 250

Operation reports of the Staff of the 40th Light Tank Brigade. Information on losses of the brigade. Fund 34980, Document List 11, File 294

Report on operations of the 39th Light Tank Brigade in the Winter War. Fund 34980, Document List 11, File 275

Rifle and Artillery Regiments of the Red Army

War Diary of the 245th Rifle Regiment. Fund 34980, Document List 12, File 410

Operation reports of Staff of the 255th Rifle Regiment. Fund 34980, Document List 12, File 439

List of names of killed and missing men of the 255th Rifle Regiment. Fund 34980, Document List 12, File 449

List of casualties of the 272nd Rifle Regiment. Fund 34980, Document List 12, File 472

Operation and battle reports of the Staff of the 274th Rifle Regiment. Fund 34980, Document List 12, File 474

War Diary of the 85th Rifle Regiment. Fund 34980, Document List 12, File 184

War Diary of the 331st Rifle Regiment. Fund 34980, Document List 12, File 525

Air photos of Summa village fortifications 1939–1940. Fund 34980, Document List 12, File 527

355th Rifle Regiment. Brief overview of the regiment's participation in Polish and Finnish campaigns. War Diary, schemes and maps. Fund 34980, Document List 12, File 552

War Diary of the 55th Motor Rifle Regiment. Fund 34980, Document List 12, File 870

War Diary of the 271st Motor Rifle Regiment. Fund 34980, Document List 12, File 880

War Diary of the 278th Rifle Regiment. Fund 34980, Document List 12, File 890

Operation reports of the 387th Rifle Regiment. Fund 34980, Document List 12, File 591

Operation reports of the 541st Rifle Regiment. Fund 34980, Document List 12, File 718

War Diary of the 541st Rifle Regiment. Fund 34980, Document List 12, File 720

Operation reports and other reports of the 733rd Rifle Regiment. Fund 34980, Document List 12, File 807

War Diary of the 364th Rifle Regiment. Fund 34980, Document List 12, File 571

Diary of deputy political worker of the 364th Rifle Regiment Ya. V. Vinogradov. Fund 34980, Document List 12, File 572

War Diary of the 461st Rifle Regiment. Fund 34980, Document List 12, File 672

War Diary of the 354th Artillery Regiment. Fund 34980, Document List 12, File 1528

Operation reports of the 101st Rifle Regiment. Fund 34980, Document List 12, File 198

War Diary of the XXIV Corps Artillery Regiment. Fund 34980, Document List 12, File 989

Ammo spending report of the 21st Heavy Corps Artillery Regiment. Fund 34980, Document List 12, File 975

Description of operations of the 609th Rifle Regiment. Fund 34980, Document List 12, File 736

War Diary of the 212th Rifle Regiment. Fund 34980, Document List 12, File 350

Rifle Divisions

Description of combat of the 90th Rifle Division at the crossing of Kiviniemi on 7–9 December 1939. Fund 34980, Document List 10, File 1562

Operation reports of units of the 90th Rifle Division. Fund 34980, Document List 10, File 1572

Description of operations of the 62nd Rifle Division. Fund 34980, Document List 10, File 1051

Operation reports of the Thirteenth Army, XXIII Rifle Corps, 8th, 136th, 142nd Rifle Divisions. Fund 34980, Document List 10, File 1040

War Diary of the 70th Rifle Division. Fund 34980, Document List 10, File 1117.

Collection of documents of the 44th Rifle Division. Fund 34980, Document List 10, File 659

Operation reports of the units of the 163rd Rifle Division. Fund 34980, Document List 10, File 3117

Operation reports, Staff of the 139th Rifle Division. Fund 34980, Document List 10, File 2572

Description of the operations of the 164th Rifle Division. Fund 34980, Document List 10, File 3209

Report on combat of the 90th Red Banner Rifle Division in war against White Finns. Fund 34980, Document List 10, File 1591

Report on combat operations of the 123rd Rifle Division. Fund 34980, Document List 10, File 2095

Other Document Collections in the Russian State Military Archives

'Short description of the fortification line of the Karelian Isthmus'. Fund 36967, Document List 1, File 414

Historical file of the 150th Rifle Division. Fund 34912, Document List 1, File 79

Bibliography

Finnish Sources

Hakala Jaakko, Santavuori Martti: Summa, Otava 1960.

Hämäläinen Walde: *Rihimiehenä talvisodan Summassa* (*Rank-and-File Man in the Battle of Summa*), Loimaa 1976.

'Kansa taisteli-miehet kertovat' ('The Nation Fought – the Men are Telling', magazine), Sanomapaino, Helsinki 1976–1985.

Kotikylämme Summa (*Our Home Village Summa*), Kotiprint Oy 2000.

Oksanen Eki: *Summan miehet* (*Soldiers of Summa*), Gummerus Kirjapaino Oy, Jyväskylä 1984.

Palmunen Einar: *Tampereen rykmentin suojapataljoona talvisodassa* (*The Guard Battalion of Tampere Regiment in the Winter War*), Kaaristo Oy, Hämeenlinna 1963.

Perkjärvi – Kannaksen seitsemin savuin sinisin (*Perkjärvi – the Crossroads of the Isthmus*), Kaaristo Oy, Hämeenlinna 1988.

Pohjamo Eino: *Verinen tanner* (*Bloody Fields: the 7th Detached Battalion in Winter War*), Kaaristo Oy, Hämeenlinna 2005.

Raunio Ari, Kilin Juri: *Talvisodan taisteluja* (*Battles of the Winter War*), Otava 2007.

Uitto Antero, Guest Carl-Fredrik: *Mannerheim-Linja. Talvisodan legenda* (*The Mannerheim Line – the Legend of the Winter War*), Gummerus Kirjapaino Oy, Jyväskylä 2006.

Unto Partanen: *Tykistömuseon 78 tykkiä* (*78 Guns of the Artillery Museum*), Kymen Painotuote 1988.

Sorko Kimmo: *Suvannon Salpa* (*The Lock of Lake Suvanto*), Otava 2004.

Talvisodan historia 1–4, (*History of the Winter War, volumes 1–4*), Sotatieteen laitoksen julkaisuja, WSOY 1977.

Hatjalahdelta Viipurinlahdelle (*From Lake Hatjalahti to the Gulf of Vyborg – the 11th Infantry Regiment in the Winter War*), Suomen Kirjallisuudenseuran Kirjapaino Oy, Helsinki 1940.

Joukko Luosto: *Voittojen Tie* (*The Road of Victories*), WSOY 1940.

Antila Olavi: *Suomi Suursodassa* (*Finland in the Great War*), Kirjaveteraanit 1992.

Timo Vihavainen, Andrei Saharov: *Tuntematon Talvisota: Neuvostoliiton salaisen poliisin kansiot* (*The Unknown Winter War: Files of the Soviet Secret Police*), Edita Publishing Oy 2009.

Kauki Tiili: *Tykistöupseeri talvisodassa* (*Artillery Officer in the Winter War*), Neirol-Kustannus, Helsinki 2006.

Russian Language Sources

E. Balashov: *Receive Us, Beautiful Suomi*, collection of documents on the Winter War, St Petersburg 1999.

E. Balashov, V. Stepakov: *Mannerheim Line and Finnish Fortifications on the Karelian Isthmus*, Nordmedizdat, St Petersburg 2000.

Fighting in Finland, collection of memories, Voenizdat, Moscow 1941.

In Snows of Finland, collection of memories, OGIZ Moscow 1941.
Finnish War 1939–1940: Joseph Stalin and the Finnish Campaign, Nauka, Moscow 1999.
'Military Chronicles', No. 5, 2005, BTV-MN, Moscow 2005.
'Frontline Illustration: Multi-turreted T-28 and T-29 Tanks', Moscow 2000.
P. Polyan and N. Sobol, *Through Two Wars and Two Archipelagos: a Human at the Roadside of War*, Rosspen, Moscow 2007.
Memories of Karl-Gustav Mannerheim, Vagrius, Moscow 2000.
P. Petrov, V. Stepakov, D. Frolov, *War in the Arctic 1939–1940*, Institute of Russia and Eastern Europe in Helsinki, 2002.

Swedish Sources
B. Geier: *Vinterkrigets Taipale (Taipale in the Winter War)*, WSOY 1941.
Jarl Gallen: *Tionde Regementet (The Tenth Regiment)*, Söderströms 1940.
Tragedier vid Summa (Tragedies at Summa), Forsbergs tryckeri, Jakobstad 2001.
Harald Ökvist: *Vinterkriget ur min synvinkel (The Winter War From My Point of View)*, WSOY 1949.

English Sources
Winter War: a Frozen Hell, William Trotter, NY 1991.

Online Sources
www.iremember.ru Veteran interviews taken by Artem Drabkin and Bair Irincheev, 'I remember' web pages
www.narc.fi Database of Finnish Army casualties in the Second World War
www.mil.fi Official web pages of the Finnish Defence Forces
www.obd-memorial.ru Database of Soviet Armed Forces casualties in the Second World War, Ministry of Defence of the Russian Federation
www.winterwar.karelia.ru Database of Winter War casualties, Petrozavodsk State University and Yuri Kilin
www.winterwar.com Sami Korhonen's web pages on Winter War
www.warheroes.ru Heroes of the Country web pages, dedicated to all men awarded with the Gold Star of the Hero of the Soviet Union

Index

217

Stackpole Military History Series

Real battles. Real soldiers. Real stories.

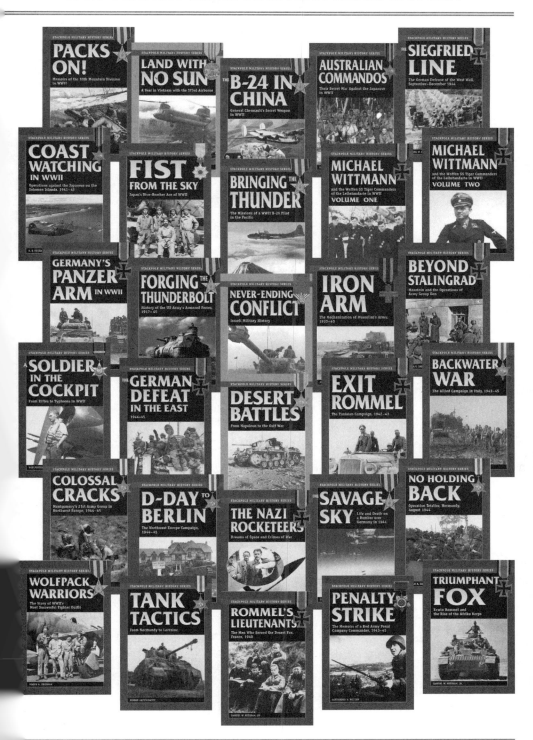

Stackpole Military History Series

Real battles. Real soldiers. Real stories.

Stackpole Military History Series

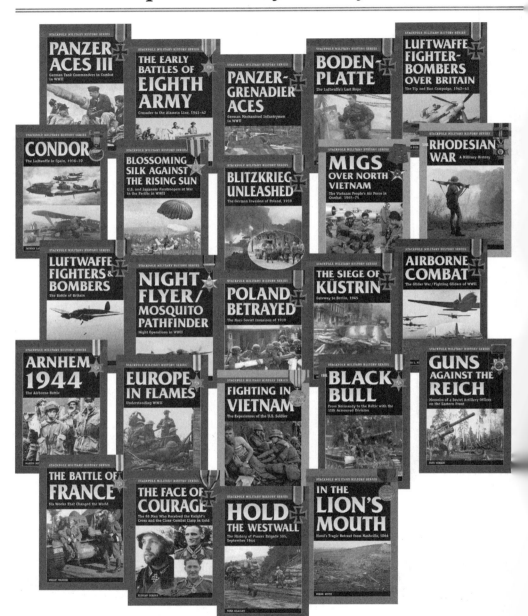

Real battles. Real soldiers. Real stories.

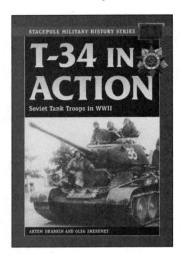

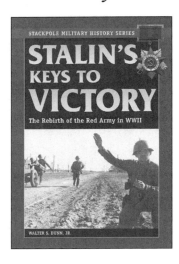

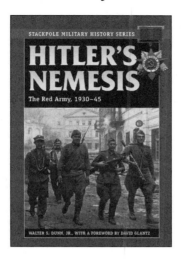

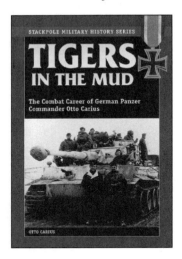

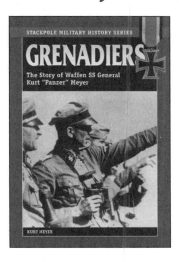

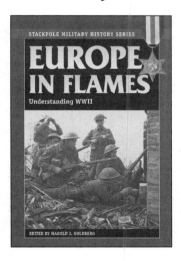

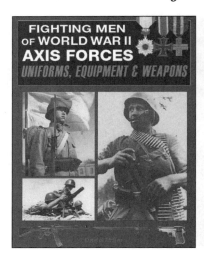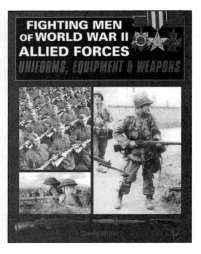